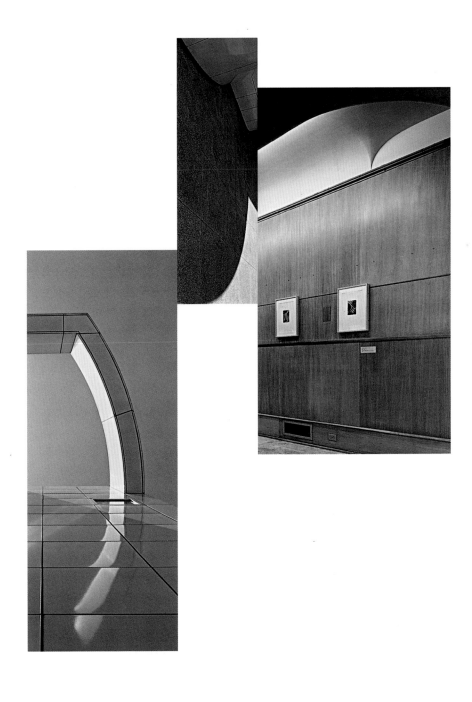

Neal Benezra

Julia Brown

David Cateforis

Teri A. Coate

I. Michael Danoff

Lea Rosson DeLong

James T. Demetrion

Deborah Leveton

Terry Ann R. Neff

Louise
Rosenfield Noun

M. Jessica Rowe

Christopher D. Roy

Franz Schulze

and

Amy N. Worthen

Published by the
Des Moines Art Center
Des Moines, Iowa

Distributed by
Hudson Hills Press
New York

An Uncommon Vision

The Des Moines Art Center

An Uncommon Vision:
The Des Moines Art Center
was published on the occasion of
the fiftieth anniversary of the
founding of the Des Moines Art
Center. It serves to celebrate
the extraordinary vision that
selected three leading architects
to create a special place and
then continues to fill that space
with equally challenging art
of the highest quality.

©1998 Des Moines Art Center
4700 Grand Avenue
Des Moines, Iowa 50312

Distributed by
Hudson Hills Press, Inc.
122 E. 25th Street
New York, New York 10010
Editor and Publisher:
Paul Anbinder

Distributed in the United States,
its territories and possessions,
and Canada through
National Book Network

Distributed in the United
Kingdom, Eire, and
Europe through Art Books
International Ltd.

Library of Congress
Catalog Number
98–72941

ISBN: 1-879003-20-1

Publication coordinated and
edited by Terry Ann R. Neff
t. a. neff associates, inc.
Tucson, Arizona

Design and typography by
studio blue, Chicago

Printed by Arnoldo Mondadori
Editore, S.p.A., Verona, Italy

Photography credits

All color plates are by Michael
Tropea, Chicago, except for the
following: Craig Anderson,
Des Moines, Boltanski, pp. 62–63
and Gauguin verso, p.117;
Ray Andrews, Des Moines, Blake,
p. 61; Cornell, p. 83; Dubuffet,
p. 105; Kelly, p. 152; Segal,
p. 246; Sherman, p. 257; Twombly,
p. 277; Warhol, p. 278; Roy essay,
figs. 4, 5, 7, 9–11; and Worthen
essay, figs. 1–6 and 10–12;
Farshid Assassi ©1996 Assassi
Productions, Santa Barbara,
California, Miss, p.195; courtesy
Joseph Helman, New York, Sultan,
p. 270; courtesy Luhring
Augustine, New York, Whiteread,
p. 285; Mary Miss, New York,
p. 194; Michael Jay Smith,
San Antonio, Texas, Moore,
pp. 200–201.

All black-and-white photographs
are by Steve Hall, ©1997
Hedrich Blessing, Photographers,
Chicago, except for the following:
Mark Tade, Iowa City, Dunlap,
p. 107; Noun essay, figs. 2 and 3;
Schulze essay, courtesy Archives,
Cranbrook Academy of Art,
Bloomfield Hills, Michigan, fig. 1;
courtesy Pei Cobb Freed &
Partners, Architects, New York,
fig. 10; Ezra Stoller, Esto Photo-
graphics, Inc., Mamaroneck, New
York, figs. 12 (©1967), 16 (©1968),
and 19 (©1948); courtesy Tyler
Photography, Des Moines, fig. 9;
©Luca Vignelli, New York, fig. 18.

Preface
I. Michael Danoff
4

Acknowledgments
M. Jessica Rowe
7

**Architectural trinity in
Des Moines**
Franz Schulze
9

**The history of the
Des Moines Art Center**
Louise Rosenfield Noun
25

**Nineteenth- and
twentieth-century works of art**
Various authors
41

Works on paper
Amy N. Worthen
297

Tribal arts
Christopher D. Roy
315

Index
329

Table of contents

Preface

The Des Moines Art Center plays against expectations. First-time visitors may have heard that the Art Center enjoys buildings designed by Eliel Saarinen, I. M. Pei, and Richard Meier. But only traversing them in person imparts the effectiveness of each of these structures conceived by three of the most innovative and renowned architects of the twentieth century: the classic and functional elegance of the Saarinen galleries (1948); the glazed soaring vault and extraordinary vistas onto the park setting upon which Pei capitalized (1968); and the variously scaled spaces in the Meier galleries which facilitate the highlighting of individual works (1985). And one actually must experience the three buildings to comprehend the effectiveness.

The collection is equally a discovery. A first-time visitor who is a museum professional may know that the holdings include extraordinary objects in the scholarly area in which that professional is working. But what elicits surprise is the consistency of the quality, work after work. This consistency is confirmed by the continual requests from museums internationally to borrow works from the Art Center.

Also surprising is the focus of the collection. There are substantial holdings of works on paper which reach back five centuries. But the collection of paintings and sculptures is restricted by policy to the nineteenth and twentieth centuries, and within that span the greatest weight primarily is American and European art of recent decades. There also is a notable collection of tribal art, mostly African.

It is not unusual for a city to support an important museum with a largely contemporary program, but almost always that city also accommodates an encyclopedic museum (e.g., New York, Chicago, Los Angeles, Minneapolis, and San Francisco). For a city's sole art museum to have so specific a focus is rare. Moreover, that focus is challenging because contemporary art makes more demands on its audience than do most other periods of art.

While the architecture and collection are each remarkable, together they strengthen one another because most of the art is historically coincident with the architecture housing it. Seeing so many signature works in so beautiful and sympathetic a setting is a unique and invigorating museum experience.

That experience actually begins outside the buildings with art that responds to the architecture and landscape. The Art Center is located just within the nineteenth-century Greenwood Park and in view of a major thoroughfare. From that thoroughfare one can see important site-specific works by Bruce Nauman – a unique bronze cast of a pyramid of animals – and Richard Serra – six large Swedish granite forms. On the opposite side of the Art Center is the major portion of the park, which unfolds with gently rolling hills and huge oaks. The Pei building's vast windows feature that vista, commencing with a historical rose garden. Farther down the park is a pond, which is the center of another site-specific work of art, a vast wetlands restoration created by Mary Miss. And in a space where the Saarinen and Meier buildings converge is an installation by Lewis deSoto.

The architecture and art out-of-doors intimate at what becomes certain when walking through the galleries: for decades the Art Center's collecting has been adventuresome. While controversy never was sought, neither was it shied away from. Purchases of works by Auguste Rodin, Jean Dubuffet, Brice Marden, and Jeff Koons were among the most controversial. But in these as in all the acquisitions, the guiding spirit has been quality. This vision begins with the Board of Trustees who have made it a charge to the Art Center's professional staff. It is a vision that has been consistent and inviolable. The Acquisition Committee must be convinced that the director is recommending for purchase a work that represents the artist at a consummate level of quality by international standards. Of course, there are those who may disagree with the judgment, but regardless it remains the museum's guiding principle in purchasing art. It also inspires collectors to donate works that fit into such a collection. There are a surprising number of art collectors in Des Moines, and in large part because of the Art Center, most of these collectors have a contemporary focus.

This guiding principle in purchasing art would have been impractical if it were not for the Coffin Fine Arts Trust, launched in time for the opening of the museum in 1948. The Coffin Trust far and away has been the major source of funds for art purchases. It was established exclusively for that purpose; operating expenditures are prohibited. Even at times when the Art Center has been hard pressed for operating funds, the collection has been able to grow.

Endowment funds derived from the Edmundson estate have never produced sufficient income to meet operating expenses. Additional support has come over the years through membership revenue, donations, bequests, and grants, including challenge grants from the National Endowment for the Humanities (1976) and the National Endowment for the Arts (1982). The first unrestricted bequest received by the Art Center came from the estate of Henry Frankel (1959); later important bequests came from Anna K. Meredith (1981) and Helen Urban (1985). The Jacqueline and Myron Blank Exhibition Fund established in 1987 helps finance the exhibitions program. The Cowles family (which includes the Kruidenier and Edwards families) has been providing support for four generations, and more recently significant endowment contributions were received from Martin and Melva Bucksbaum, and Pioneer Hi-Bred International, Inc. The museum relies on other sources of money, both public and private. In the early 1950s the City of Des Moines began making annual contributions; suburban communities followed in the early 1970s. These subsidies ceased in 1987 when the Art Center began receiving a share of the hotel/motel tax proceeds.

The Art Center offers more than the marriage of remarkable architecture and art. When the doors first opened in 1948, educational programs were integral and continue so to this day. Saarinen, who designed the esteemed Cranbook Academy of Art in Bloomfield Hills, Michigan, also designed the still bustling Art Center classrooms. Courses for all ages continue to be taught primarily by artists residing in this region. Many of Des Moines's adult residents not only visited the galleries as children, but took classes; today their children attend classes. These early bonds are continuously repaid in devoted volunteer support, financial contributions, and general good will. Rounding out the educational act-ivities are endowed lectures, concerts, films, and poetry readings.

The Art Center's commitment to education reaches far and wide into the community. Programs for children at risk and their families are ongoing activities. Scholarships allow classroom participation to be enjoyed by many. Teen docents involve their families and peers. Visiting artists and Art Center faculty and educational staff work in concert with neighborhood community centers, social-service agencies, and libraries.

Employing artists from this region as teachers is one of the ways in which the Art Center interacts with area artists. As well, the Art Center presents a major annual exhibition that traditionally has drawn works from around the State. From time to time works from these exhibitions enter the collections.

The combination of unified and sustained trustee and staff vision focused on quality; available funds for purchases; contributions from inspired donors and volunteers; the emphasis on works by living artists; viewing those works in extraordinary buildings contemporary with the art; and a zealous educational thrust have been and remain the driving forces that make the Art Center a model regional museum of international significance.

I. Michael Danoff
Former Director

Acknowledgments

From the beginning An Uncommon Vision has been a collaborative undertaking: it incorporates the results of numerous specialized studies, and it reflects the knowledge and opinions of experts in many fields. The instrumental roles that every trustee, staff member, volunteer and donor – past and present – have played in the growth of the collections and guidance of the Des Moines Art Center over the decades is evident throughout the pages of An Uncommon Vision. This book is impressive evidence of their judgment and dedication, but credit must go to I. Michael Danoff, whose role as director of the Art Center and passion for art provided the fundamental inspiration for this publication.

There was extensive collaboration in the choice of works and writing of the essays and entries for this book. We would like to express our appreciation to Louise Rosenfield Noun, a key voice in the rich history of the Art Center, who formulated an illuminating essay chronicling this institution's past. Franz Schulze's research about the Art Center's extraordinary architecture provides valuable insights and new information. Amy N. Worthen had the challenging task of providing, in one essay, an overview of approximately 3,000 examples of art on paper, highlighting particular works, and interweaving the strengths of the collection into the history of prints. And Christopher D. Roy's treatment of the Art Center's collection of tribal arts examined the role of particular objects within the context of their social value and usage.

The individual entries were prepared by a team of authors, most of whom are or were intently involved with the Art Center. These include three former directors, Julia Brown, I. Michael Danoff, and James T. Demetrion, and former curator Neal Benezra. In addition to myself, the Art Center's curatorial staff wrote entries, and they are: Lea Rosson DeLong, Teri A. Coate, Deborah Leveton, and Amy N. Worthen. David Cateforis and Terry Ann R. Neff prepared entries as well.

The editing of all the written material and its preparation for publication is Terry Neff's achievement. The institution and I are especially indebted to her. As mentor to this publication, she brought standards of editorial responsibility that provided a foundation of the highest quality. Without her enthusiasm, patience, and continuing encouragement, it would have been impossible to complete the publication.

To studio blue, a design team consisting of Kathy Fredrickson and Cheryl Towler Weese, I express gratitude for creating a superb design without sacrificing clarity and bringing a mastery of expertise to the production process.

To Paul Anbinder of Hudson Hills Press, I want to state how much his commitment to museum publishing is appreciated. We thank him for his support on this project.

In the course of more than three years' planning, many people have assisted in a variety of ways. Credit must be shared with numerous staff who, despite many other demands on their time, contributed to this book. My thanks especially go to C. Rita Luther, administrative assistant, who prepared multiple manuscript versions of the one hundred twenty entries and the five major essays. Rose Wood, registrar, and Geoffrey Dare, assistant registrar, spent substantial time working with authors and the photographers. Mary Morman-Graham, art librarian, provided essential support in research and documentation for several authors, and Susan Burgess, executive assistant, also assisted the project.

The extraordinary quality of the collections and caliber of architecture could not have been shown to such advantage without the photographs of the works of art taken by Michael Tropea of Michael Tropea Photography and photographs of the buildings taken by Steve Hall of Hedrich Blessing Photographers.

The Art Center is indebted for the early support of a grant from the National Endowment for the Arts. Also, this project received a handsome contribution from Sotheby's. Substantial donations from Carolyn S. and Matthew Bucksbaum, and from the Gardner and Florence Call Cowles Foundation, Inc. and the Kruidenier Charitable Foundation, Inc. have permitted us to do a book that does justice to a half-century of achievement.

Finally, these acknowledgments would not be complete without heartfelt gratitude to Melva Bucksbaum, who provided the major funding for this book from its early stages to conclusion. Through her confidence and generosity, the Art Center was able to take a fresh look at this institution and sustain this unique publication.

M. Jessica Rowe
Acting Director

Architectural trinity
in Des Moines

Franz Schulze

1

The pivotal moment in the history of the architecture of the Des Moines Art Center occurred on March 22, 1945, when the institution's trustees received Eliel Saarinen's latest and final proposal for the design of the building. Saarinen, seventy-two at the time, was an internationally renowned figure, widely recognized earlier in the century in his native Finland and more famous still during the years following his immigration to the United States in 1923 (fig. 1).

He was effectively the only architect subject to serious consideration for the Des Moines commission after his name was brought up in the center's councils early in 1944. The job did not, however, come easily into his hands, nor was it a certainty even after he submitted his last scheme. The center was a new entity, long anticipated but as yet without material form or professional focus. An organization known as the Des Moines Association of Fine Arts had operated off and on since 1916, offering the city exhibitions of art whenever it could. But a far more substantial creation was at last within reach. In the will of James D. Edmundson, a wealthy, self-educated Iowan who died at ninety-five in 1933, well over half a million dollars had been provided for the erection and maintenance of a museum, as well as the acquisition of artworks appropriate to it. The canny Edmundson, knowing how devalued his assets were during the Depression, when he drafted his will, also stipulated that his funds were to be held in trust until ten years after his passing.

The time had come. World War II was still raging in 1943, but the prospect of an Allied victory was nearly a foregone conclusion, and the leading citizens of Des Moines were ready to draw up plans for a building appropriate to a brave new postwar world.

Saarinen had attracted local attention several years earlier, in 1939, when his work was shown in the galleries of the Fine Arts Association. The featured exhibit was his design for the Smithsonian Art Gallery (fig. 3), a project that won first prize in a highly publicized national competition. It was a strikingly Modernist effort – long, low, flat-roofed, and rigorously abstracted, a marked divergence from the Neoclassical look that dominated the architecture of Federal Washington at the time. While Congress never voted the funds for it, it advanced Saarinen's name within the profession that had already been virtually unanimous in honoring him for another unbuilt work, his second-prize-winning proposal for the 1922 Chicago Tribune building competition, and for the brilliantly realized complex of schools, museum, library, and residences in Bloomfield Hills, Michigan, known collectively as Cranbrook Academy.

If the Smithsonian Art Gallery impressed itself favorably on a number of influential Des Moinians, it had an opposite effect on others.

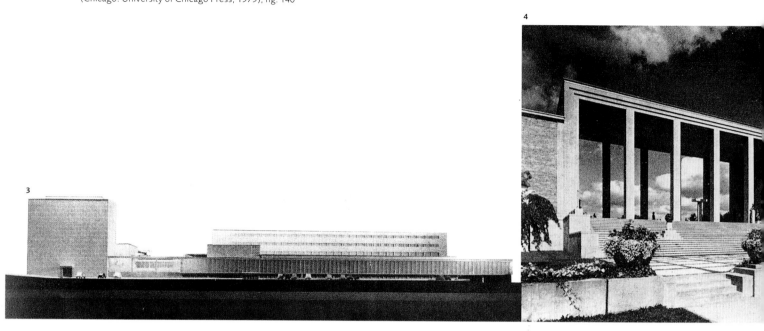

The 1940s, it is worth remembering a half-century later, was the decade in which American culture had its most affecting encounter with the Modernist point of view that originated mostly in Europe. The war thrust this country not only into the center of international politics, but into a confrontation with the global arts as well. The legion of foreign masters in all fields who sought refuge in the United States seized the attention of native artists and audiences alike. Battle lines were drawn, separating converts to the new Modernism from conservatives more attached to tradition.

The debate was stirred up among the citizens responsible for creating the new art center. In the preliminary planning stages, the Edmundson trustees approached several architects, all of whose proposals were only briefly considered, thus leading to the first contact with Saarinen. It was a move not reached unanimously. One of the trustees found the exterior of the museum at Cranbrook "hideous,"[1] and even after Saarinen submitted his first plan for the center, it was met in some quarters with unalloyed hostility, several trustees likening its Modernistic look to that of a factory and others complaining "how terrible they thought [it] was; that it was all right for Hollywood, but not for Des Moines; that Saarinen was a Nazi at heart and we would not be regimented in this country."[2]

Happily these proved to be minority sentiments. The acceptance of Saarinen's final plan on that decisive day in March 1945 not only certified him as the architect of the building, but signaled that the Des Moines Art Center had ruled against "an imitation of Greek, Gothic or English architecture," committing itself instead to "the best type of architecture of the period in which the museum is built…. Any style different from what we are used to may seem strange at first, but this building will be judged by succeeding generations, and it must satisfy them or it will soon be obsolete."[3]

In its half-century of existence, the center's steadfast support of that principle is manifest in the continued integrity of Saarinen's structure as well as the merit and compatibility of the two additions by architects of equal stature, I.M. Pei in 1968 and Richard Meier in 1985. What amounts to a collaboration among three independent and strong-minded spirits has resulted in one of the most arresting examples of museum architecture in the United States. A further concurrence derives from the relationship between the outstanding trio of buildings and the center's art collection, which ranks with the best of its counterparts in American museums of comparable size. The response of public and experts alike has confirmed that the act of viewing first-rate painting and sculpture in a surpassing architectural environment at Des Moines is an experience more compelling than the sum of its parts.

Eliel Saarinen, Des Moines Art Center:
first scheme, comprehensive layout with
theater and amphitheater, 1944; photograph
taken from Christ-Janer, fig. 165

Eliel Saarinen was granted a major advantage from the outset in the site of his new structure. Greenwood Park, a handsomely hilly, wooded acreage, prompted him to build on the crest of its gentle slopes, thus guaranteeing the museum optimal visibility to anyone approaching west on Grand Avenue from downtown Des Moines. Saarinen also accommodated his design to several of the wishes of his clients, most notably that "the building should be low so as to hug the ground and become part of the existing landscape."[4] The instruction seems to have been easy for him to follow, since he adhered to the shallow profile and flat roof of the Smithsonian Art Gallery project, thus reinforcing the desired sense of horizontality.

The flat roof is one of the hallmarks of Modern architecture, especially of the species that became known as the International Style: a lean, rectilinear, ornament-free manner that dominated the early Modern movement in Europe during the 1920s and began to transform architecture in the United States at about the time Saarinen commenced working on the Art Center. While he yielded somewhat to the International Style in Des Moines, he never qualified as one of its devotees. Even in the late additions at Cranbrook, finished in the early 1940s, the most palpably Modernist passages still acknowledge tradition in the form of abstract ornamental reliefs and classicizing columns (fig. 4).

One of Saarinen's preliminary schemes for Des Moines illustrates this predisposition (fig. 5). It features a colonnaded entry on the east, reachable by a double flight of formal stairs, an image obviously indebted to the propylaealike gateway that links museum and library at Cranbrook. The drawing of the Des Moines building makes it appear horizontal enough, but not so low as the finished structure; moreover, a blocklike tower shown to the south was never realized. There is also the suggestion of a flat, smoothly dressed wall, very unlike the cladding of Lannon stone shown in a drawing of the final building.

The stone was another request of the trustees met by Saarinen. Even though he had never employed it in any of his previous work, he seemed at home with it, probably because his partner (and son-in-law), J. Robert F. Swanson, who worked with him at Des Moines, had used Lannon stone in an earlier building, the Flynn Memorial at Belle Isle, in Detroit. Indeed anyone exploring the grounds around the museum might presume that Saarinen was the designer of the engaging axial walkway that leads southward and downward from the museum to a lagoon (fig. 6). The path is flanked by a row of pylons in the same Lannon stone as the building. It is punctuated by a small clearing surrounding a spherical sundial that rests, like the earth in the ancient Hindu myth, on the back of a tortoise said to be the second avatar of Vishnu, which supported the world while gods churned the seas. It is a charming piece of whimsy, typical of

Eliel Saarinen, Des Moines Art Center: early
perspective drawing (by Saarinen), 1944;
photograph taken from Christ-Janer, fig. 166

6

7

the pleasure Saarinen took in figurative decora-
tion, and together with the stone, it is enough
to suggest that the pathway was done either
by him or someone faithful to the manner he
employed in this building.

This turns out a faulty presumption. Photographs
of the pylons complete and intact before ground
was cleared for the Art Center prove that the
building bowed to the pylons, not the other
way around.

In the plan of his own building, Saarinen
remained free to stray from the constraints of
axiality as surely as to follow them. The aforementioned preliminary scheme of the center discloses a rambling layout which, though later
modified, endures to this day. In its very informality it represented a bold departure from the
institutionally corseted look that had long been
taken for granted in American museum design. It
is shown in an early drawing (fig. 7) as a U-shaped
organization of foyer, galleries, and an auditorium
addressing a reflecting pool that provides the
visitor with a diverting moment of visual relax-
ation as it surveys the pathway to the south.
Eastward from the fly tower over the stage of
the auditorium, the education wing would have
curved slightly to the south before jogging
sharply, still southward, and ending in an outdoor theater. In built form the plan contains most
of the original spaces and preserves the overall
directions, although the latter have been
tamed somewhat by right angles and straight lines

(fig. 8). With the theater removed, the school
wing is still bent, but northward now, to embrace
a parking lot. One explanation for the modesty
of the final form relative to the more ambitious
preliminary scheme would be an unforeseen
reduction in the budget. A more purposeful
alternative was offered up in the July 1949 issue
of Architectural Forum: "Early in its planning,
there was much discussion of the basic problem:
whether this center should be a monumentally
formal and conspicuous structure in the urban
organism or whether it should be an informal
home institution for art activities, imbedded in
the verdure of the park."[5] The two possible
explanations can coexist. If by eliminating
the colonnade and lowering the profile of the
building Saarinen saved money, he also achieved
the ends the trustees had enunciated in their
final prospectus.

In any case, what the visitor encounters today
is not only Saarinen at his most sensitive, and
programmatically responsive, but a building
changed hardly at all from the one that viewers
saw in June 1948 when the center was opened
to the public. The auditorium has found a new
home in the Pei addition, but its consequent
replacement by galleries has increased the space
for the exhibition of paintings, drawings, and
prints and created a more generously propor-
tioned interior plan.

Eliel Saarinen, Des Moines Art Center:
entrance gallery, 1948

Eliel Saarinen, Des Moines Art Center:
final drawing, plan of main floor, 1944; photograph taken from Christ-Janer, fig. 168

8

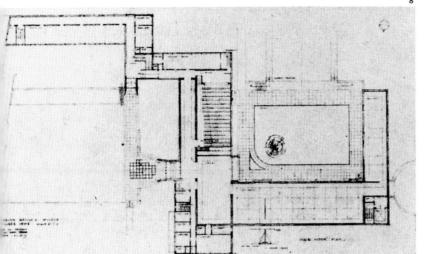

9

The volume and detailing of the Saarinen foyer set the tone for all that follows even now (fig. 9). An amplitude of space is kept free of the weight of monumentality by the warmth of rift-grain oak walls whose panels are joined by lineaments just bold enough to recall Saarinen's constitutional inclination toward ornament. Directly across from the entry is a tall glass wall enclosing a door that leads west to the shimmering reflecting pool. It supplies most of the natural illumination of the foyer, while a measure of artificial light washes the walls from cunningly designed coves in the ceiling. The main galleries, which bend west, then again south, are similarly lit, with additional candlepower from downlighting canisters. These rooms accommodate most of the art on public view at any one time, and one is less conscious of their considerable length than of the lively paths threaded through them by panels freely but judiciously placed at right angles to their main axes. Short frontal and diagonal views of the works mix with longer perspectives in a happily unforced arrangement that helps each painting and sculpture retain its individuality rather than lose it in the gathering company of its neighbors. And again, the materials: walls variously covered with plaster, monk's cloth, and concrete block, and floors of wide-planked oak more rugged than standard hardwood yet more in keeping with the informality of the place.

Reaching the end of the west gallery, the visitor in the years prior to the Pei addition would have made his way clockwise back around the U-shape toward the entry, tempted to interrupt his perambulations to exit the north bank of galleries, or the foyer, to tarry at the reflecting pool. The openness of this courtyard area introduces a note of serenity to the whole, although there is drama there too, in the form of a single artwork: a massive, tautly energetic figurative bronze by the Swedish émigré Carl Milles, Man and Pegasus. It is another reprise of Cranbrook, where at the head of a long descending series of pools Milles had earlier placed another piece, Europa and the Bull, drawn from the mythology so dear to the hearts of the two Scandinavian friends and colleagues.

The remaining portion of the Saarinen structure is the education wing, which houses a tidy, disciplined row of studios serving the needs of children and adults alike. Its inclusion in the program fulfilled a special personal priority of the architect that developed in his years of teaching at the University of Michigan in Ann Arbor and at Cranbrook Academy. He not only allotted it a spacious floor area, but sited it at the center's southeast flank, where it extends with maximal visibility toward Grand Avenue.

Saarinen lived only two years after completing his building. It served its public well enough that nearly two decades passed before the need for additional space and technically upgraded functions grew pressing enough to be acted upon.

I. M. Pei, 1996

10

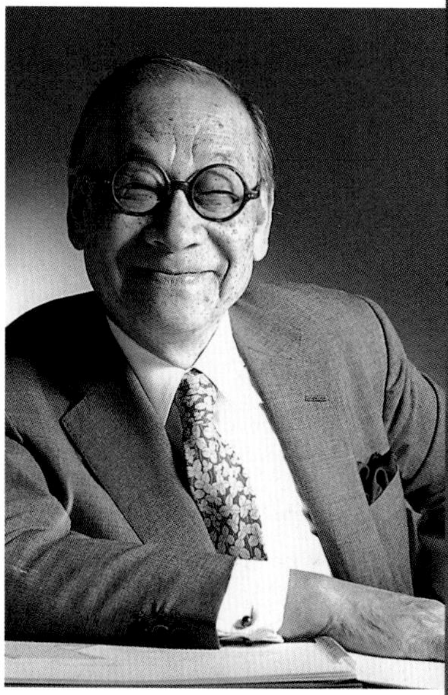

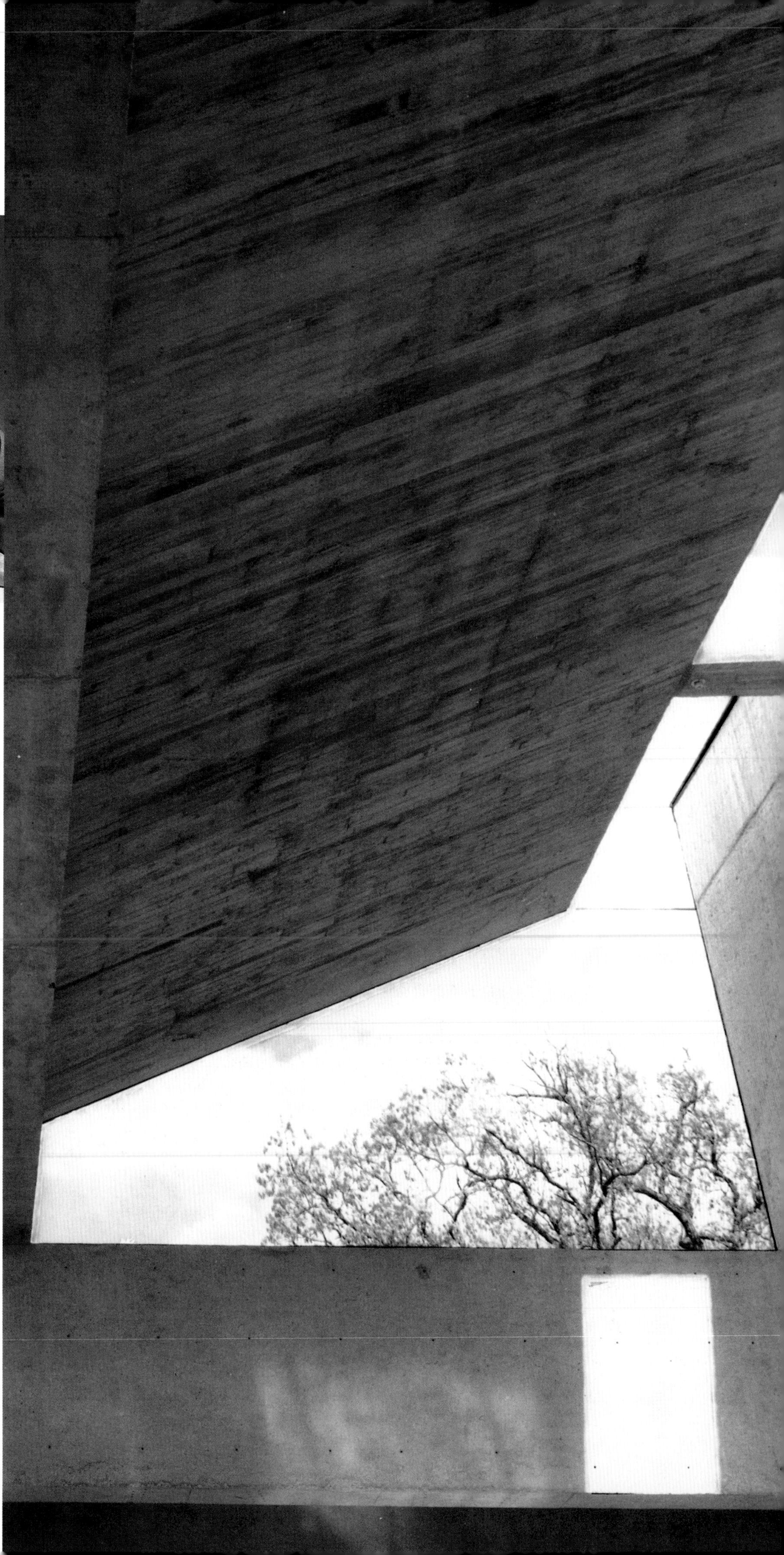

I. M. Pei, National Center for
Atmospheric Research, near Boulder,
Colorado, 1961–67

Des Moines Art Center, I. M. Pei
wing: detail of interior with butterfly-
sectioned roof, 1968

The 1960s were an appropriate time for the expansion. American artists as a collective had responded so enthusiastically to their postwar lessons in Modernism that within a generation they had taken over the leadership of the international art world. Abstract Expressionism grew into the dominant movement of the 1950s and Pop Art together with a second major wave of abstraction maintained the new momentum. While these developments were initially associated with painting, sculptors asserted themselves in short order, and a similar scenario was acted out in architecture.

As this period of American artistic success crested, the Des Moines Art Center elected to build a full-scale new wing, not only to keep pace with the quickened national tempo, but specifically to exhibit sculpture, a medium whose three-dimensionality required walk-around space. The commission went to I. M. Pei, a native Chinese educated in America who became one of the most favored designers of art museums in the 1960s and succeeding decades (fig. 10). Like the Everson Museum of Art in Syracuse and the Herbert F. Johnson Museum of Art at Cornell University in Ithaca, New York, the Des Moines Art Center grew out of Pei's famous design for the huge National Center for Atmospheric Research, constructed between 1961 and 1967 on the slopes of the Rocky Mountains near Boulder, Colorado (fig. 12). NCAR is a complex of stern concrete forms so organized that an interplay of walls and lintels framing deep indentations produces a massive, asymmetrical solid geometry.

The Des Moines wing is smaller, but it is composed with a comparable emphasis on fullness of scale, a property appropriate to its function. Since one of the most identifying features of international postwar art is its tendency toward large size, the exhibition of sculpture called for nothing less than a setting of comparably generous dimensions.

The Pei wing was built across the axis that runs from the reflecting pool to the pylon-flanked pathway on the south. Thus it fills in Saarinen's U-shaped plan, completing a square and facilitating a circular tour of the interior. It is two stories in height, with access from the Saarinen building to a roofed upper court, a tall space that overlooks the lower court from a balcony transverse to the wing's long axis. The part of the lower court directly beneath the upper is occupied by the new auditorium.

This is the barest description of the plan, none of it doing justice to the effect of the whole work, to the concerted logic of its function and the related inventiveness of its articulation. By building on ground that drifts downward from the Saarinen courtyard, Pei managed to create two levels of space without overlording the older structure. Since his addition is largely concealed on the Grand Avenue approach by the original building, the best view of it is gained from the north edge of the reflecting pool, which itself has been reconstituted (fig. 13). Now at a depth of six

13

14

inches rather than the three feet Saarinen assigned it, it is shallower, safer, and cleaner, with a pavement of cobblestones that radiate outward and impressively from the base of the Milles sculpture. Here, on the north apron of the pool, the Pei facade fills one's field of vision. Its pattern of straight-line geometry recalls the NCAR complex, but its individuality is secured by a contrasting rounded protrusion that extends boldly forward into the court. It is an element effective in the most fulfilling architectural sense for it provides a moving formal contrast to both the rectilinearity and planarity of the wall from which it emerges, while functioning as the housing of the stairway that leads with ease and convenience from the upper court to the corridor bordering the auditorium downstairs.

The Pei interior is arguably the most moving passage in the entire center (fig. 14). Again, it does double duty, as a building form unto itself and a showcase for artworks. Nothing about it is more memorable than the way natural light has been made an expressive component of the interior space. Pei has designed a V-shaped, butterfly-sectioned roof (fig. 11) that admits copious quantities of light, but indirectly, with the result that the exhibited objects, while always fully discernible, present themselves in shifting aspects as the sun moves across the sky. An astonishing sensuosity makes itself felt here, as sculptural matter – stone, steel, wood, mixed media – changes and seems to come alive. Architecturally, moreover, a similar transformation occurs on the surfaces of the walls, floors, and ceiling.[6]

Pei's handling of these last structural components, as well as his overall way with illumination, recalls Le Corbusier's famous definition of architecture as "the masterly, correct and magnificent play of masses brought together in light."[7] The effect produced by the balcony comes to mind, not only in the exhilarating explosion of space that the downward view sets off, but in the light that enters through the great southern windows. A long footbridge on the west flank of the space (fig. 15) as a whole connects the balcony to the fetching circular stair leading downward to the lower court. The stair is just visible enough from the opposite end of the bridge to charm the viewer into examining it, whereupon walking down it seems the only sensible thing to do. And even before reaching the intimately scaled stair, he will have been struck by the magnitude of the vertical window in front of him, through which the old formal path leading to the lagoon can be seen and visually traced.

Another stair at the north edge of the lower court beckons him upward again, its angle echoing the huge double tilt of the roof and adding diagonals to the lively exchange already taking place between horizontals and verticals.

The auditorium remains to be explored, and there Pei used consonances and contrasts to typically good effect (fig. 16). The round-ended projection booth, reminiscent of the aforementioned

Des Moines Art Center, I. M. Pei wing:
detail of interior, 1968

Des Moines Art Center,
I. M. Pei wing: detail of interior,
sculpture gallery, 1968

Des Moines Art Center, I. M. Pei wing:
auditorium, 1968

15

16

staircase-extension into the reflecting pool, is a
convexity opposed here by the flanking concave
niches at the top of the auditorium steps that
function as conversation pits for intermission
audiences.

Inside and out, the walls are built of bushham-
mered concrete in keeping with one of the stylistic architectural tendencies of the 1960s,
brutalism, a term that stood with implied affirmation for the kind of consciously coarse masonry
used here. It might seem, then, that Pei would be
at expressive odds with Saarinen, whose natural
inclination was more nearly one of gentleness
and refinement. But the two manners harmonize,
not only in tonality, but because the Lannon
stone in the hands of Saarinen and his partner,
Swanson, provided a model of rough texture
that links the older to the newer building with no
apparent discord.

The exterior of the Pei addition makes much the
same potent impression as the interior. Its principal face, on the south, features a composition of
horizontal and vertical members framing deeply
shaded window indentations. The image projected, especially at night when light from within
turns the wall into a perceived plane, may recall
the geometric abstractions of the painter Piet
Mondrian, although some critics more mindful of
the architectonic character of the whole structure have suggested a more direct connection to
the massing of the buildings Le Corbusier put
up in India shortly before the Des Moines wing
was designed.[8]

Des Moines Art Center, Richard Meier
north wing: detail of west
elevation, 1985

17

Surely Le Corbusier is cited by nearly everyone writing
about the work of the architect who in 1985
added a third major component to the design of
the Art Center. Richard Meier (fig. 18) gained
national attention as a member of the so-called
"Whites," a group of five younger Americans
whose creative reworking of the Corbusian style
of the 1920s was documented in a 1972 exhibition at New York's Museum of Modern Art. Meier
has consistently maintained his stylistic alle-
giance to the Swiss-French master, as his use of
curves and straights mixed on a high-keyed
palette at Des Moines attests. Nonetheless, his
addition to the Art Center (fig. 17) is personal
enough to be recognizable as his own and trace-
able to one of his previous works.

He had such a linkage in common with his prede-
cessors at Des Moines. Just as Saarinen derived
his design largely from his earlier Smithsonian
Art Gallery project, and Pei returned to the
motifs of his NCAR complex, Meier drew several
crucial formative ideas from his widely heralded
1983 High Museum of Art in Atlanta (fig. 19).
There, in an extraordinary gesture, Meier organized the plan into four quadrants, partially
separating one from the other three. The space
created by the division was opened into a four-
story-high atrium bordered by ramps that give
onto galleries and auxiliary spaces. The similarities this program bears to Meier's work at Des

Richard Meier, High Museum of Art,
Atlanta, 1983

Moines are palpable. Most obviously, he has separated the parts into three fully distinct structures that attach to the Saarinen-Pei building at points close to existing axes. One of the parts, moreover, which includes the atrium, is especially indebted to the High Museum model.

These resemblances notwithstanding, Meier's effort at Des Moines grew out of conditions specific to its setting. The 28,000 square feet required in the commission implied a large addition, which, if treated as a unit, would have overpowered all it was meant to unite with. Bearing this in mind, Meier joined a wing of modest dimensions, containing gallery, storage, and service space, to the west wing of the Saarinen building, and insinuated a restaurant block into the northwest corner of the courtyard. Thus the remaining structure, intended to house the permanent collection and temporary exhibitions of contemporary art, could be free of other functions and restricted to a comfortably manageable size relative to its neighbors.

The architect made what he called a conscious effort to keep his three structures deferential to the original Saarinen building, even isolating the largest of them at a distance to the north that required a connecting, glass-enclosed corridor. Nonetheless, Meier's inventive way with the

massing of his building elements is hard to miss. In the largest of them, the north structure, an almost dizzying intricacy of contours, with looping, sinuous curves moving both vertically and horizontally against an assortment of rectilinearities, relies greatly for stabilization on the cubic granite block that rises above its dependencies to anchor the whole (fig. 20). The pyramidal cap of the block acts as a foil to the concavely sectioned roof of the Pei addition, while the atrium within is dominated by a staircase that performs a sweeping quarter circle (fig. 21), providing for very tall works and leading as well to a series of peripheral exhibition halls, rooms, even crannylike areas. The granite cladding of the block is counterposed against the bright, porcelain-coated metal skin of the dependencies. Balconies and patios are added on the outside of the building, with each side of the elevation compositionally unique.

The formal relationship of all three Meier wings is ensured by the use in each of a central cube encased in curvilinearly defined volumes. It is a kinship sufficient to avoid any conflict in differences of scale, especially in the contrast between the north wing and the smallest, the little restaurant-meeting room volume that is tucked into the corner of the courtyard. The intimate grace of the latter structure adds to its sociability, with further credit going to the decision to place it at that very spot. For the view out the curving window-wall discloses the pool, the Milles sculpture, the Pei addition, and part of the east wing of the Saarinen building (fig. 22). The works of the

20

21

sculptor and the three architects are united here,
a confluence appropriate to a space that makes
the pleasures of eating, drinking, and repose all
the more refreshing.

With the completion of Eliel Saarinen's design in
1948, the Des Moines Art Center established a
significant Modernist alternative to the traditional
architectural concept of the small American art
museum. That special rank has been underscored
in the later additions by I.M. Pei and Richard
Meier, each effort distinguished in its own right,
and both, together with the Saarinen original,
adding up to a complex as enduringly elegant as
it is demonstrably innovative. Yet the very distinction of the center's architecture has made the
art it is meant to serve all the more compelling:
the nineteenth- and twentieth-century painting
hanging in the amiable atmosphere of the
Saarinen structure; the large scale of the sculpture – and the painting – that enjoy the expansive
space of the Pei wing; the challenging variety of
contemporary expression that fills all levels of the
Meier. At the outset of its second half-century,
Des Moines continues to occupy a singular place
in any transcontinental museum tour.

Des Moines Art Center: view of
Richard Meier restaurant-meeting
room (center) with I. M. Pei wing (left)
and Eliel Saarinen wing (right)

22

1   Fred W. Hubbell, a trustee of the
    Edmundson Memorial Foundation,
    letter to fellow trustee Forest
    Huttenlocher, October 24, 1944.
2   Forest Huttenlocher, letter to fellow
    trustee J. N. Darling, January 9, 1945.
    Huttenlocher attributed these opin-
    ions to trustees Paul Beer and F. W.
    Hubbell of the foundation's building
    committee. Historian Louise Rosenfield
    Noun, in a letter of July 20, 1996 to the
    author, reported that she later met Paul
    Beer at the 1948 opening of the Art
    Center. Beer had apparently changed
    his mind about Saarinen. Noun: "I
    asked him how he liked the building.
    'The man is a genius,' he said."
3   **Studies of Historic Iowa Architecture
    Part 2: Des Moines Art Center** (Ames,
    Iowa: Engineering Research Institute,
    Iowa State University, Ames, Iowa, July
    1975), p. 8, reporting on the minutes of
    the special meeting of the Edmundson
    Memorial Foundation trustees,
    November 7, 1944.
4   Ibid., p. 7, reporting on the minutes of
    the annual meeting of the Edmundson
    Memorial Foundation trustees, June 6,
    1944.
5   **Architectural Forum** 91, 1 (July 1949),
    pp. 67–69.

6   In a conversation with the author,
    August 22, 1996, David Kruidenier,
    a trustee of the Art Center, recalled a
    visit to I. M. Pei's office in 1966 at
    which the architect was offered the
    Des Moines commission. "He took out
    a piece of tracing paper on the spot,"
    Kruidenier reported, "and in ten or
    fifteen minutes had sketched a plan
    and elevation so close to the final prod-
    uct that the sheer act of creativity left
    me breathless."
7   Le Corbusier, **Towards a New
    Architecture** (Paris: Editions Cres,
    1923), trans. Frederick Etchells
    (London: Architectural Press, 1927),
    p. 31.
8   See "Des Moines Art Center: Ein
    Museum mit drei Architekten,"
    Baumeister (Munich), January 1987,
    pp. 52–57.

The history of the
of the
Des Moines Art
Center

Louise Rosenfield Noun

2

James D. Edmundson plaque by Christian Petersen, c. 1948. The inscription, as specified in Edmundson's will, reads: "This art museum was founded by a citizen of Des Moines who bequeathed funds for its establishment as a gift to the citizens of Des Moines and to the people of his native state."

1

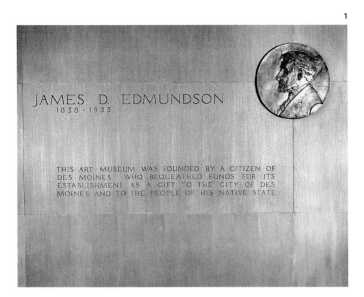

THE DES MOINES
ASSOCIATION
OF FINE ARTS
FOUNDED 1916

HOURS OF OPENING
WEEKDAYS 12 N. TO 5 P.M.
WEDNESDAYS UNTIL 9 P.M.
SUNDAYS 2 P.M. TO 5 P.M.
CLOSED ON HOLIDAYS

FREE OF CHARGE

Antecedents. The opening of the Des Moines Art Center on June 2, 1948 meant the culmination of more than three decades of planning and work on the part of a group of women and men who looked forward to having a museum in the city. Spurred by the revelation that seventy-eight-year-old James D. Edmundson (see fig. 1), a wealthy citizen, planned to bequeath funds for such an institution, the Des Moines Association of Fine Arts was established in 1916 under the leadership of J.S. (Sanny) Carpenter, a bridge builder who was the leading art collector in the city (see fig. 2). The purpose of the association was to bring exhibitions to Des Moines and to acquire works of art to be placed in the future museum. Initial funds came from a grant of $1,500 from the Greater Des Moines Committee, a group composed of business leaders in the city. Annual membership dues of $100 were set aside for the purchase of works of art, and the dues of members paying smaller amounts were used to cover operating expenses. The Des Moines Public Library located at First and Locust provided a gallery on the second floor for touring shows booked by Carpenter.

The first exhibition sponsored by the Fine Arts Association consisted of 300 contemporary paintings by French and Belgian artists which had been shown two years previously at the Panama-Pacific International Exposition in San Francisco. This exhibition filled all available space at the library and was viewed by large crowds. At the end of the first year of operation, the association had forty-eight patron members, but found itself without sufficient funds to cover operating costs. The following year, with the help of the Des Moines Women's Club, the Greater Des Moines Committee, and the Chamber of Commerce, the association was able to bring four exhibitions to the city. From that time until the early 1930s, the association, under Carpenter's guidance, continued to bring several exhibitions each year.

Most of the works shown were by living Americans who were relatively well established, and considered modern, that is, vaguely Impressionist, but not avant-garde. Neither American nor European Modernist works were exhibited. It was from these exhibitions that purchases were made, not only by the association but by private individuals as well. The association's first purchase was Woodland Brook, a painting by Edward Redfield, acquired in 1917. From that time until 1930 the association purchased twenty-two more oils, the most notable being Christ Walking on the Water by Henry Ossawa

Entrance to the Des Moines Association
of Fine Arts Gallery at 610 1/2 Walnut
Street, c. 1940.

In 1941 the WPA took over management of the Des Moines Association of Fine Arts Gallery at 610 1/2 Walnut Street and the name changed to Des Moines Art Center. Photograph courtesy Des Moines Art Center.

3

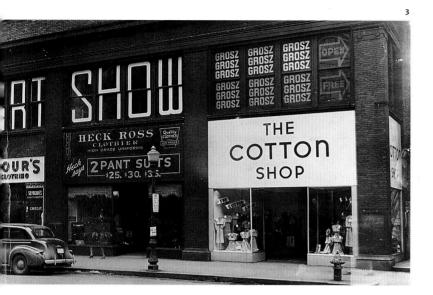

Tanner, acquired in 1921, and Ballet Girl in White by Robert Henri, acquired in 1927. All these works, along with a few drawings and prints and one sculpture, were eventually given to the Des Moines Art Center. A number of purchases made by association members also eventually went into the Art Center's collection; for example, the very fine The Hour of Tea by Frederick Carl Frieseke, which was among eighteen paintings given by Florence Carpenter in 1941 in memory of her recently deceased husband, and A Path at Ste. Brelade by Théodore Van Rysselberghe, a 1964 bequest of William and Edith King Pearson.[1] The prize of the Carpenter collection was George Bellows's Aunt Fanny, which was purchased from Mrs. Carpenter with Edmundson funds in 1942. Sanny Carpenter bought this painting in 1920 directly from the artist while the paint was still wet on the canvas.

Only six paintings acquired by the Fine Arts Association have stood the test of time and remain in the Art Center's permanent collection. With the exception of one painting that was sold in 1951, the remaining sixteen were sold at auction in 1990 during Julia Brown Turrell's directorship. Eight of the artists whose paintings were sold are still represented in the collection by works considered superior in quality.

Activities of the Des Moines Association of Fine Arts came to a halt with the onset of the Depression in the early 1930s, but in 1938 a group of members wishing to keep the association alive until the museum became a reality, launched a successful membership drive. The second floor of an old two-story building (reached by an outside stairway) at 610 1/2 Walnut Street was rented (fig. 3). Galleries and studios were constructed with labor donated by the painters' and carpenters' unions and materials furnished by local businesses. Paul Harris was hired as the association's first professional director. The gallery opened in the fall of 1938 with an exhibition of work by Des Moines artist Russell Cowles and one of fifty prints by Works Project Administration (WPA) artists. Other exhibitions during Harris's tenure (1938–40) included prints by Käthe Kollwitz, Old Master drawings, Daumier lithographs, and photographs by Louis Hine. An exhibition of ten winning designs in a competition for a new Smithsonian Art Gallery in Washington, DC included the entry of Eliel and Eero Saarinen and served to introduce the work of this father-son team to Des Moines. No works of art were purchased during Harris's tenure.

In March 1941 the WPA took over management of the gallery in cooperation with the Des Moines Association of Fine Arts. It was renamed the Des Moines Art Center and its program was greatly expanded. Art instruction for both children and adults became, for the first time, an important part of the gallery's activities – as reflected in its new name. WPA sponsorship lasted until sometime in 1943.[2] The Des Moines Association of Fine Arts continued to operate the Walnut Street quarters until 1945, when it voluntarily dissolved and turned over its assets to the Edmundson Art Foundation, which had been established under the will of James D. Edmundson who died in 1933.

Edmundson bequest. James D. Edmundson's will provided $300,000 for the erection of a museum building; $200,000 for an endowment fund; and $100,000 for the purchase of works of art "for exhibition, free of charge for admission, for at least three days in each week including Sunday, and all legal holidays." Edmundson also left the remainder of his estate, after payment of certain other bequests, for unrestricted museum purposes. Because his estate contained more than 8,500 acres of farm land which was depressed in value, Edmundson provided that no museum funds could be distributed for at least ten years after his death. This waiting period, followed by a delay in construction caused by World War II, meant that the Art Center was not completed until June 1948. After payment of construction costs, the Edmundson bequest to the Art Center amounted to more than a million and a half dollars.

Edmundson, a reclusive lawyer, real-estate investor, and scholar, was born in a log cabin near Burlington in 1838 when Iowa was still a territory. He lived in Council Bluffs for many years before moving to Des Moines at the turn of the century. His will named thirty-five men, any nine of whom were empowered to form a corporation bearing his name, to receive and administer the museum funds. This corporation was organized in 1935 under the name of the Edmundson Memorial Foundation with Jay N. Darling, noted conservationist and cartoonist, as president. The corporation currently operates under the name of the Edmundson Art Foundation, Inc., with a self-perpetuating, rotating board of twenty-five members. Former board members serve as honorary members with no power to determine Art Center policy.

The Edmundson will stipulated that the museum could not be built east of West Fourteenth Street unless the smoke nuisance in Des Moines, caused by heating with soft coal, had sufficiently abated so that there was no danger of injury from this source to the building or its contents. This provision caused the Edmundson trustees to abandon plans to build on property on East First Street which had been acquired by the city as a museum site. In 1940, at the request of the trustees, the city designated land in Greenwood Park for the building. John Woolson Brooks, a Des Moines architect, was asked to draw preliminary plans. Four years later, after lively and often heated discussion about the style of architecture for the new museum, the trustees hired Eliel Saarinen, the noted Finnish architect, to design the structure.

In planning the museum, the trustees wisely decided to make it more than an institution for preserving and showing works of art. In addition to exhibition galleries, the building had an auditorium for lectures and the performing arts; a library; and a meeting room with kitchen facilities for use by community groups.[3] The Saarinen plans also provided for a two-story education wing with studios for printmaking, painting, ceramics, and other arts.

In 1945 Paul Parker, an artist who was director of the Colorado Springs Fine Arts Center, was hired as director of the Des Moines Art Center. His job was to help with developing plans for the museum, establishing policies, and preparing for the opening of the new building. In 1946 the trustees created the Des Moines Art Center Association, a subsidiary board which was to be responsible for membership recruitment and for operation of the museum. This board, headed by Florence Cowles Kruidenier, was composed of former board members of the Des Moines Association of Fine Arts. The Edmundson trustees, however, retained control of finances, the selection of personnel, and the acquisition of works of art.

Boys looking at Mary Cassatt's La Toilette
at an Art Center opening, 1948.
Photograph by Frances Shloss, courtesy
Des Moines Art Center.

5

Early controversies. The Art Center opened in Greenwood Park in June 1948 with a large exhibition of nineteenth- and twentieth-century European and American art, and a special section devoted to the work of Iowa artists (see fig. 4). However, management problems quickly overshadowed this high-quality show. The Art Center Association felt it lacked sufficient authority to function satisfactorily and, as a consequence, asked that it be amalgamated with the Edmundson board. The Edmundson trustees, fearing that the operating board was too sympathetic to modern art for their generally conservative taste, and reluctant to have women as fellow board members, rejected the proposal. The problem of a single board was solved when all the members of the operating board resigned, thus forcing the trustees to assume responsibility for the center's operation. The trustees soon found that they needed female volunteers to help run the membership campaign, and in 1950 the first women were added to their board.

Concurrent with the 1948 controversy over the two-board setup was a serious disagreement between Paul Parker and the Edmundson trustees over the director's authority relating to acquisitions of works. While museums generally acquire works of art only on the recommendation of their directors, the Edmundson trustees, distrustful of Parker's taste for modern art, refused to follow this procedure. When they accepted a gift of a painting without consulting him, Parker resigned. He also cited the two-board structure as an unworkable situation. Since Parker's departure, the Edmundson trustees have followed accepted museum practice for acquisitions: the director presents proposed gifts or purchases to an acquisitions committee for consideration and then reports the committee's recommendations to the board for final action.

Funds for the purchase of art were available from two sources: the Edmundson bequest of $100,000 for art acquisitions, and the bequest of Winnie Ewing Coffin who died in 1937 (fig. 5). Coffin's will provided that the major part of her estate be put into a trust, the income from which was to be used for the purchase of works of art in memory of her husband, Nathan Emory Coffin. Her will explicitly stated that no part of the bequest be applied toward operating costs. The Coffin bequest amounted to $750,000 and has increased substantially since that time.

6

Acquisitions and exhibitions. In the early years of the
Art Center, there was considerable tension
between those who wanted to build a collection
with works of art representative of the past and
those who believed that the Art Center should concentrate on twentieth-century art. Parker recommended that about half of the money available for
acquisitions "be spent on the work of living artists,
mostly American, and the other half on works of
the past 150 years."[4] He observed that paintings
by important Old Masters were too expensive for
the museum to collect and he argued against the
purchase of minor older works, stating that "if a
work is of small stature when it was created, the
addition of centuries will not enhance the quality."
However, no substantial funds for acquisitions
were made available to Parker.

Richard F. Howard, a Harvard-trained art historian
who succeeded Parker in 1948, had been involved
with the US Army's program of repatriating art
confiscated by the Nazi government in Germany. In
contrast to Parker, Howard recommended that not
more than $5,000 a year of the Edmundson fund be
used to purchase works, primarily American, from
exhibitions shown at the Art Center. Coffin funds
should be designated to "purchase objects…other
than contemporary art with the aim of making the
Coffin Memorial a small cross-section indicative
of the history of art…."[5] The first Coffin fund purchases were made in 1949 when more than twenty

works – including ancient Egyptian sculpture, a
Byzantine medallion, medieval sculpture, ecclesias-
tical accouterments, a Deruta plate, and a Native
American jar – were acquired in accordance with
this objective. These pieces, some of value and
others questionable, have since been deaccessioned
and sold. During Howard's brief stay at the Art
Center, the familiar bronze, Man and Pegasus, by
the Swedish sculptor Carl Milles, was installed in
the pool adjacent to the museum. This work was
the gift of Florence Call Cowles, an artist in her
own right who was the wife Gardner Cowles, Sr.,
owner of The Des Moines Register.

Howard was succeeded in 1950 by Dwight Kirsch,
an artist who was director of the Sheldon Museum at
the University of Nebraska (fig. 6). His reputation
was built on the high quality of the contemporary
American art that he bought for the Sheldon.
Kirsch's eight-year administration at the Art Center
brought much-needed stability and greater focus
to its acquisitions program. His purchases concentrated primarily on nineteenth-century European
and twentieth-century American art with an
emphasis on painting and sculpture. Among the
significant works of older contemporary Americans
acquired with Edmundson funds during Kirsch's
tenure were Alexander Calder's mobile Black
Spread, Yasuo Kuniyoshi's Amazing Juggler, and
Edward Hopper's well-known Automat. Purchases
made with Coffin trust funds were almost entirely of
European origin: Auguste Rodin, Camille Pissarro,
Gustave Courbet, Honoré Daumier, and Francisco
Goya. The Goya painting, a full-length portrait cost-

ing $130,000, was purchased in large part to satisfy those who thought the Art Center should own a work by an important Old Master which would dazzle the public. This work only partially served its purpose, and when the Art Center declined the offer of a group of minor Old Master works from the Kress Foundation, a policy of acquiring mainly nineteenth- and twentieth-century works was implicitly affirmed.

During the Kirsch administration a group consisting mainly of contemporary works on paper was put together with funds received in memory of his wife, Truby Kelly Kirsch. The collection was further enhanced when Rose Frankel Rosenfield donated $25,000 in honor of Kirsch to be used for the purchase of recent art: works by eighteen artists, including George Grosz, Matta, Ben Nicholson, and Ben Shahn, were purchased.

Gifts of art from private individuals at this time tended to center around prints, the decorative arts, and works by Iowa artists. The most important exception was a small but select group of works (including prime examples by Brancusi, Gauguin, Kokoschka, and Matisse) that John and Elizabeth Bates Cowles formally donated to the Art Center between 1952 and 1964. Although many of these works were not finally transferred until the 1970s and 1980s, because of the tax laws then in effect, the gifts gave further evidence that the museum's collection was growing not only numerically but qualitatively as well.

Dwight Kirsch retired as director in 1958 and Dennis Peter Myers, his successor, remained only one year. Thomas Tibbs, who had previously been director of the Museum of Contemporary Crafts in New York and of the Huntington Galleries in West Virginia, began his eight-year tenure at the Art Center in 1960. Tibbs believed it was important to broaden the scope of the museum, and before officially starting work he had a seventeenth-century Dutch landscape painting (purportedly by Jacob van Ruysdael) sent to the museum for consideration. Although his recommendation was counter to the policy adhered to under Kirsch, the acquisitions committee, hesitant to reject the new director's recommendation, reluctantly approved the purchase. Despite the fact that questions about the authenticity of the work were immediately raised, Tibbs, with the consent of the president of the board of trustees, chose to ignore them and the picture was purchased without further investigation. It was later determined to be a heavily restored work by a minor figure and was subsequently deaccessioned and sold for a fraction

of its original cost. This was the last "Old Master" painting purchased by the Art Center.

Tibbs believed that the public would view contemporary art more sympathetically if it were seen in relation to the art of ancient and "primitive" peoples whose art had affinities to the abstract forms used by modern artists. Consequently, the Art Center acquired examples of African, Arabian Pre-Islamic, Oceanic, and Pre-Columbian art through Coffin funds and other sources. Although there were some first-rate pieces among these works, they have never seemed particularly compatible with the museum's collection as a whole.

Among the key works acquired during Tibbs's administration were Stanton MacDonald-Wright's Abstraction on Spectrum (Organization 5) which represents the artist at the height of his powers, Jean Arp's sensuous marble sculpture Torso Sheaf, and John Marin's oil Mid-Manhattan. A small stone sculpture by John Storrs was paid for with the last of the Edmundson acquisition fund, leaving the Coffin trust as the only unrestricted source for museum purchases. Significant gifts entering the Art Center's collection during Tibbs's tenure include a Gilbert Stuart portrait of George Washington donated by the George Olmsted Foundation; art objects and paintings from the estate of William and Edith King Pearson, and paintings from Florence Cowles Kruidenier and James and Dorothy Schramm.

The museum also underwent an expansion during Tibbs's administration with the addition of the I.M. Pei wing to the south of the Saarinen building. This wing includes the Cowles upper and lower sculpture courts, the Levitt Auditorium, the Meredith Gallery, and the Maytag Reflecting Pool. With the building of this addition, the auditorium in the Saarinen building was converted into the three A.H. Blank Galleries designed by Des Moines architect Charles Herbert.

In 1968 Tibbs took a museum post in California and the following year James T. Demetrion, head of the Pasadena Museum of Art, became the Art Center director. During Demetrion's fifteen-year tenure in Des Moines, the Art Center became an internationally respected institution because of the depth and wide range of his scholarship and the superb quality of his acquisitions. Since the center already had a respectable collection of early twentieth-century art, Demetrion recommended a policy of acquiring vanguard post-World War II art, especially American, as the primary area of concentration.

With the exception of several sculptures purchased hurriedly during the last year of Tibbs's administration to help fill the newly built Cowles Sculpture

Court, Coffin trust funds had not previously been expended for works by the younger generation of artists. With the adoption of the new acquisitions policy, that situation changed dramatically. However, when it soon became apparent that there was not sufficient income to acquire major works by first-generation Abstract Expressionists, Demetrion turned to the next generation of artists, selecting major works by Richard Diebenkorn, Robert Irwin, Jasper Johns, Ellsworth Kelly, Kenneth Noland, Robert Rauschenberg, Frank Stella, William Wiley, and others. Also acquired during Demetrion's administration were key works by European artists, including Francis Bacon, Jean Dubuffet, and Alberto Giacometti. A Director's Discretionary Fund established by the Gardner and Florence Cowles Foundation for the purpose of acquiring works by less established or less well-known artists enabled Demetrion to purchase a chalk drawing on blackboard by Joseph Beuys as well as works by Robert Arneson, Irving Petlin, Susan Rothenberg, and Charles Simonds. David Smith's sculpture Zig II was acquired through other funds supplied by the Cowles foundation.

A 1975 bequest from Edith M. Usry provided funds for the purchase of "art not commonly called modern." A late letter-rack painting by John Frederick Peto was acquired with the Usry bequest as well as John Singer Sargent's important oil Portraits of Edouard and Marie-Louise Pailleron, which was purchased with the help of additional contributions from Peder and Ellen Maytag Madsen, and Anna K. Meredith. With the 1983 bequest of Mildred Meredith Bohen, the Art Center received representative pictures by Emile Bernard, Eugène Boudin, Marc Chagall, Gabriele Münter, and Pierre-Auguste Renoir. Funds from the estate of Anna K. Meredith, who died in 1981, made possible the acquisition of Frank Stella's spectacular Interlagos.

Funds from the deaccessioning and sale of decorative art objects and paintings went for the purchase of a number of diverse works, including a "Veil" painting by Morris Louis, one of Claes Oldenburg's most famous watercolors, a hand-colored lithograph by Edvard Munch, and Grant Wood's classic Birthplace of Herbert Hoover (the last purchased jointly with The Minneapolis Institute of Arts). Among the gifts received during Demetrion's directorship were an oil by Sam Francis donated by Jeanne and Richard Levitt, and paintings and prints given by Louise Rosenfield Noun. A number of pieces of African art given by

Irma and Julian Brody, and fifty-one German Expressionist prints donated by John Huseby were forerunners of major bequests from these donors in 1992 and 1994, respectively.

Among the important exhibitions organized by Demetrion were "Egon Schiele and the Human Form, Drawings and Watercolors," which traveled to the Columbus Gallery of Fine Arts (Ohio) and The Art Institute of Chicago (1971); "Paul Klee, the Bauhaus Years" and "Twenty-five Years of American Painting" (1973). The last exhibition was in honor of the twenty-fifth anniversary of the Des Moines Art Center. Other noteworthy Demetrion shows include "European Art – Postwar Decade, 1945–1955" (1978); and "Giorgio Morandi" (1982), which traveled to the San Francisco Museum of Fine Arts and The Solomon R. Guggenheim Museum in New York. Another important exhibition during the Demetrion years was "The Etchings of Jacques Bellange" (1975), curated by Amy N. Worthen of Des Moines and Sue Welsh Reed of the Boston Museum of Fine Arts. Quadrennial collectors' exhibitions selected by Demetrion offered opportunities for individuals and corporations to acquire art at reasonable prices and resulted in raising the number and quality of private collections in the community.

In 1983 the architect Richard Meier was engaged to design gallery wings to the north and west of the Saarinen building and also the restaurant that is adjacent to the pool area. At this time the library located at the north end of the museum was moved to the school wing to make room for the museum shop.

Demetrion resigned from the Art Center in 1984 to take the position of director of the Hirshhorn Museum and Sculpture Garden in Washington, DC. His successor, David Ryan, former director of the Modern Art Museum in Ft. Worth, stayed at the Art Center for slightly over a year. The highlight of his tenure was a retrospective exhibition of the work of Robert Arneson organized by the Art Center's curator, Neal Benezra. In 1986 Joan Simon of New York, at the suggestion of Acting Director Peggy Patrick, served as consultant to the board of trustees. Simon organized an exhibition of signs by Jenny Holzer which was the artist's first museum exhibition.

No history of the Des Moines Art Center would be complete without special mention of Peggy Patrick, who retired in 1986 after forty years of service. She worked as a volunteer in the museum the year it opened, and in 1950 joined the education staff as a teacher in the education department. In 1971 Director James T. Demetrion promoted her to the position of assistant director. Because the staff was small during her years at the Art Center, Patrick performed a multiplicity of jobs, including serving as interim director during vacancies in the directorship.

Julia Brown Turrell (now Julia Brown), senior curator at the Los Angeles Museum of Contemporary Art, succeeded Ryan in 1987. Turrell brought to the Art Center the critical eye of a younger generation of curators inspired by Postmodernism. Her broad vision of art embraced the Conceptual and the intuitive as well as an interest in the environment, urban design, and architecture. With the exception of two boxes by Marcel Duchamp, all of the acquisitions selected by Turrell were produced in 1970 or later. These include paintings by Anselm Kiefer, Elizabeth Murray, and Robert Ryman; sculptures by Louise Bourgeois, John Chamberlain, Eva Hesse, Donald Judd, Joel Shapiro, and Deborah Butterfield, the last a gift from the Principal Financial Group. Red Grooms's piece based on the Iowa State Fair was initiated by Turrell, but commissioned after Turrell's resignation by Interim Director M. Jessica Rowe. Funds for this project came from Rose Lee and Marvin Pomerantz and the National Endowment for the Arts. Turrell also acquired important print portfolios by Cy Twombly and Francesco Clemente, and an installation of eighty-four photographs by Lewis Baltz, which was a gift from the artist. The Baltz photographs marked a change in Art Center acquisition policy: individual photographs or works involving the medium of photography would now be considered.

Turrell also commissioned the first site-specific works for the Art Center. These include the Sol LeWitt wall drawing in the Cowles Sculpture Court; and two sculptures on the museum grounds: Animal Pyramid by Bruce Nauman; and Standing Stones by Richard Serra. Nauman's photo-collage study for Animal Pyramid was purchased with funds from Melva and Martin Bucksbaum. This gift represents only a small part of the generous (and often anonymous) support that Melva Bucksbaum has given and continues to give to the Des Moines Art Center. The Serra work, consisting of six rough-hewn granite blocks, was given by the Kruidenier family in memory of David S. and Florence Cowles Kruidenier.

Exhibitions curated by Turrell during her tenure at the Art Center include "Waxworks" by Peter Shelton, Conceptual Art by Wolfgang Laib, and photographs by Jo Ann Callis. The Callis and Shelton shows were cocurated with Associate Curator Cornelis Butler. An innovative exhibition of architecture for children consisted of five play spaces built and exhibited at the Art Center from designs by five American architects chosen by Turrell. Instructions for making these structures were sold by the museum shop. Two traveling exhibitions curated by Turrell were a major exhibition of twenty-five sculptures by Joel Shapiro which went to the Baltimore Museum of Art and the Miami Art Museum; and photographs of Lewis Baltz, shown at eight additional venues including the Los Angeles County Museum of Art; the Musée de l'Art Moderne, Paris; the Fotomuseum, Winterthur, Switzerland; and the Amerika Haus, Berlin.

Extensive sale of deaccessioned works during Turrell's administration resulted in a sizable fund for new acquisitions. Associate Curator Deborah Leveton was responsible for the efficient and responsible way in which these sales were handled.

In 1987 Turrell suggested that the museum collection be extended into the twenty-seven-acre public park behind the Art Center through the placement of site-specific works. Although the board approved this innovative idea, it met with vociferous and determined protests on the part of the public. "Friends of Greenwood Park," an organization formed to fight the project, evidenced a deep distrust of the museum and a decided dislike of modern art. According to their literature, they feared that the park would be polluted by "sculptures of a non- or anti-traditional type," proving that Des Moines is "arts-dumb or deluded." Three thousand citizens signed petitions opposing the project. After lengthy negotiations, the Art Center and the City of Des Moines came to an agreement whereby sculptures would be sited in the park on a case-by-case basis, with each project being approved individually.

To date the only proposal constructed is Greenwood Pond: Double Site, an environmental work by Mary Miss, which was completed in the fall of 1996. The project, which covers six acres and includes wetlands, prairie, and woods, features pathways, terraces, an observation tower, and a pavilion which serves as a warming house for ice skaters in winter and an open-air shelter in summer. The completed project has met with enthusiastic public approval and the opposition has faded away.

Funding for Greenwood Pond: Double Site came from the National Endowment for the Arts, Melva and Martin Bucksbaum, Carolyn and Matthew Bucksbaum, the Des Moines Founders Garden Club, and also six individuals, foundations, and business enterprises. The project represents a unique collaboration between the artist, the Art Center, The Science Center of Iowa, the Des Moines Founders Garden Club, the Des Moines Parks and Recreation Department, the Iowa Natural Heritage Foundation, and the Polk County Conservation Board. Credit for making this collaboration work must go to M. Jessica Rowe, associate director of the Art Center, who labored tirelessly to keep the project on track.

I. Michael Danoff, the most recent director of the Des Moines Art Center, assumed his position in Des Moines in the fall of 1991. Danoff, former director of the San Jose Museum of Art, formally established acquisition priorities based on filling gaps in the Art Center collection. Works by Magdalena Abakanowicz, Mario Merz, and Gerhard Richter augment the representation of European art. American Minimalist works by Robert Mangold, Brice Marden, and Agnes Martin were added, as were Figurative Expressionist paintings by Philip Guston and Julian Schnabel. Other significant acquisitions include Alfred Leslie's large charcoal on paper of 1968, three works by Dennis Oppenheim, a Franz Gertsch woodcut, and seven photographs by Cindy Sherman, one of which is a gift from Joan Simon.

Works of a younger generation of artists dealing with social and political issues such as racism, sexism, and consumerism add a new dimension to the Art Center collection. These include artists Ashley Bickerton, Nayland Blake, Jeff Koons, Glenn Ligon, Kiki Smith, Carrie Mae Weems, Lorna Simpson, and Tony Oursler. A construction by Iowa artist Jane Gilmor deals with issues

Painting studio in the upper level of the education
wing, Des Moines Art Center, c. 1965.
Photograph courtesy Peggy Patrick, Des Moines.

relating to children with cancer with whom she worked at the University of Iowa hospitals. Important gifts entering the collection under Danoff's directorship include works by Helen Frankenthaler and Dorothea Rockburne donated by Helen Urban, thirty-six prints by Susan Rothenberg given by Mary and John Pappajohn, a Grant Wood oil donated by Ted Lee, a Max Ernst bronze given by Watson Powell, Jr., and James Rosenquist lithographs given by Louis E. Schneider. Anastasia and Paul Polydoran have generously given several works from their collection, and Louise Rosenfield Noun has donated important works by women such as Eva Hesse, Lee Krasner, and Olga Rozanova.

Exhibitions organized by Danoff include paintings by Peter Halley and a show consisting of five installations by artists Barbara Bloom, Ann Hamilton, Nam June Paik, Robert Ryman, and James Turrell. Temporary site-specific installations by Betye Saar and by Lewis deSoto are indicative of Danoff's efforts to reference issues of diversity in Art Center exhibitions.[6] Other exhibitions under Danoff's directorship include the major

show "American Indian Parfleche: A Tradition of Abstract Painting," guest-curated by Gaylord Torrence;" The Berlin Artists of the Weimar Era," guest-curated by Louise Rosenfield Noun; and one-person exhibitions of Iowa artists Rita McBride and Will Mentor, curated by Deborah Leveton.

Finally, during Danoff's tenure the Art Center saw new focus on public relations and marketing. In 1996 the center undertook and completed a major deferred maintenance program which required a temporary curtailing of program expenses. It is also notable that the Art Center successfully overcame significant flooding in 1993, and a fire that affected the Saarinen and Pei buildings in 1996.

Since Danoff resigned his position at the Art Center in November 1997, the acting director, M. Jessica Rowe, has carried on an active and innovative program overseeing the center's fiftieth anniversary events and establishing new curatorial positions. Now, proud of a fifty-year history that is distinguished by enlightened and adventuresome building and acquisition policies, the Des Moines Art Center is confident that it will continue to be an important asset to the community during the next half-century.

Works on paper collection. The Des Moines Art Center has a collection of more than 3,000 works on paper representing a variety of artists ranging from Albrecht Dürer to Kiki Smith. With the exception of a large group of prints purchased with Edmundson funds in 1950 from the estate of Florence Carpenter, print purchases have generally been made either with memorial funds or with gifts designated especially for the purchase of prints. Designated funds include a gift in the 1940s from Benjamin A. Younker, and a 1961 bequest from Rose Frankel Rosenfield. In 1972 a group of seventeenth-century Dutch and nineteenth-century painter-etcher prints collected by her sister, Jennie May Gabriel, was received from the estate of Grace E. Gabriel. John Huseby, who died in 1994, left the Art Center 388 prints, many of them reflecting his interest in French nineteenth-century printmaking, especially lithography. Including previous gifts and a few prints purchased from his estate, the Huseby collection numbers 519 works.

Education department. The Art Center school, which opened with the original Saarinen building in 1948, was intended to offer instruction of the highest quality, on a par with professional schools, with distinguished working artists serving as the studio faculty (**see fig. 7**). Adult classes were offered in painting, design, drawing, sculpture, weaving, ceramics, and printmaking, as well as a variety of topics in art history and art appreciation. Visiting artists, scholars, and critics gave lectures and a full range of children's classes was offered after school, on Saturdays, and during the summer. A limited scholarship fund for high-school students was funded by the Des Moines Junior League in 1953, and three years later, an extensive scholarship program for children in elementary through high school was instituted under the leadership of Hans van Weeren-Griek, the acting director while Dwight Kirsch was on extended leave. This program was funded by the Art Center until 1974 when area schools began assuming the cost.

In 1957 the first administrative positions for the school were created, and by the 1980s the education department had expanded to four full-time staff. By that time the education department had become responsible for a wide variety of additional programs, including gallery talks, film series, music programs, special workshops, and lecture series. In recent years the education mission has been redefined to include the entire program of the museum, including exhibitions, interpretation, and publications. A fund established in 1976 in memory of Margaret Ann (Dudie) Ash enables the Art Center to offer an annual lecture by a nationally prominent artist.

A unique feature of the education program was the artist-in-residence position which existed from 1949 to 1990. In exchange for a stipend and an on-premises studio, the artist-in-residence taught classes during the two or more years of the appointment. In 1966 a second residency position in ceramics was created. From 1952 to 1972 the Art Center also had a summer visiting artist program with nationally prominent painters presenting classes during a six-week residency. The Jean Charlot mural over the stairs in the school wing was painted with the help of local artists when Charlot was a guest artist in the summer of 1956. Since 1990 the Art Center has limited visiting artists to semester and one-year appointments.

Current community engagement efforts of the education department include family museum visits for children from low-income areas in cooperation with the Des Moines Public Schools, and classes and museum visits for children at various social-service agencies. An effort is also being made to increase the cultural diversity of children and adults involved in Art Center activities. Some classes qualify for college credit in area schools, and internships offer college students the opportunity to learn about museum operations. An important part of the education department is the training of volunteer docents in a year-long program that prepares them to lead tours of children and adults.

The Art Center library was initially stocked with books transferred from the art department of the Des Moines Public Library and for a number of years it was funded with proceeds from Arts and Ends sales. The library now has more than 14,000 volumes and subscribes to thirty-five art periodicals. It also has extensive back files of periodicals as well as files on individual artists.

Member activities. A Junior Art Museum sponsored by the Junior League of Des Moines was a feature of the Art Center program from 1953 to 1979. This program operated under the supervision of the education department with the assistance of Junior League volunteers who helped arrange exhibitions and served as docents.

An annual art fair, known as **Art in the Park**, where artists can display and sell their products, was for many years managed by volunteers. From a small sale of art by faculty and students in the lobby of the Art Center in 1950, the fair expanded both in size and number of participants, first to the parking lot in front of the building, and then in 1969 to the park behind the museum. Due to the demand for more exhibition space as well as damage to the park caused by large crowds in wet weather, the fair was moved to the Varied Industries Building at the Iowa State Fair Grounds in 1992, though it continues to be called **Art in the Park**. Attendance in 1997 totaled 22,270, with 200 participating artists.

The Members Council, which has traditionally been a volunteer organization for Art Center activities, once had full responsibility for **Art in the Park** and for hosting exhibition openings. However, the art fair is now under professional management and openings are the responsibility of the Art Center restaurant. The council still hosts some Art Center events, such as the Holiday Open House, special events on the first Friday of each month, and assists with **Art in the Park.**

The Des Moines Art Center Print Club was organized in 1981 by a group of members interested in the study and collecting of prints. The program includes lectures at monthly meetings, visits to local collections and artists' studios, as well as tours to out-of-town museums and print fairs. Gifts from Lois and Louis Fingerman fund an annual lecture. The club also purchases a print each year to add to the Art Center's permanent collection.

1 Although the Art Center building
did not open until 1948, the board
of trustees had been in existence
since 1935.
2 The exact date is not known because
the Art Center has no records of the
WPA administration. They probably
were sent to the National Archives.
3 In December 1960 the meeting room
was taken over by the Museum Shop,
and in 1983 it was remodeled into
administration offices.
4 Untitled manuscript, June 1946.
5 Board minutes, July 12, 1949.
6 The Bohen Foundation subsequently
donated one of the deSoto installations
to the Art Center.

Nineteenth- and twentieth-century works of art

Various authors

Purchased with funds from the Edmundson
Art Foundation, Inc.; Des Moines Art
Center Permanent Collections, 1992.36

Thirty-five figures, burlap and resin,
each 54 inches high (137.2 cm)

magdalena abakanowicz

Polish, born 1930   **Flock II,** 1990

Magdalena Abakanowicz's life and art were deeply affected by early influences, which included playing alone as a child on the land of her family's estate outside of Warsaw and witnessing the violent takeover of that estate by German troops. Following the war Abakanowicz was schooled as an artist in her native Poland. She entered the Academy of Fine Arts in Warsaw in 1950 and in 1955 won a prize for painting. About this time she became interested in fiber as an alternative to traditional fine art. She sees fiber "as the basic element constructing the organic world on our planet... it is from fiber that all living organisms are built – the tissue of plants, and ourselves. Our nerves, our genetic code, the canals of our veins, our muscles. We are fibrous structures."[1]

With her extraordinary successes at the First International Biennial of Tapestry in Lausanne, Switzerland in 1961 and the São Paolo Bienale in 1965, Abakanowicz became the single most influential artist working in fiber during the 1960s and 1970s. In the early 1970s she made a series of works using fiber that was wrapped, stitched, and molded, rather than woven. Among these were figures, which have constituted the artist's core image since that time.

The Des Moines Art Center's **Flock II** consists of thirty-five sculptures of standing human figures. To create this work, the artist made a plaster cast from one person, filled it with wax, and lined it with burlaplike material dipped in a gluey medium. She applied a synthetic resin and then another layer of sacking and glue. The impregnated fiber hardened so that it could be removed and the figure could stand on its own. This process was repeated for each figure, using the same cast.

Abakanowicz has often made works consisting of a group of images, stating that she feels "overawed by quantity where counting no longer makes sense. By unrepeatability within such a quantity. By creatures of nature gathered in herds, droves, species, in which each individual while subservient to the mass retains some distinguishing features."[2]

She has related the specific history and circumstances of this particular work: "Lukas was fourteen years old, fascinated by my work; he liked to visit my studio. One day he agreed to be cast. It is very hard to stand under the pressure of plaster that makes the body heavy in an unusual, unnatural way. He moved and the cast was not very good. Nevertheless, I decided to use it, but I had to elaborate every figure, carefully pulling the hands backwards so that each one got a resolute and courageous expression. I made twelve figures and stopped.

After a year I found the figures in my attic and felt the necessity to create a large group of these 'ragazzi' [boys]. I asked Lukas to come to my studio and we made several casts of his body in standing and reclining positions. The result was not good at all. I decided to elaborate each figure separately, taking only some features from the cast. Each figure is a shell-like negative of the bulk of the body – thin and delicate. I gave them shapes of columns or tree trunks or stalagmites or stalactites with surfaces of broken rocks or cocoonlike. If one looks at them carefully, they are as figurative as they are abstract. **Flock II** is a statement about the power of silence."[3]

The artist, who is married but has no children, has written: "In my belly, life was never conceived. My hands shape forms, seeking confirmation of each individual specimen in quantity. As in a flock subordinating the individual, as in the profusion of leaves produced by a tree."[4] IMD

Purchased with funds from the bequest
of Edith King and William W. Pearson;
Des Moines Art Center Permanent
Collections, 1984.9

Oil on Masonite, 32 x 32 inches
(81.3 x 81.3 cm)

joseph albers

American, born Germany, 1888–1976   **Study for Homage to the Square**, 1967

Although Joseph Albers is best known for the extended group of paintings titled "Homage to the Square," he did not paint his first work in the series until 1950, when he was sixty-two years of age. Born in Bottrop, in Germany's industrial Ruhr region, Albers was educated in Berlin, Essen, and Munich, before entering the Bauhaus in Weimar in 1920. After finishing coursework he taught at the Bauhaus, and he also completed work in stained and sandblasted glass and in furniture, as well as other design projects. When the Bauhaus closed in 1933, Albers immigrated to the United States and taught at Black Mountain College in North Carolina; Harvard University; and, beginning in 1950, at Yale University.

Albers began to paint in earnest only after his arrival in the United States. In evolving the approach to painting that reached its highest achievement in the "Homages," one work, **Gate** (1936; Yale University Art Gallery), was of exemplary importance. The painting consists of floating planes of modulated color, with a luminous white rectangle resembling an architectural passageway hovering in the center. As if to counter the ethereal quality of the composition and the color, Albers applied oil directly to the Masonite sheet. This rough texture suggested Albers's love of Pre-Columbian architecture, a source that resonates strongly in the "Homages."

When Albers began the "Homages," he conceived a format restricted to four concentric squares; soon he began to work with three alternate formats, each featuring three concentric squares. Albers made careful studies of colors and color combinations prior to arriving at the selection and order of the hues for each painting. Within these rigorously limited compositional alternatives (which vary only in relative size) and this highly systematic approach to color, Albers was able to make work of great formal and poetic beauty.

While the three-square "Homages" often emphasize strong, structural color relationships, Albers achieved perhaps his most subtle and lyrical effects in the four-square paintings. The Des Moines Art Center's **Study for Homage to the Square** features two framing bands in dark green. Nearing the center, there is a shift toward a luminous blue, with a pale and evocative green in the middle. The allusion to an architectural gateway or passage is strong, as is the quality of soft poetic light emanating from the center. NB

NASAL OFFICER

REGULAR CRACKER TO BOOT

LOKO KLOWN

Director's Discretionary Fund
from the Gardner and Florence Call Cowles
Foundation; Des Moines Art
Center Permanent Collections,1980.4
Glazed ceramic, 37 inches high (94 cm)

robert arneson

American, 1930–1992   **Klown,** 1978

A groundbreaking West Coast artist, Robert Arneson was a native of the San Francisco Bay Area. He attended the California College of Arts and Crafts and Mills College in Oakland, before becoming an influential professor of sculpture at the University of California, Davis in 1962. Arneson began his career as a craftsman and ceramist making functional vessels on a potter's wheel. Influenced virtually simultaneously by the expressionist work in clay being made in the late 1950s in Berkeley by Peter Voulkos, and by the irreverent neo-Dada attitudes then very much in the air, Arneson began to transform himself into a sculptor. While he continued to work with clay, he began to question the limitations of pure craft and to comment sardonically on the historical uses of clay in the production of functional objects.

After joining the Davis faculty, Arneson made work with a devastating and often bawdy sense of humor. Funky toilets, telephones sprouting breasts, typewriters and toasters bearing fingers, all characterize his art of the mid-1960s. In the following decade, Arneson focused obsessively on portraiture, making work that paid satirical homage to favorite modern artists and contemporary colleagues. Self-portraiture became a principal concern, as Arneson created images of himself in the form of death masks, pedestal and bust portraits, and a wide variety of invented guises. During the 1970s he depicted himself as a chef displaying his baked ceramic goods, balancing a stack of bricks atop his head, or as a classical herm with genitals exposed.

Throughout this work Arneson displayed a wicked sense of humor, and he often found himself simultaneously praised by critics as a gifted ceramist and sculptor, but also dismissed as a mere stand-up comic. And yet, like a great comic, Arneson employed self-parody as a vehicle of profound self-expression, and this, in essence, is the subject of the Art Center's **Klown** (1978). Festooned in a skin-tight mask, an oversized bright orange ear, and an extravagant collar joined in the center by a bow tie in the form of genitals, **Klown** satirizes Arneson's own critical self-image among "serious" art critics. A cunning wordsmith, Arneson riddled the pedestal bust with characteristically self-deprecating inscriptions resembling graffiti. NB

Marble, 44 1/2 x 25 1/2 x 16 1/2 inches
(113 x 64.8 x 41.9 cm)

jean arp

Swiss, 1886–1966   **Torse Gerbe (Torso Sheaf),** 1958

"Music, poetry, sculpture are the real world, in which forests can still grow, mountains can still stand unmutilated, and people can still exist unquantified…,"[1] declared Jean (Hans) Arp, who aspired to a new principle of order through his art and poetry. Arp was a lyrical poet and a gentle man who embraced peace and nature. His contributions to psychological explorations are as important as his contributions to problems of formal order. Alfred H. Barr, Jr., founding director of The Museum of Modern Art in New York, proclaimed him "a one-man laboratory for the discovery of new form."[2] Arp is one of the seminal figures in twentieth-century art, and as a founder of the Dada movement, played a leading role in the development of European art before World War I.

With Arp's prestigious 1954 sculpture prize at the Venice Biennale, came a broader public recognition of his work. This popularity improved his financial situation and allowed him to have a number of his sculptures cast in bronze and carved in marble, many of which until then had existed only in plaster. Considerable praise has been focused on a small portion of the artist's prodigious output created during his last twenty years: curvaceous sculptures of white marble and of bronze. It was during this period that the Art Center's spiraling white marble sculpture **Torso Sheaf** was carved.

Arp worked in two concurrent but sharply different abstract styles: one geometrical and the other biomorphic, based on organic forms of nature. **Torso Sheaf**, completed in 1958, is a dazzling example of Arp's biomorphic form. The rounded, irregular shapes allude to nature's universal processes of growth and decay. Floral imagery found fertile soil in Arp's imagination along with the archetype of the torso. "From a sailing cloud a leaf emerged to the surface. The leaf changes into a torso. The torso changes into a vase. An immense navel appears. It grows, it becomes larger and larger."[3] This formal vocabulary and the theme of natural metamorphosis became the basis of his life's work.

Torso Sheaf appears at first to be a budlike sprout, but then glides into a statuesque, eloquently undulating form in flux – flowing, swelling into a sensuously round female torso, upright in posture, symmetrical, limbless, and featureless. In **Torso Sheaf**, Arp has brought together the qualities of the serene and sensual, and has fused landscape with the human figure in an extraordinary manner – as if the earth was rising and becoming human.

This sculpture was completed during the decade following the death in 1943 of Arp's wife, Swiss artist Sophie Taeuber. Arp was devastated and never fully recovered from this loss. He ceased sculpting for four years, but wrote moving poems and essays about Taeuber. When Arp returned to the human figure, it became the image of his longing for a state of otherworldly peace and tranquility.

Arp was born in Strasbourg in 1887. He studied at art academies in Strasbourg, Weimar, and Paris. In 1909, disillusioned by conventional art training, he turned to literature, composing poems. His fluency in French and German and his love of language gave rise to a bilingual literary production astonishing in its quality and extent. His French poems and prose fill a 669-page anthology, and his collected German poems have been published in three volumes. By the outbreak of World War I, he was engaged in intensive contacts with the international avant-garde. He married Sophie Taeuber, who was both his muse and his financial support. By her example and through their famous collaborative works, she strengthened his commitment to abstract art and his conviction that art could be a manifestation of immaterial values. Arp died in 1966 in Basel. MJR

Purchased with funds from the Coffin Fine
Arts Trust; Nathan Emory Coffin
Collection of the Des Moines Art Center,
1980.1

Oil on canvas, 60 1/2 x 46 1/2 inches
(153 x 118.1 cm)

francis bacon

British, 1909–1992   **Study after Velásquez's Portrait of Pope Innocent X,** 1953

In 1650 Diego Velásquez, the greatest of all Spanish painters, was commissioned by Pope Innocent X to paint his portrait. Now situated in the Galleria Doria Pamphili in Rome, the painting is not only comparable to earlier portrayals of popes by Raphael and Titian, but is ranked among the finest portraits ever painted by any artist.

Three hundred years later Velásquez's papal masterpiece became an inspiration – indeed, an obsession – for the British painter Francis Bacon, even though he knew it only through reproductions. From 1949 to 1971 he painted forty-five canvases with the pope as his theme, nearly all of them based on the Velásquez. Nine of those works were completed in 1953 alone, including **Study after Velásquez's Portrait of Pope Innocent X,** which is considered by most critics to be Bacon's definitive statement on the subject. Painted early in the year, it was soon followed by a series of eight works depicting the pope in various moods: pensive, grinning, screaming, threatening, etc. Each of the eight was given a generic title (**Study for Portrait**), followed by a Roman numeral. All nine pictures are roughly the same size (60 x 46 inches) and, perhaps coincidentally, not too different in this respect from the Velásquez (55 x 49 1/2 inches).

In the Des Moines painting, Bacon has retained the basic composition of his model, but the differences in the two are striking. Bacon has overlaid the composition with thinly painted black and violet vertical strokes suggesting a transparent drape or curtain through which one views the pope in his private anguish. However, these verticals yield to curved strokes that rush in from the bottom of the painting; they function as lines of force and a base that provides support for the legless figure. Whereas the seventeenth-century work depicts a person of authority, who sits confidently on his capacious throne and is obviously in command of any situation, Bacon's personage is constricted and hemmed in by the yellow tubular element that surrounds him. The back rest of his throne is narrow and adds to the feeling of compression.

But it is the scream that is the most unsettling aspect of the painting. Although the most famous scream in modern art was painted in 1894 by the Norwegian Edvard Munch, Bacon's acknowledged source was the Russian film classic **The Battleship Potemkin** (1922) by Sergei Eisenstein. The memorable scene at the Odessa steps in which the nurse cries out as she is shot in the eye through her pince nez made a lasting impact on Bacon, and it is that scream along with the broken eyeglasses that the artist incorporated in a few of his pope paintings, including the Art Center's.

What is so frightening about Bacon's representation is that the scream does not emanate from some common Everyman crossing a bridge, as in the Munch, but rather from someone whom we associate with supreme authority and control. This anomaly of impotence in those whom we believe to embody power is a part of what gives the painting its tension and strength. Unique to the Des Moines canvas are the red drops of paint splattered like blood across the lower part of the picture and onto the pure white surplice worn by the Bishop of Rome.

In later years Bacon was extremely critical of these paintings, saying that he had come to "regret" and even to "hate" them because the Velásquez was a "perfect" painting that could not be added to. Despite his protestations, Bacon's pope paintings have become his signature works. They confirm the artist's belief that "the greatest art always returns you to the vulnerability of the human situation."

Francis Bacon was born in 1909 in Dublin, of English parents. He was self-taught. He died while visiting Madrid in 1992. JD

Purchased with funds from the
Coffin Fine Arts Trust; Nathan Emory Coffin
Collection of the Des Moines Art Center,
1981.60

Oil on canvas, 44 1/2 x 57 1/2 inches
(113.7 x 146.1 cm)

william bailey

American, born 1930   **Migianella Still Life,** 1976

William Bailey's works are part of the resurgence of realism in American art beginning in the 1960s. But Bailey's realism is not related to the photograph or to contemporary life; rather it joins a long tradition that finds in common objects timeless beauty and mystery. Bailey has been compared to artists such as Chardin, Zurbarán, Piero della Francesca, and Ingres in his ability to render objects in a way that lifts them beyond everyday associations to an enduring realm of classical substance. As in the works of these Old Masters, the light is even and luminous, falling on the objects in a way that makes them seem concretely solid but also abstract and even poetic. In comparison to Giorgio Morandi, the twentieth-century Italian artist with whom he has often been compared, Bailey's paintings are highly refined and finished, with little suggestion of the painting process.

Bailey's still lifes employ a repertoire of objects that can be recognized from painting to painting; usually, as in the Art Center's **Migianella Still Life**, they are simple ceramic vessels along with eggs and metal forms. They are objects without specific cultural associations and are neither overtly narrative nor symbolic. They are arranged on top of a simple table or chest against an apparently blank background in a roughly horizontal composition with little depth. The spatial relationships among the objects, their support, and their background seem at first to be logical and clear, but prolonged looking

reveals subtle shifts and ambiguities. Here, for instance, we seem to look slightly downward onto the chest top while the objects are observed at eye level. In realizing these differences, the viewer finds the still life changing from an inert, passive situation to an engaging and mutable one.

Bailey was born in Council Bluffs, Iowa. He attended the University of Kansas (1951) and received both his Bachelor of Fine Arts (1955) and Master of Fine Arts degrees (1957) from Yale University, where he was a student of Joseph Albers. After service in the Army (1951–53), he lived in Europe before returning to begin teaching at Yale (1957–62, 1969–79) and at Indiana University (1962–69). He was dean of the School of Art at Yale in 1974–75, and in 1979 was named Kingman Brewster Professor of Art there. He maintains a home in Umbria in Italy, and the title of this painting refers to a partially destroyed fifteenth-century castle nearby.[1] Although he is best known for his still lifes, Bailey also produces evocative figure studies, two of which (**Head and Torso, 1983**) and (**Head, 1980**), are in the Art Center collection along with a 1976 lithograph of a still life (**Still Life No. 4**). LRD

**Purchased with funds from the
Edmundson Art Foundation, Inc.;
Des Moines Art Center Permanent
Collections, 1942.1**

Oil on canvas, 44 ¹/₂ x 34 ¹/₄ inches
(112.1 x 87 cm)

george bellows

American, 1882–1925   **Aunt Fanny (Old Lady in Black)**, 1920

George Bellows is associated with the first progressive years in the development of a genuinely "American" style, helping to organize both the formative 1910 Exhibition of Independent Artists and the Armory Show of 1913, and also as a founding member of the Society of Independent Artists in 1916. At Ohio State University (1901–1904), Bellows distinguished himself in both art and sports – interests that he was later able to integrate in some of his best-known paintings. He subsequently studied at the New York School of Art under Robert Henri, whose convictions were of great impact and whose friendship became lifelong, and who brought Bellows into the circle of painters known at The Eight.

Despite remaining in New York and his involvement and closeness with his colleagues, especially Henri and John Sloan, Bellows was never actually a member of The Eight. He shared their interest in America's East Coast and especially its urban sites and inhabitants, however, and was a prolific painter of a tremendous range of subject matter which includes landscapes, seascapes, and portraits as well as the crowds and sporting events with which he is most identified. In all his paintings there is an intense energy and physicality, manifest in the strong and decisive brushwork that enlivens a certain conservatism rooted in its absence of abstraction. Bellows was productive as well in printmaking and as an illustrator. When he died of neglected appendicitis at the age of only forty-three, his career was at its height.

The Art Center's **Aunt Fanny (Old lady in Black)** holds a special place in the collection: it was the first painting acquired, in 1941, even before the museum was built. A bridge builder and collector from Des Moines, J.S. (Sanny) Carpenter, saw the unfinished painting in Bellows's studio in 1920 and decided to purchase it; it was subsequently acquired by the Edmundson Art Foundation. It has been reproduced in **Time** magazine and other publications.

Aunt Fanny is a portrait that had special meaning for Bellows as well. The sitter, his mother's sister, was called Fanny although her real name was Elinor. She came to live with the Bellows when George was born, helping to care for him until she married and moved to California. This portrait was done on a summer visit in 1920. It shows Bellows in his fully mature mastery of a direct and forthright realism, marked by his characteristic vigor. The sitter's arresting gaze gives a telling glimpse into her personality, as do the large, firmly clasped hands. Head and hands are emphasized not only by their strongly modeled contours, but are highlighted through Bellows's use of sharp color contrasts. The portrait earned awards for Bellows in 1921 when it was exhibited in New York at the National Arts Club and at The Art Institute of Chicago. TRN

joseph beuys

German, 1921–1986   **Energie Plan for the Westman,** 1974

Perhaps the most important and influential German artist of the post-World War II period, Joseph Beuys was born in Kleve in northwest Germany in 1921. He entered the German military in 1940, serving first as a radio operator and ultimately as a fighter pilot flying missions over Italy, Yugoslavia, Poland, and the Soviet Union. He was wounded five times during the war, most seriously in 1943 when he was shot down in a snowstorm over the Crimea. Beuys was discovered by nomadic Tartars, who covered him in fat to regenerate his body warmth, and then wrapped him in felt to retain the heat. Fat and felt would serve as signature materials in Beuys's later work, acting as both autobiographical markers and more complex symbolic objects.

Following the war, in 1947, Beuys enrolled at the Staatliche Kunstakademie in Düsseldorf where he studied until 1951. He returned to that institution as professor of sculpture in 1961, a position that he would hold until 1972, when he was dismissed following numerous controversies concerning his teaching. For Beuys, art, politics, and teaching were inseparable, and his idealistic model of a "social sculpture" remains exemplary for many European artists to this day.

Lectures and actions formed principal elements of Beuys's work and his pedagogy, and these, combined with his great skill as a draftsman, constituted a highly original aspect of the artist's practice. From the 1960s onward, Beuys illustrated his lectures with diagrams drawn in chalk on blackboards. Perhaps the earliest instance of Beuys creating a blackboard as part of an activity and then retaining it both as a document of the event and also as a finished work, occurred with **Eurasia** (1966).

In January 1974 Beuys traveled to the United States for the first time, and his month-long speaking tour included stops in New York, Chicago, and Minneapolis, during which he gave lectures that came to be called "Energie Plan for the Westman." The work in the Des Moines Art Center collection bears this same title, and it was made by Beuys during a lecture at the Minneapolis College of Art and Design on January 17, 1974. The "Energie Plan" had occupied the artist since 1972, when he cofounded the Free International University for Creativity and Interdisciplinary Research in Düsseldorf following his dismissal from the academy. The spontaneous diagram that Beuys produced is filled with notations concerning the role of art in the larger sphere of human social, political, and environmental activity, and exemplifies the artist's lifelong endeavor. NB

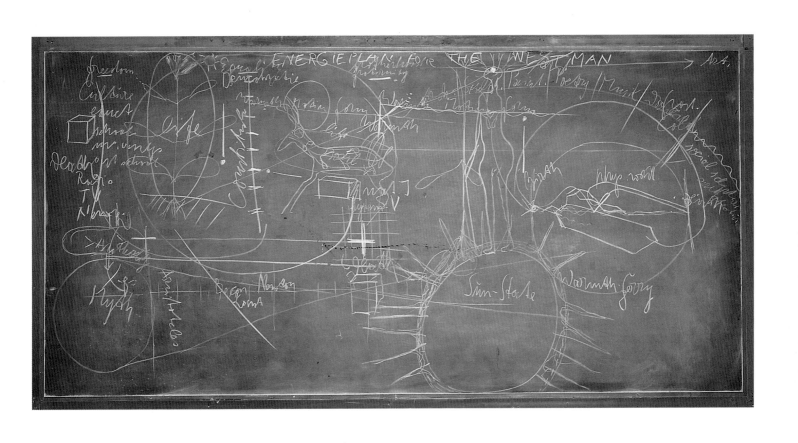

Purchased with funds from the Edmundson
Art Foundation, Inc.; Des Moines Art
Center Permanent Collections, 1994.334

Mixed media, 90 x 89 ¹/₂ x 20 inches
(228.6 x 227.3 x 50.8 cm)

ashley bickerton

American, born 1959   **Tormented Self-Portrait (Susie at Arles) No. 2,** 1988

Ashley Bickerton was born in 1959 in Barbados, West Indies. In 1982 he received his Bachelor of Fine Arts degree from the California Institute of the Arts, Valencia, and in 1985 he completed the Whitney Museum Independent Studies program in New York. For four years in the early 1980s, Bickerton was the studio assistant for the painter Jack Goldstein. He subsequently joined the distinguished group of artists at Sonnabend Gallery in New York and devoted himself full-time to his own work, which consists of both sculptures and paintings, some of the latter meticulously rendered.

Ashley Bickerton's **Tormented Self-Portrait (Susie at Arles) No. 2** is a self-portrait expressed through the logos of products personally significant to the artist – his preferences in clothing, hobbies, medicine, the media, and so forth. Bickerton stated that this work is about "seeing myself through the products I used,"[1] and focused the viewer's attention on his being an artist. The title references Vincent van Gogh, who made "tormented self-portraits" in Arles. Bickerton

even stated, "My piece says as much about myself as a self-portrait of van Gogh's did about him."[2] "Susie" is a generic person Bickerton used in referring to works he made since the early 1980s.

This work also is expressive of the times in which it was made, the "go-go" 1980s when consumerism was charging full steam ahead and yuppies were in the limelight (aspects of the times also seen in the work of Jeff Koons). The silkscreen technique, machine-like craftsmanship, and use of industrial metal in **Tormented Self-Portrait** all reinforce the fascination with manufactured consumer objects. But the work also has many physical references to being an art object. On one side is a pouch containing gloves for handling the work when it needs to be transported, and there are even instructions printed on the pouch stating the purpose. Rolled up on the bottom is a cover that can be used to protect the face of the work in transit. There are handles on the side for carrying the work, and mounting instructions on the two flat plates – upper left and right – that attach it to the wall. Another pouch contains spare hardware. The boldly indicated dating for the work – "SEASON 87/88" – refers to the so-called "art-world season"

in which the work was made. (The handles, hardware, etc. are not actually meant to be used.)

Tormented Self-Portrait has been reproduced internationally in the periodicals **Flash Art, Kunstforum International, Art and Auction, The Journal of Art, Art in America**, and in Bruce D. Kurtz's book **Contemporary Art: 1965–1990**. Prior to its purchase by the Art Center, it was exhibited at the Stedelijk Museum in Amsterdam, the Whitney Museum of American Art in New York (1989 Biennial), and The Art Institute of Chicago in the exhibition "Affinities and Intuitions: The Gerald S. Elliott Collection of Contemporary Art." The Art Center's painting by Robert Mangold also came from the Elliott collection. A smaller companion work with a white surface entitled **Tormented Self-Portrait (Susie at Arles)** is in the collection of The Museum of Modern Art, New York. IMD

Purchased with funds from the Edmundson
Art Foundation, Inc.; Des Moines Art
Center Permanent Collections, 1993.11

Nylon and steel, 78 ¹/₂ x 25 x 14 inches
(199.4 x 63.5 x 35.6 cm)

nayland blake

American, born 1960   **Untitled,** 1993

Nayland Blake grew up in New York and received his Bachelor of Fine Arts degree from Bard College (1982) and his Master of Fine Arts degree from the California Institute of the Arts (1984). He then settled in San Francisco, but relocated to New York in 1996.

In an article in **The Village Voice** (April 3, 1993) that praised the one-person exhibition at Matthew Marks Gallery in which the Art Center's work first was presented, the writer noted: "Blake explores ideas about whiteness, blackness, identity, role playing and drag...." Blake himself has said about his work: "art making is a type of analysis, it's a way in which I can figure out my relationship to the world that I live in."[1]

Blake works in a variety of media, including drawing and performance art, but most often in sculpture. The Des Moines Art Center's work has a relationship to the hand-puppet figures that the artist has made and sometimes used in performances. But the figure in **Untitled** is life-sized and, instead of being animated by inserting a hand, the entire body would be required. The work really is not intended to be worn, but it has a kinship with costumes as well as puppets. Blake has made several similar life-sized suits, but only this one is from so delicate and airy a material.

The figure is evocative and ambiguous. It has what may be interpreted as a phallus, but it also has nearly identically shaped inside-out pockets and a tail, thus calling into question what any of these forms may be. The ambiguity is further complicated by similar protrusions on the head, which appear to be floppy ears, and therefore relate this work to a series of bunny images that the artist has made for several years.

The ears are part of a mask or hood with crossed slits for eyes and but the tiniest suggestion of a mouth, as though silenced. For some viewers the hood and appendages suggest tribal or mythological images. For others the hood recalls the costume traditionally worn by members of the Ku Klux Klan.

A striking feature of the work is the skinlike quality of the fabric, the dark skin of a person of color: if one were to don this sculpture, then that is what one would become (it is likely of significance that the artist's father is black and his mother is white). To become a person of color would likely expand the horizons of one who is not, demonstrating that so often attitudes and behavior towards others are constructed by surface appearance rather than by core being. This resonant work also implicitly suggests that gender sometimes is ambiguous. For while the sculpture does appears to be a male figure, it is constructed from a material most commonly associated with women's hosiery. IMD

Purchased with funds from the Melva and Martin
Bucksbaum Director's Discretionary Fund for
Acquisition and Innovation; Des Moines Art Center
Permanent Collections, 1988.1

Oxidized copper with candles,
80 x 102 x 12 ¹/₄ inches
(203.2 x 259.1 x 31.1 cm)

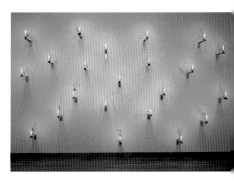

christian boltanski

French, born 1944   **Les Bougies (Candles),** 1987

Christian Boltanski's complex installations deal with memory, death, and identity, both personal and cultural. His role as an artist is that of a shaman or quasi-religious figure, provoking meditations on the meaning of life as actually lived or as recalled, whether rightly or falsely. Common materials and reproductions express his speculations about modern culture, especially its reliance on images more than reality.

The Art Center's **Candles** consists of narrow metal ledges that extend a few inches from the wall and bear figures cut from metal sheets with candles in front of them. When the candles are lit in a darkened room, the figures projected against the wall enlarge and appear to move or dance as the flames flicker. A triangular network of light and shadow arises, suggestive of an alpine landscape, with the mysteriously dynamic figure-shadows at the apex. The spindly, primitive-looking forms suggest cave drawings or children's art. Many carry objects that appear to be battle gear, some are in dance or perhaps defensive positions, some have wings, and all possess skeletal heads. Sculptures that at rest appear slight or insignificant now loom as potent, unsettling shadow images.

Many references exist for **Candles** and similar pieces: Indonesian or European shadow puppets, the illusions of reality in Plato's Cave, or early humans contemplating their world and their own natures by firelight. The sculpture also conjures up dark childhood fears and relates such memories to adult apprehensions about death and the unknown. Certainly one association is with the candles of religious settings and ceremonies. An early installation of this piece, in 1986, was in the church of La Salpêtrière in Paris where Boltanski realized that the work might be seen at first less as a "work of art" than as a compelling image. "The fascinating moment for me is when the spectator hasn't registered the art connection, and the longer I can delay this association the better."[1]

Candles also relates to Boltanski's personal biography. His Catholic mother hid his Jewish father beneath the floor of their house in Paris during the Nazi Occupation; Boltanski was born around the time of the Liberation. His father's experience and his own concerns with the complexities of dual cultures account in part for Boltanski's interest in multiple layers of meaning in sorrow, fear, loss, memory, and death. Downplaying his materials in order to emphasize the spiritual or emotional character of his work, Boltanski uses "poor" materials or unrefined substances such as the oxidized copper of the Art Center's work. He has

explained, "Artists have the power to transmute lead into gold, to make something splendid out of nothing. They are the last alchemists. If I often use poor materials, it is because the emotion develops in a kind of inverse ratio to the poverty of the object and its effective impact."[2]

Boltanski's early years and artistic training are somewhat obscure, since he is deliberately vague about his own history. He began to work in the late 1960s, influenced by European movements such as Nouveau Réalism and Fluxus, and American Pop artists, such as Andy Warhol, who use actual objects to blur the boundaries between life and art. Marcel Duchamp's focus on the ambiguity of reality, the subjective nature of artistic interpretation, and the definition of the artist as a person more of ideas than of technical skill, as well as Joseph Beuys's identification of the artist as a shaman, further affected Boltanski's development. He has produced films, performances, mail art, and artist's books, in addition to sculptures and installations. LRD

Purchased with funds from the National
Endowment for the Arts and the Coffin Fine
Arts Trust; Nathan Emory Coffin Collection
of the Des Moines Art Center, 1989.4

Wood and paint, 74 x 96 x 18 inches
(188 x 243.8 x 45.7 cm)

louise bourgeois

American, born France, 1911   **The Blind Leading the Blind,** 1947–49

Louise Bourgeois's work is characterized by intensely personal, occasionally even viscerally discomforting imagery. It draws on her own psychological history, but addresses universal human experiences such as fear, vulnerability, anger, sex, and familial relationships. Her form ranges from an evocative biomorphism, especially in the later work, to the sparely geometric. Throughout her long career, beginning in the 1930s, she has never been firmly connected to any specific movement or style, always maintaining a distinctive, if not isolated, position in American art. Both Surrealism and Feminism relate to her work, but neither accounts completely for its formal and expressive scope.

Bourgeois's early life is intimately connected with her art. She was born in Paris in 1911. Her family owned a prosperous tapestry business and her childhood exposure to weaving influenced her art, particularly during the 1930s and 1940s when she used a Cubist grid in much of her work. More important was the psychological tension within the family, especially between her passionate, easily angered father and her calm, nurturing mother. Her feelings, especially about her father, have provided Bourgeois with an enduring source of subject matter and emotional intensity. Her preoccupation with themes of sexual anxiety, with the role of women in both sexual and domestic

situations, and the frustration engendered by them all, began to emerge in the late 1940s and associated her later on with Feminist art. Perhaps in reaction to these early insecurities, her education at the Sorbonne (1932–34) was in mathematics and geometry, whose precise structuring became an element in her early works. By 1934 Bourgeois turned to art, training primarily in Cubist-dominated studios including the Ecole des Beaux-Arts and the Académie de la Grande-Chaumière, where she met Fernand Léger, Roger Bissière, and André Lhote, among others. In 1938 she married the American art historian Robert Goldwater and moved to New York, where she studied with Vaclav Vytlacil at the Art Students League. Her artistic career has been spent entirely in the United States where, after working steadily for two decades, she became a prominent figure starting in the 1970s.

The Blind Leading the Blind dates from the beginning of Bourgeois's sculpture career. Before that she produced paintings and prints, in a geometric Cubist style. In New York she affiliated herself with the American abstract artists, but soon added the influence of Surrealism, which she encountered primarily through the émigré European artists who congregated in New York during the war years. Perhaps her most prophetic early images were the "Femme-Maison" (Woman House) paintings in which the heads and upper torsos of women were replaced by houses. This concept – so fundamental to later Feminist imagery – is linked

with the earlier geometric and Cubist work by her early sculpture, such as **The Blind Leading the Blind.**

Bourgeois's first solo sculpture exhibition in 1949 at the Peridot Gallery included the first version of **The Blind Leading the Blind.** Although it was likely destroyed, Bourgeois produced at least six others in wood. The Art Center piece is painted pink (a color Bourgeois described as "anti-art") with ten pairs of legs (as is the work also known as **C.O.Y.O.T.E.** in the National Gallery of Australia, Canberra). Others are painted in various combinations of red, black, purple, and dark brown with six or seven pairs of legs. One interpretation for this important series is that it derives from Bourgeois's visit as a very young child to her father in a hospital at Chartres during World War I where she saw him and others lying in rows of beds. The title may also reflect her feelings about that war. The phrase has its origin in the Gospel of Matthew where Jesus warns that when "the blind lead the blind, both shall fall into the ditch." She may also have had in mind Pieter Bruegel's 1568 painting of the same title, which is probably a comment on the religious conflicts of his day. Other accounts associate the series with the "Femme-Maison" series or with the artists' recollections of tables where fears and resentments about her father were acted out. **LRD**

Gift of Elizabeth Bates and John
Cowles; Des Moines Art Center Permanent
Collections, 1960.22

Polished bronze with stone base, from an
edition of 3, 24 inches high (61 cm); stone,
11 7/8 inches high (30 cm); overall,
35 7/8 inches high (91 cm)

constantin brancusi

Romanian, 1876–1957   **Maiastra,** 1912

This monumental and heroic sculpture representing the magic bird from Romanian folklore embodies a theme that fascinated Constantin Brancusi from 1910 into the 1940s. The folk tale has many variations and crossed many cultural boundaries, but in each version a miraculous golden bird with mystical power and a luminary nature helps mortals triumph over wickedness and achieve good.[1] Enamored with birds and with the idea of soaring in flight, Brancusi said, "All my life I have sought the essence of flight. Flight! What bliss!"[2] For him, flight proclaimed joy because it symbolized ascension, transcendency of the human condition, and freedom.

Brancusi explored this theme progressively and his first eight bird sculptures (completed c. 1910 to 1915) are titled **Maiastra.**[3] The Art Center's bronze is the only one of the series of four made in 1912 that is signed and dated by the artist: "C. BRÂNCUSI, PARIS 1912." The intermediate abstractions of the subject were called **Golden Bird** (1919–20), and the last phase includes the various versions of the famed **Bird in Space** (1923–40s).[4]

The first cast of **Maiastra,** now in The Tate Gallery, London, was placed by Brancusi on a column more than eleven feet high in colleague Edward Steichen's garden in Voulangis, near Paris. Brancusi presumably conceived **Maiastra** to stand on a column pedestal, like the birds that stand on wooden pilasters in Romanian peasant cemeteries – symbols of the eternal soul.

The Art Center's bronze is one of the largest of the eight versions of **Maiastra,** with the bird's distinctly articulated leg and tail noticeably longer. It measures twenty-four inches high and rests on a saw-toothed pattern, limestone base of eleven inches. The base's zigzag shape suggests a sensation of upward motion, like a bird flapping its wings.[5] **Maiastra's** swelling chest, arched throat tapering up from the body, and slight cleft in the beak provide an unmistakable sense of an uttered cry – as in one Romanian version of the magic bird that could resurrect the dead with its glorious song.

Following the example of Brancusi's original installation in Steichen's garden, this simple, majestic bird is posed on top of a dark wooden plinth – a splendid, powerful creature transcending the compressed, severely geometric form beneath it. The smoothly polished, flowing forms of the bird sharply contrast with the soft-textured surface of the stone base. It is this contrast of form and material that evokes a powerful sense of transformation, from something earthy and somber into something exalted and radiant.

Brancusi played a pivotal role in developing the shifting and expanded identities that sculpture has assumed today. His reputation was built mainly in the United States, beginning in 1913 when his work caused a sensation at the Armory Show.[6] His influence, however, was international, and was felt by Henry Moore, Amedeo Modigliani, Isamu Noguchi, and Jean Arp, all of whom have work in the Art Center's permanent collections.

Born in 1876, in a farming village in Romania, Brancusi studied at the School of Arts and Crafts in Craiova and the National School of Fine Arts in Bucharest, where he had his first public exhibition. In Bucharest he received a fine arts degree, then left for Paris – a trip taken largely on foot, according to legend. He died in Paris in 1957. MJR

Gift of the Principal Financial Group;
Des Moines Art Center Permanent
Collections, 1987.1

Painted steel, 84 x 96 x 52 inches
(213.4 X 243.8 X 132.1 cm)

deborah butterfield

American, born 1949 **Untitled (Hoover),** 1986

Deborah Butterfield sees her sculptures of horses as metaphorical self-portraits.[1] **Untitled (Hoover)**, the Art Center's surprisingly lifelike image of a horse assembled from rusting metal rods and crumpled sheets of steel, conveys an affecting mixture of nobility and humility, confidence and vulnerability, that speaks as much to the human as to the equine condition.

Born and raised in San Diego, Butterfield attended San Diego State College (1966–68) and the University of California, San Diego (1969), before enrolling at the University of California, Davis to earn her Bachelor of Arts (1972) and Master of Fine Arts degrees (1973). Butterfield taught art at the University of Wisconsin, Madison from 1974 to 1977, and then moved to Bozeman, Montana, where she taught at Montana State University (1977–86). Since 1986 Butterfield has spent her summers in Montana and her winters in Hawaii.

A lover of horses since childhood and now an accomplished dressage rider, Butterfield considered studying veterinary medicine before turning to ceramics. She bought her first horse while at the University of California, Davis, and started sculpting horses in 1973. These early, life-sized sculptures, modeled in plaster over a steel armature and painted with

muted hues of blue, pink, orange, and black, are realistic representations of mares. "My previous knowledge of horse art," Butterfield recalls, "was soldiers on war-horses going off to kill people. I wanted to do these big, beautiful mares that were as strong and imposing as stallions but capable of creation and nourishing life. It was a very personal feminist statement."[2]

Dissatisfied with the overly literal quality of her plaster horses, Butterfield began in 1976 to work with mud and sticks, sacrificing realistic detail for a more basic sculptural evocation of the horse's essence. A further transformation occurred in 1979 when she began to use discarded fencing, steel, sheet metal, and other scrap materials to build her horses, participating in a modern tradition of assemblage stretching back to Picasso and David Smith.

The pieces of scrap that make up Butterfield's horses retain associations with their former, functional lives while also serving a new, artistic purpose. "When I walk past my pile of junk, I am inspired by things I see. It has to do with finding and identifying objects of interest that I can work with. Working with junk is a way of recognizing a quality of line and appropriating it to my sculpture."[3] Butterfield works spontaneously with her materials, shaping, joining, subtracting, and adjusting until she achieves an effective composition – one that simultaneously reveals its structure,

narrates the process of its construction, and achieves a remarkable resemblance to a living horse.

Every one of Butterfield's constructed horses has a distinctive personality; many are in fact "portraits" of the artist's own horses. **Untitled (Hoover)** was inspired by a horse Butterfield bought near Des Moines while she and her husband, the sculptor John Buck, were visiting friends in Iowa. Butterfield recalls that "this horse...took my breath away – he looked like he was straight out of the Tang Dynasty.... We had him shipped home and John named him Hoover, partly because of the remarkable size of his feet. He is seventeen hands, part Appaloosa and possibly Percheron – massive and his dappled gray and spotted coat is nearly white. He broke a hind leg and I nursed him back to health, though he now has to deal with arthritis. At any rate, his whole character and presence are so like the Tang horses and he is a constant joy and inspiration. I am thrilled that his portrait is back in Iowa."[4] D C

Purchased by the Carl Weeks Memorial
Fund; Des Moines Art Center Permanent
Collections, 1990.22–.27

Installation of six bronze sculptures,
dimensions varied

michael peter cain

American, born 1941 **Nature Takes Delight in Nature: Seed of the World –
Forming Process – #s 10, 15, 23, 30, 35, and 46**, 1989

The sculptures in Michael Peter Cain's "Seed of
the World – Forming Process" series are simple, elegant works of Modernist anthropomorphic abstraction. Stylistically descended
from the work of artists such as Jean Arp
and Henry Moore, Cain's sculptural variations
of natural and manmade forms are readily
accessible and comprehensible. Their intimate
scale and traditional materials are a further
link to earlier sculpture.

An assertive restlessness, an intensity, in
the sculptures belies their diminutive size.
From 1967 to 1973 Cain was a founding
member of Pulsa, a seven-member team of
artists and engineers who created very large-
scale, high-tech interior and exterior installations using light and sound. Cain's "Seed of
the World – Forming Process" works have
the same result, but through opposite means.
Pulsa utilized state-of-the-art technology
and materials to challenge conventions of
art-making from the outside; these works
now question artistic traditions from within.
Also, while Pulsa sought to change the world
by imposing art onto it, Cain now tries to
deconstruct it and, through sculpture, create
a new world. Here Cain does not want simply to respond to the world, but to use his art
to criticize, improve, and restructure it.

The title of this series, "Seed of the World –
Forming Process," indicates the artist's
theme of genesis. Specific works reveal a

direct figurative basis for the abstracted forms.
"Seed of the World – Forming Process" #10,
for example, holds direct reference to a
seed, although that of a peach rather than
the apple of the Garden of Eden.

Images of reproduction and nurturing are
also essential elements in Cain's projected
world. "Seed of the World – Forming Process"
#30 is strongly indebted to the multibreasted
goddess figures created to assure fertility
and abundance. Cain's sculpture is more
androgynous, however, and its form could
also be derived from male reproductive
anatomy.

Numerous additional elements suggest the
creation of a world. Images as diverse as
the pair of lions in "Seed of the World –
Forming Process" #15 and the brain in #23
congregate in readiness to populate Cain's
new world. "Seed of the World – Forming
Process" #35 even accounts for the production of sculpture. While it may be read as
a fetus being nurtured in the womb, the work
also refers to bronze-casting technique.

In 1990 the Art Center presented a one-person exhibition of Cain's work. The six
sculptures in the collection were selected
from that exhibition, and combined by
the artist into an installation titled **Nature
Takes Delight in Nature**. DL

Purchased with funds from the Edmundson
Art Foundation, Inc.; Des Moines Art
Center Permanent Collections, 1952.15

Painted steel, 68 x 144 inches high
(172.7 x 365.7 cm)

alexander calder

American, 1898–1976   **Black Spread,** 1951

Alexander Calder, the "father of the mobile," originated sculptures that move in space according to the delicate balance of their elements and the ambient currents of air. The descendant of two generations of sculptors, Calder was born in Lawnton, Pennsylvania. Perhaps to distinguish himself from his father, Alexander Stirling Calder, and his grandfather, Alexander Milne Calder, young "Sandy" Calder studied mechanical engineering. After graduating in 1919 with a Master of Engineering degree from the Stevens Institute of Technology in Hoboken, New Jersey, he worked at jobs ranging from draftsman and logger to firefighter and freighter hand. In 1923 Calder enrolled at the Art Students League in New York, where he studied for two years.

In 1925 Calder spent two weeks sketching people and animals at the Ringling Brothers Barnum and Bailey Circus in Florida. His observations of the circus acts kindled a love of spontaneity, suspense, playfulness, drama, humor, acrobatics, and motion – all of which remained at the core of his work. Settling in Paris from 1926 to 1932, Calder next turned to making his first "mobile"

sculptures – wood and wire animals that moved in lifelike fashion when he pulled on strings. He exhibited these animated toys and later, when he returned to the United States, he designed "action toys" for a toy firm. Calder was a prodigious worker and by 1943 received his first retrospective exhibition, at The Museum of Modern Art in New York; he subsequently exhibited all over the world.

Calder's "mobiles" (a term coined by Marcel Duchamp) have occasionally used motors to impart movement. However, his best-known works, like the Art Center's **Black Spread**, seemingly move by themselves. **Black Spread** not only occupies space, but interacts with it. The black, organic forms unify the sculptural whole, while each part reacts independently. Negative space becomes an aspect of the visual experience. By cutting out parts of certain forms, Calder made negative space a part of the positive shape, giving the form additional complexity and a light, weightless feeling. Calder explained the process of calculating the weight balance required in mobiles: "I begin with the smallest and work up. Once I know the balance point for the first pair...I anchor it by a hook to another arm, where it acts as one end of another pair of scales, and so on up. It's kind of an ascending scale of weights and counterweights."[1]

Calder's shapes are biomorphic forms similar to those used by Jean Arp and Joan Miró. For the most part, they are playful, reminiscent of natural forms – fish, animals, leaves, flowers, planets, and stars. His use of strong primary colors came as a direct result of a visit to Piet Mondrian's New York studio in 1930. While Mondrian was among the few people Calder credited as an influence on his work, the ideals of Constructivism and Dadaism played a significant part in his artistic development. Ingenious and witty, Calder's wire and metal shapes in motion – and their commanding counterparts, the "stabiles" – seem to embody what is most positive in the American spirit. Calder did what few artists in the twentieth century have accomplished: create art that inspires millions of people worldwide to appreciate contemporary sculpture. **MJR**

Pastel on paper, 25 1/8 x 20 3/4 inches
(63.8 x 52.7 cm)

mary cassatt

American, 1844–1926   **Nicolle and Her Mother,** c. 1900

Born in 1844 to a prominent family in Allegheny City, Pennsylvania (now part of Pittsburgh), Mary Stevenson Cassatt was one of the first American women to challenge convention and pursue art as a profession. From 1861 to 1865 she studied art at the Pennsylvania Academy of Fine Arts in Philadelphia, and then set sail for Europe where she had traveled extensively with her family between 1851 and 1858. In 1871 the Franco-Prussian War forced Cassatt to return home, but she returned to Europe one year later, visiting Spain, Belgium, Holland, and Italy, before settling in Paris in 1874.

Cassatt quickly came under the influence of Impressionism, responding to the spontaneous directness and freedom of this radically new style. Edgar Degas became an important mentor and comrade to Cassatt.

"An enduring professional and personal relationship developed between the two. They shared the attitudes of the class to which they belonged and were fastidious to the point of snobbery. Both witty and acerbic, they respected each other's talent and intelligence and shared a common aesthetic: both were passionately committed to drawing."[1]

Degas deeply influenced Cassatt's work by teaching her to use pastels for drawing and soft-ground etching and aquatint for printmaking. He also suggested the theme of mother and child, a subject that subsequently dominated her career. In 1877 Degas invited Cassatt to join the "Indépendants," as the Impressionists were then known. She participated in the fourth, fifth, sixth, and eighth Impressionist exhibitions between 1879 and 1886.

Members of Cassatt's family, including children, often visited her in France and provided the majority of the sitters for her paintings. She portrayed them engaged in the everyday activities of bathing, having tea, reading, playing, or embracing, all the while keeping her own presence anonymous, a practice used frequently by the Impressionists.

In addition to family members, Cassatt often used neighbors and their children as models, and on rare occasions she also accepted commissions. The figures in the Art Center's **Nicolle and Her Mother** were residents of Mesnil-Théribus, a village near Cassatt's summer home in the Oise country, not far from Paris. This pastel was created during the prime of her career and is a marvelous example of the closeness between a mother and child that Cassatt was able to depict. Although the two figures do not look directly at each other, their heads are turned slightly

toward one another and Cassatt has unified their bodies into one rounded form. The figures emanate a feeling of contentment and peace.

A counterproof of **Nicolle and Her Mother** is in the collection of the Belgrade Museum, Hungary. To create the counterproof, a piece of thin paper was laid on top of the original pastel drawing and rubbed from the back. Some of the chalk was transferred to the sheet, creating a mirror image of **Nicolle and Her Mother**. Cassatt then added more pastel to the original drawing to enrich the portions of the medium lost to the counterproof.

At the turn of the century, Cassatt's eyesight began to fail. Her subsequent works have a softer look and the children appear older (and therefore able to pose for longer periods of time). In 1912 Cassatt underwent her first operation for cataracts on both eyes. Blindness forced her to cease painting at the start of World War I, and she died of diabetes in 1926. TAC

Mildred M. Bohen Collection of
the Des Moines Art Center, 1983.12

Gouache on paper, 24 $^5/_8$ x 19 $^3/_8$ inches
(62.6 x 49.2 cm)

marc chagall

French, born Russia, 1887–1985   **Les Amoureux (The Lovers),** 1926

Marc Chagall is one of the twentieth century's best known and most prolific artists. He lived for almost a century and worked in a variety of mediums, creating paintings, drawings, prints, stained-glass windows, scenery and costumes for theatrical productions, and even the mural on the ceiling of the Paris Opéra.

Chagall was born in Vitebsk, Russia in 1887. He was the oldest of nine children in a Hasidic Jewish family. After taking private art lessons in Vitebsk for a year, Chagall attended the Imperial School for the Protection of Arts in St. Petersburg in 1907. He left Russia for Paris in 1910, carrying little money and only a few paintings and drawings. In Paris, Cubism was flourishing, and his style began to undergo rapid changes from Modernist influences. Chagall was especially interested in Robert Delaunay's style of painting, called Orphism, which maintained recognizable imagery and incorporated brilliant colors. But throughout his career Chagall maintained a unique style; while he experimented with elements of numerous Modernist styles, including Surrealism and Expressionism, his work remained outside rigid stylistic categorization.

Chagall had his first major exhibition at the Der Sturm gallery in Berlin in 1914. A year later he returned to Vitebsk and in 1919 he founded the Vitebsk Academy, an art school that emphasized Modernism and counted among its staff the Russian Constructivists El Lissitsky and Kasimir Malevich. Chagall left the Soviet Union in 1922, living for a short time in Berlin but then returning to Paris.

In 1923 Chagall received his first of three projects from the important Parisian art dealer and publisher Ambroise Vollard. These commissions to illustrate literary works occupied him for the next sixteen years. He worked on Gogol's **Dead Souls** from 1923 to 1925; La Fontaine's **Fables** from 1927 to 1930; and the Old Testament from 1930 to 1939. During this period, Chagall traveled extensively, visiting Egypt, Palestine, Holland, Italy, England, Spain, and Poland for inspiration. He would continue to illustrate literary works throughout his career.

While he was working on the Vollard commissions, Chagall would often take a break to paint individual gouaches on paper. The Art Center's **The Lovers**, from 1926, is one of these works. In addition to themes of Chagall's Russian-Jewish heritage, images of simple people performing everyday tasks, and especially of people expressing love for one another, are frequent in his work. In **The Lovers**, a young couple shyly embrace

and touch one another, oblivious to the world around them. As in this work, Chagall frequently set scenes in front of windows looking out over rooftops. Also typical of his style is the disproportion of scale between the figures and the other objects in the space, such as the vase of flowers. The reduction in size of the figures and their placement in a corner, neatly defined in their own space by the couch, emphasizes their intimacy and concentration on one another.

The flying figure, another repeated image in Chagall's work, is a symbol of love. It is neither Cupid nor an angel, but a symbol of benevolence specific to Chagall. "The image of weightlessness...carries with it a poetic charge of overwhelming simplicity and power."[1]

Chagall lived in Paris until the Nazi Occupation, when he fled to New York, where he remained until 1950. He then returned to France, where he lived for the rest of his life. During the 1940s and 1950s, commissions "poured in and he found himself launched on an international career. Thanks to his exceptional energy, he was able to respond to its demands, remaining active as a painter until the age of ninety-seven."[2] TAC

Purchased with funds from the
Coffin Fine Arts Trust; Nathan Emory
Coffin Collection of the Des Moines
Art Center, 1987.9

Painted and chromium-plated steel,
65 x 68 x 42 inches
(165.1 x 172.7 x 106.7 cm)

john chamberlain

American, born 1927   **Vandam Billy,** 1981

John Chamberlain was influenced in his early years by the welded steel sculpture of David Smith, whose work he was introduced to at The School of The Art Institute of Chicago, where Chamberlain studied between 1950 and 1952. Chamberlain subsequently studied and taught at the experimental Black Mountain College in North Carolina (1955–56) before moving to New York in 1957. Almost immediately he began incorporating into his sculpture parts of scrapped automobiles, and by 1959 he was using these crushed and welded parts exclusively. Chamberlain exhibited frequently throughout the 1960s in both one-person and group shows, and had a major mid-career retrospective at The Solomon R. Guggenheim Museum in New York in 1971.

Chamberlain's aggressive, gestural sculpture parallels in many ways the Abstract Expressionism of the New York School painters, especially Willem de Kooning and Franz Kline. But Chamberlain's appropriation of the automobile as his source and material makes an insistent point of reference to America's car culture, and thereby to popular culture and Pop Art. Like the Pop artists, Chamberlain was interested in blurring the lines between art and life by mining mass culture for its "low art" irony, but also for its freshness and undeniable power, no matter how material or vulgar. The automobile is the epitome of American popular culture. Although he has explored using different materials for his sculpture, for example, urethane foam and melted plexiglass, and has also investigated painting, photography, film, and video, his automobile-derived metal work has remained Chamberlain's signature contribution.

The Des Moines Art Center's **Vandam Billy** is a massive work that sits directly on the floor of the gallery. It is unpretentious in its lack of formal presentation, yet its very bulk in the visitor's path makes clear that it is a presence to be reckoned with; at five-and-one-half feet high and even wider, it is obstacle as well as object. Despite its considerable mass, however, **Vandam Billy** manifests a certain friendliness and rollicking good humor, as evidenced in its cheerfully colored sections and its affectionate, companionable title. **TRN**

Gift of Florence L. Carpenter; Des Moines Art
Center Permanent Collections, 1941.9

Oil on canvas, 29 x 36 ⅛ inches
(73.7 x 91.8 cm)

william merritt chase

American, 1849–1916   **Still Life with Fish,** c. 1908

William Merritt Chase epitomizes the successful American artist at the end of the nineteenth century. Not only were his paintings esteemed critically and commercially, but he was also one of the preeminent teachers of his period. His style throughout his career was characterized by a lively, energetic brush stroke that produced an animated, sometimes sparkling, surface, whether in dark or light tones.

Born in the Midwest, in Williamsburg, Indiana, Chase grew up in Indianapolis where he received his earliest training, with Benjamin F. Hayes. He studied briefly at the National Academy of Design in New York (1869–70) and then worked professionally in St. Louis before leaving on his first trip to Europe in 1872. He enrolled at the Royal Academy in Munich where he studied with Wilhelm Leibl and Karl van Piloty. He joined other American students such as Frank Duveneck and John H. Twachtman who also traveled throughout Europe studying the Old Masters in museums. Chase was particularly influenced by Hals and Tintoretto, and later by Velásquez and Manet, all of whom were noted for their brilliant, painterly

brushwork. When he finished at the academy, Chase was offered a professorship, which he declined in order to return to the United States where he set up his studio in New York. He then embarked on one of the most successful careers in American art, much of it spent teaching at several schools, including the Art Students League, the Brooklyn Art School, the Pennsylvania Academy of Fine Arts, and at his own Chase School, from 1896 to 1908.

Although Chase produced genre, landscape, and portrait paintings, the subject matter of the Art Center picture, a still life with fish, was a common one for the artist. The dark tone of **Still Life with Fish** reflects the Munich manner Chase learned as a student and which he maintained intermittently throughout his career. It also reveals the enduring effect of his study of Dutch still-life paintings of the seventeenth century. But he also responded to Impressionism in the 1880s, and his palette could be a light-filled one of vibrant, clear color. This kind of eclecticism was characteristic of Chase. Although he drew the line at the acceptance of early twentieth-century modern styles, he was the teacher of many students who went on to become important artists, such as Georgia O'Keeffe, Edward Hopper, and Charles Demuth (all of whom are represented in the Art Center's collection). **LRD**

Purchased with funds from the
Coffin Fine Arts Trust; Nathan Emory Coffin
Collection of the Des Moines Art Center,
1970.18

Wooden box construction with
assemblage, 14 ¹/₄ x 7 ³/₄ x 4 inches
(36.8 x 19.7 x 10.2 cm)

joseph cornell

American, 1903–1972   **Untitled (Pour Valéry),** c. 1955

Nearly all of Joseph Cornell's box constructions –
an art form that he virtually invented – are
intimate in scale, and a sizable number of
them contain movable elements that require
the viewer's participation to activate them.
Balls, marbles, metal rings, chains remain
inert until one picks up a box, tilts it, and
causes the objects within to roll and slide;
the resulting sounds become part of the
overall effect. Some boxes have drawers to
pull or lids to lift. Some house cordial glasses
or compasses or pharmaceutical bottles or
glass "ice" cubes that beg to be removed
from their places for closer examination and
in the process reveal what may lie inside
or beneath them. Many, such as the Art
Center's **Untitled (Pour Valéry)**, include colored sand that can be made to flow in a pre-
scribed manner or shifted about to suit the
viewer. "Toys for adults," they were called,
but these are toys with poetic impulses, toys
of metaphysics. And, like many toys, just
one person at a time can "play" with them.

Habitat Group for a Shooting Gallery, however, is not a toy, neither for adults nor for
children. True, the title conjures up the gaiety of a boardwalk or a county fair, and numbers from a lotto game are affixed on or next
to each of the brightly plumed cutout birds.
But though bits of paper and colored feath-
ers lie at the bottom, one is not tempted to
handle the box, because it depicts the after-
math of an act of extreme violence. In that
respect this construction is relatively rare in
the artist's oeuvre.   continued on page 85

Purchased with funds from the
Coffin Fine Arts Trust; Nathan Emory Coffin
Collection of the Des Moines Art Center,
1975.27

Mixed media, 15 1/2 x 11 1/8 x 4 1/4 inches
(39.4 x 28.3 x 10.8 cm)

joseph cornell

Habitat Group for a Shooting Gallery, 1943

The viewer's eyes are first attracted to the red and blue macaws, then to the other two exotic birds, and next to the red, yellow, and blue splotches that stain the white background. A bullet has pierced the glass that had provided protection for the habitat group, and the parrot in the middle of the composition has been shot; its head and the surrounding area are splattered with red. A disk used in the bingo-related game of lotto and bearing the number 12 – the lowest of the four numbered disks in the box – has been placed on the perch of the wounded bird. As in lotto, its number has been called, its number is up.

The box was created in 1943 while World War II was raging. France had already fallen, and one becomes aware that the most prominent collaged elements on the background are French: postage stamps, the name of a famous department store, street addresses, a city square. The temptation to equate the wounded parrot with France is considerable and, once that step is taken, then the remaining feathered creatures may represent the other Allies in Europe: Great Britain, the Soviet Union, and the United States.

Certainly Cornell's title does not suggest the specificity of the above interpretation. But eleven years later, in 1954, Cornell made another construction featuring a bullet hole and shattered glass. The later box is sparser than the Art Center's; it contains a solitary, orange-crested white cockatoo resting on its perch with the bullet hole in the glass by its head and with spatters of paint against the background. The title given to this work by the artist is **Isabelle Dien Bien Phu**. The 1954 defeat of French forces in the Vietnamese city of Dien Bien Phu marked the end of French colonialism in that Southeast Asian country. A map of Asia and the East Indian Ocean is collaged on the back of the box along with a portion of a newspaper article reporting that 2,000 Foreign Legionnaires stationed at the French outpost "Isabelle" made a suicidal attack on Dien Bien Phu in a futile attempt to recapture the city. Such literal explication is highly unusual in Cornell's works, but it lends reinforcement to the supposition that **Habitat Group for a Shooting Gallery** may be less about an attack on civilization in general than about an attack on the civilized world as represented by the four leading Allies in the West in World War II.

Joseph Cornell was born in Nyack, New York in 1903. He was self-taught as an artist. He died in 1972 in Flushing in the borough of Queens, New York. JD

Purchased with funds from the Coffin Fine
Arts Trust; Nathan Emory Coffin
Collection of the Des Moines Art Center,
1962.20

Oil on canvas, 18 ¹/₄ x 21 ³/₄ inches
(46.4 x 55.2 cm)

jean-baptiste-camille corot

French, 1796–1875   **Ville-d'Avray – L'Etang et les maisons Cabassud (The Pond and
the Cabassud Houses at Ville-d'Avray)**, 1855–60

The influence of Jean-Baptiste-Camille Corot on subsequent painting has been far-reaching. A calm, ascetic character, Corot was spectacularly innovative in his approach and was among the first to paint directly out-of-doors, in a distinctively French style called **plein-air**. He was considered during his life to be "the greatest landscape painter of our time."[1]

The public's admiration and Corot's fame were built upon landscape paintings in which amorphous trees and dim pools are veiled in the mist of dawn or evening. The Art Center's **The Pond and the Cabassud Houses at Ville-d'Avray** is characteristic of Corot's silvery, seductive, gray-green scenes. It possesses the obvious, almost sentimental, poetry that became Corot's best-loved quality.

Corot repeatedly used motifs that were inspired by his visits to Ville-d'Avray, near Versailles and close to the home Corot occupied for the greater part of his life. Along the road to Ville-d'Avray stood large houses called Cabassud. The road, rue du Lac, became known as Corot's road, and its splendid view of the pond and the houses turned out to be a boundless source of images. He regularly came back to paint this site at different stages in his career, but "never twice in the same manner."[2] On these frequent returns he was absorbed in thoughts and studies of nature.

The Art Center's painting is linked to two others: **Ville-d'Avray – L'Etang, la maison Cabassud et le bout de la propriété Corot** (Musée du Louvre, Paris) and **Ville-d'Avray** (private collection). Unlike the other views, the Art Center's painting presents the rue du Lac largely concealed by a cluster of slender birch trees. In the foreground of this wistful scene, the sunlight illuminates a tender moment wherein a woman pauses at the water's edge, her back turned to the viewer as she kneels down absorbed with a child. It is springtime and the filmy quality of the foreground foliage is gradually replaced by a rendering of reflected light that establishes the tranquil pond and the graceful houses as the primary theme. The delicately handled sky, with its softly modulated clouds, suggests that Corot was accurately transcribing his responses to nature: his masterful treatment of trees and the effects of light relied on working from nature. Here he systematically applied the Neoclassical formula for a landscape composition: the right side filled by foliage, the left side open to the horizon.

Corot was born in 1796 over the Parisian shop of his mother, a successful milliner. After studying at the college in Rouen, he briefly apprenticed as a draper. In 1817 his family bought a country home at Ville-d'Avray, where Corot used his bedroom as a studio. He became devoted to Neoclassical painting, initially studying under Michalon, then in the studio of Jean-Victor Bertin, who introduced him to the work of Nicolas Poussin and instilled in him a desire to paint in Italy, where Corot developed his early landscape style. Using a small allowance from his family, Corot embarked on his own successful career. He died at Ville-d'Avray in 1875. **MJR**

Purchased with funds from the Coffin Fine
Arts Trust; Nathan Emory Coffin
Collection of the Des Moines Art Center,
1958.1

Oil on canvas, 36 ½ x 58 ¾ inches
(92.7 x 149.2 cm)

gustave courbet

French, 1819–1877   **La Vallée de la Loue (Valley of the Loue),** 1865

Gustave Courbet was an audacious painter and personality, willing to challenge French academic painting and offer instead a new brand of realism based on subject matter drawn from ordinary life and presented in a style of execution noted for its directness and vigor. Courbet's influence on the subsequent generation of Impressionist painters was tremendous. He was acclaimed for his iconoclastic originality, his innovative application of paint with a palette knife, and also for his direct engagement of real and recognizable locations in the French countryside. He was equally radical in his politics, and after the fall of the Commune of Paris in 1871, spent time in prison. In 1873 he fled to Switzerland, where he lived and worked until his death in 1877.

Courbet is known as a realist painter, yet his landscapes and seascapes have a heroic monumentality that is in essence Romantic. The heavy, inexorably rolling waves of the seascapes in particular have a physicality and an elemental character – in part the product of Courbet's rough application of paint – that goes much deeper than simple observation of nature. Even in his figure paintings, Courbet's work is frequently much more complex than it appears at first glance. Often the subject is allegorical, with attendant props and attributes that have a symbolic as well as logical place within the composition.

By the mid-1860s, when the Des Moines Art Center's **Valley of the Loue** was painted, Courbet was at the height of his fame and influence. The painting exemplifies the solid construction of simply massed forms that characterizes Courbet's landscapes. A rising hill sweeps up from the banks of the Loue River, filling the middle ground of the composition with an intense and deep green. Ponderous dressed stones, the remains of some abandoned medieval ruin, rest on top of the rise, forming a cap of unimaginable weight and density. A brilliant blue sky lightened with flecks of white clouds forms an equally saturated but more lighthearted backdrop to the countryside. Indeed, it is as if Courbet wished to make a literal distinction between earth and air, finding equivalents in paint for the weightiness of the former and the atmospheric insubstantiality of the latter.

Despite the outrage that greeted Courbet's monumental painting **Burial at Ornans** (1849–50), which was roundly castigated even by such enlightened critics and colleagues as Eugène Delacroix for its "hideous" and "common" people and presentation, Courbet for decades maintained his position at the forefront of vanguard French painting, losing this distinction only when Edouard Manet and the Impressionists emerged as new targets for the art conservatives' anger. However, even during the 1850s, when his artistic notoriety was at its height, Courbet had a following for his less controversial, though no less inventive, landscapes and portraits. **TRN**

Purchased with funds from Mr. and Mrs. Richard T.
Fisher, the Gardner and Florence Call Cowles
Foundation, the Dr. and Mrs. Peder T. Madsen Fund, and
The Jacqueline and Myron Blank Charitable Trust;
Des Moines Art Center Permanent Collections, 1977.23

Oil on canvas, 32 x 40 inches
(81.3 x 101.6 cm)

ralston crawford

American, born Canada, 1906–1978   **Worth Steel Plant,** 1936

Ralston Crawford was born in St. Catharines, Ontario, Canada in 1906, but grew up in Buffalo, New York. After high school, where he excelled in art, Crawford planned to study commercial design at Pratt Institute in New York. An enrollment error prevented him from entering, however, so he hired on to a steamship. After six months at sea, Crawford decided to study painting at the Otis Art Institute in Los Angeles, and disembarked in California in early 1927.

Crawford spent only two terms at Otis, and by fall 1927 was instead attending The Pennsylvania Academy of Fine Arts in Philadelphia. Although most of Crawford's training was in figurative painting, he studied extensively with Hugh Breckenridge, a Modernist abstract painter who emphasized strong color; Crawford's work would always reflect this influence. He was also exposed to modern art through the collectors Albert Barnes and Earl Horter. Through Barnes, Crawford learned of Cézanne's emphasis on structure, which informed all of Crawford's subsequent work. Horter introduced him to slightly older colleagues in Pennsylvania, Charles Sheeler and Charles Demuth. Crawford would share their interest in crisply rendered landscape painting emphasizing industrial imagery. The term the three artists became categorized by is Precisionism, and the Art Center's painting, **Worth Steel Plant**, is a strong example of this style.

Crawford lived in New York during the Depression, from 1931 to 1935. He struggled amidst his first experiences with teaching, short-term employment with the Public Works of Art Project, and burgeoning political activism advocating support for artists, as well as pursuing his own art. Thanks to affluent in-laws, he also was able to honeymoon in Europe, attending two different art academies in Paris and visiting museums in France, Italy, Spain, and Switzerland.

Landscape dominated Crawford's oeuvre. He was inspired in particular by rural structures, such as barns, and scenes of wharfs and ships. When Crawford moved to Exton, Pennsylvania in 1935, his concentration shifted to industrial imagery. He began developing the flat, simple, strongly colored paintings of ice plants, grain elevators, roofs with water towers, ships, breweries, coal elevators, gas tanks, and bridges for which he would be known throughout his career.

The paintings from 1935 to 1938, such as **Worth Steel Plant**, have a somber and brooding aspect. Here the uncharacterized, flat plant is bulky and dark, and where the noise and activity of manufacturing are expected, stillness is found. The doors are black and forbidding, the smokestacks inactive. This "eerie, forlorn stillness" has been attributed to Crawford's lingering interest in Surrealism from his European travels and his friendship with the American Surrealist O. Louis Guglielmi.[1] In 1938, however, a shift

occurred in Crawford's work. While an artist-in-residence in Maitland, Florida, he became more interested in light, and without changing subject matter the somber weight of his previous work gave way to a brighter airiness. He developed an interest in photography as well, and began to photograph sites prior to painting them. This practice led to an increased attention to detail in his later paintings, which remain elegant in their crispness, but lose some of the mystery of the earlier images. Crawford also began exhibiting his photographs independently.

Crawford served in the Army Corps of Engineers during World War II. In 1946 **Fortune** magazine commissioned him to observe and paint the atomic bomb tests at Bikini Atoll. This experience was profound for Crawford: his images became torn, twisted, and fragmented, leading to a much higher degree of abstraction which he would pursue for the rest of his career.

Although based in New York, Crawford traveled extensively throughout the United States, exhibiting his work, teaching, and lecturing. In addition to continuing to paint, he became fascinated with New Orleans, and produced an important series of photographs of the jazz milieu and musicians of that city. DL

Oil on wood panel, 13 ½ x 10 inches
(34.3 x 25.4 cm)

honoré daumier

French, 1808–1879   **Le Liseur (The Reader),** c. 1863

Honoré Daumier portrayed with inexhaustible zeal one of the most politically turbulent periods of history: the revolutions, uprisings, riots, and wars that transformed Europe during the nineteenth century. A master of political and social illustration, Daumier reacted to the social and economic struggle that pitted industrial capitalism and the bourgeoisie against the widely impoverished masses.

Daumier was born in Marseilles in 1808. His father was a glazier by trade, but a poet by ambition. Both father and son shared a passion for books. In his father's modest library, Daumier became familiar with the thoughts of the philosopher and political theorist Jean-Jacques Rousseau, whose maxims seem to have influenced his thinking. Even though the elder Daumier never gave up his dreams of literary fame, he insisted that Daumier go to work and learn a vocation at age twelve. Entering the process-server trade, Daumier found himself in the kind of sordid place so skillfully rendered by Balzac and Dickens, and this brief, dismal experience left a profound impression on him.

By the mid-1820s, Daumier made his first friends in the art world while attending one or two small academies where students worked before a model without instruction. As a young artist, he was inspired by the English school of satirical artists: Hogarth, Gillray, and Rowlandson. All that was worth drawing in Paris was right under his nose: in a railway carriage, a cellar, a butcher shop, or a law court. He immersed himself in the squalor and detail of everyday life. Celebrities of bourgeois France were often portrayed by Daumier with a vengeance that metaphorically impaled them upon his lithographic crayon.

The diffusion of Daumier's satirical prints has caused them to overshadow the rest of his work. Indeed only twice in his life was Daumier able to give his time entirely to drawing and painting, rather than producing images designed for mass reproduction. The first occasion was just after the 1848 revolution, when press censorship put him out of work. The second was after 1860, when he was fired for a time by the Paris daily paper **Le Charivari**. It was during this second period, considered Daumier's most inventive and technically mature, that the Art Center's **The Reader** was painted.

Daumier's painting style has been compared to that of Eugène Delacroix, whose distinct power and fluidity of line he admired. Daumier had a superb command of drawing that enabled him to define his figures first with a small brush and then later assimilate these outlines into built-up forms using semitransparent pigment.

The Reader, vivid in its dark tonal structure, is natural and unpretentious in expressing the gravity of the subject's concentration. The painting is an intimate view of a simple human being thoughtfully absorbed in his book. The subject's balding head dominates the picture – only a low-relief plaque of a man's profile competes for the viewer's attention. His vigorous physiognomy and sensitive mouth are modeled with power and sureness. The luminous head is painted in dramatic light and with overlapping pigments and glazes. The red-edged, soft-bound book, held open by both hands, is placed in partial light with a single application of paint. A single brush stroke gives individual form and expression to the hands.

A fervid caricaturist, Daumier was also capable of a quiet, concentrated study. Compositions such as **The Reader** recall an extensive group of paintings of varied formal and psychological relationships between individuals engaged in cultivated, urbane activities such as reading, singing, looking at works of art, attending theater, or playing cards, chess, or checkers.

Before it was purchased for the collections, **The Reader** was brought to Des Moines in 1958 as part of the Art Center's "Tenth Anniversary Exhibition." MJR

**Bequest of Mildred M. Bohen;
Des Moines Art Center Permanent
Collections, 1983.9**

**Watercolor and pencil,
20 3/4 x 26 1/2 inches (52.7 x 67.3 cm)**

andré derain

French, 1880–1954   **The Nymphes,** c. 1905–1906

Abandoning his study of engineering in favor of a career as an artist, André Derain became one of the leading French avant-garde painters of the early twentieth century. At the Académie Julian in Paris in 1898, he met Maurice Vlaminck, who was also from Derain's hometown of Chatou, and the two began sharing a studio in 1900. Derain, Vlaminck, Albert Marquet, and especially Henri Matisse achieved fame – and initial notoriety – at the 1905 Salon des Indépendants, where the group was dubbed "Les Fauves" or "Wild Beasts," in reaction to their bold, "savage and primitive" painting style.

Derain went on to a long and distinguished career as an artist, marked by numerous exhibitions and honors, explorations into sculpture, and set and costume design, notably for Sergei Diaghilev's Ballets Russes, as well as his two-dimensional work on canvas and paper. Nevertheless it is his earlier years, especially his Fauve period (until 1908) and his subsequent investigations into the art of Paul Cézanne (until 1912), that were his most inventive and distinct period. It was during these Fauve years that the Art Center's watercolor **The Nymphes** was painted.[1]

The Nymphes is a textbook example not only of Fauvism, with its brilliant and unrealistic palette, loosely sketched forms, and rhythmic composition, but it also highlights a subject common at the turn of the century: the theme of ideal existence. Originating clearly in the work of Cézanne and with other late nineteenth-century French artists such as Pierre Puvis de Chavannes and Paul Gauguin, the theme explores the idea of a rural Arcadia peopled by harmonious groups of men and women pursuing their leisure. They are usually nude, usually female, and frequently bathers. This idea of unspoiled harmony between humankind and nature allowed artists to create an intriguing hybrid: neither landscape nor history painting nor even the traditional mythological scene or "fête champêtre." The new theme was especially apt for the Fauves: romanticizing the simple life lived in a hospitable, even perfect, natural world, it was eminently suitable to an equally fresh, uninhibited, "artless" and "primitive" approach. Derain was even briefly inspired during this period to turn to watercolor, the medium of spontaneity, instead of oil.

The Des Moines Art Center's dazzling watercolor features a landscape conceived in five rough, horizontal bands of color: black, blue, yellow, green, and red, against which are the verticals of a fence incomplete on both sides, six extremely active, polka-dotted trees, and four sketchy, rather delicate female nudes. The heavily saturated landscape seems almost to shelter the nymphes, whose lightness is the product not only of the artist's sensitive pencil, but also the whiteness of the paper shining through the transparent watercolor of their forms. TRN

Gift of Dorothy and James S. Schramm;
Des Moines Art Center Permanent
Collections, 1961.49

Oil on canvas mounted on a honeycomb
support panel, 30 x 27 inches
(76.2 x 68.3 cm)

richard diebenkorn

American, 1922–1993   **The Table,** 1956–57

One of America's leading painters of the second half of the twentieth century, Richard Diebenkorn grew up in San Francisco and entered Stanford University in 1940. During service in the US Marines in 1943–45, he was able to visit major museums of modern art on the East Coast, an experience that would sustain his painting throughout his life. Diebenkorn continued his studies following the war in 1946, entering the California School of Fine Arts (today the San Francisco Art Institute), where he would later teach. Although he would subsequently study at the University of New Mexico in Albuquerque in 1950–51, and teach at the University of Illinois in Urbana in 1952, most of the rest of his life was spent in California.

Throughout his long career Diebenkorn worked in series. Early on he grouped paintings beneath titles corresponding to the places where he lived; for instance, the "Albuquerque" paintings (1951–52), the "Urbana" paintings (1953), and the "Berkeley" paintings (1954–55). While these series were all abstractions, in the mid-1950s Diebenkorn

embarked on a sustained period of figurative, still-life, and landscape painting that would last until 1967. In so doing, Diebenkorn pursued an approach to painting initiated earlier by his Bay Area friends and colleagues Elmer Bischoff and David Park, both of whom had recently abandoned abstraction for the figure. The freedom with which these painters alternatively pursued figuration and abstraction characterized Bay Area painting, and distinguished these artists from the influential examples provided by Clyfford Still and Mark Rothko, both of whom were active in San Francisco in the years following World War II.

The Des Moines Art Center's **The Table** (1956–57) is a fine and characteristic example of Diebenkorn's painting at this time. What he accomplished in the years 1956–67 was a conjunction of the painterly qualities of his earlier abstraction with a compositional vigor suggested by his subjects. While many of his still lifes of the period focus on objects resting atop a table – plates, scissors, and eating utensils – Diebenkorn concentrated here on the table itself, a strong geometric form firmly placed within a sunny interior space. Diebenkorn set the table before a window and – like Henri Matisse in many of his interior scenes – included a view out the window to the landscape beyond.

continued on page 98

Purchased with funds from the Coffin Fine
Arts Trust; Nathan Emory Coffin
Collection of the Des Moines Art Center,
1975.21

Oil on canvas, 93 x 81 inches
(236.2 x 205.7 cm)

richard diebenkorn

Ocean Park No. 70, 1974

Diebenkorn's interest in Matisse was lifelong,
and he visited a retrospective devoted to the
French painter when it was shown at the
University of California, Los Angeles in 1966.
In that same year Diebenkorn moved to
Los Angeles to teach at UCLA. He settled in
Ocean Park, a section of Santa Monica
fronting on the beach. The following year he
abandoned representation and began to
experiment with canvases devoted to broad
areas of carefully composed color. Large
and luminous, these paintings formed the
nucleus of Diebenkorn's next series, the
"Ocean Park" paintings. These paintings
were influenced equally by Matisse's brilliant structuring of large fields of color, and
Diebenkorn's own response to a Los
Angeles cityscape filled with gauzy color
and firm urban lines. The Art Center's **Ocean
Park No. 70** is among the best works in
the large series: beneath a high, golden horizon line are vast vertical expanses of mauve,
off-white, and red color. Throughout,
Diebenkorn's soft handling of paint yields to
a substructure of horizontal, vertical, and, in
particular, diagonal strokes, the skeletal
geometry over which the bright surface of
painted skin is applied. **NB**

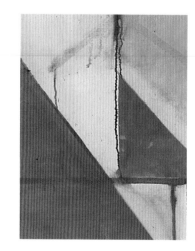

Purchased with funds from Rose F. Rosenfield;
Des Moines Art Center Permanent
Collections, 1958.21

Oil on canvas, 20 x 28 inches
(50.8 x 71.2 cm)

arthur dove

American, 1880–1946   **Corn Crib,** 1935

Arthur Dove was among the earliest American painters to move decisively in the direction of abstraction. By 1910 he had painted a significant number of abstract canvases, declaring the intention of his visualization through their titles (**Abstractions Nos. 1–6**). Color is the dominant element in Dove's compositions, and he used it to enhance form and line, extracting the essential spirit from an object or situation. He believed each object had a certain configuration that captured its spirit or inner image in an objectively perceived shape. He said in 1912: "Yes, I could paint a cyclone.... I would show the repetition and convolutions of the rage of the tempest. I would paint the wind, not the landscape chastised by the cyclone."[1]

In 1903 Dove graduated from Cornell University and left for New York City to become a successful magazine illustrator, a career that he ultimately abandoned. Four years later he ventured to Europe for eighteen months and was brought into contact with modern art: Fauvism in France was at its height; Cézanne's memorial exhibition had just been held, and Picasso's **Les Demoiselles d'Avignon** was recently completed. Throughout the following decades, remarkable interactions of the artist's life are documented in voluminous correspondence between Dove and Duncan Phillips and

Alfred Stieglitz. A philanthropist, art collector, and the founder of The Phillips Collection (the first modern art museum in the United States), Phillips became Dove's sole patron and critical supporter. Dove's career was also nourished by Stieglitz, a forceful advocate for Modernism in the United States. From 1910 until his death in 1946, Stieglitz provided financial support, periodic exposure through his galleries, and an artistic climate that nurtured the development of Dove's mature style.

Dove's deep love of nature emerged and evolved during his boyhood in Geneva, New York, located in the heart of the Finger Lakes region at the northern tip of Seneca Lake. He moved back to his hometown from Long Island in 1933 and lived on the family property through 1938 while desperately trying to salvage what remained of the family fortune. Images of dense peach orchards, barnyards, and lush pasture around Geneva permeate his most evocative and intense paintings from the 1930s. As Georgia O'Keeffe said of her friend, "Dove comes from the Finger Lakes region. He was up there painting, doing abstractions that looked just like that country, which could not have been done anywhere else."[2]

Painted after Dove and his wife, the artist Helen "Reds" Torr, settled in Geneva, the Art Center's **Corn Crib** favors irregular, roughly circular shapes swelling outward with halos of modulating color, like many of Dove's extraordinary paintings from the late 1920s

and 1930s. The shapes suggest an inherent growth and explosive energy equivalent to the universal rhythm or life force that he felt existed in the world. He wrote, "I have come to the conclusion that one must have a means governed by a definite sense beyond geometric repetition. The play or spread or swing of space can be felt with this kind of consciousness."[3]

In the foreground of **Corn Crib**, concentric bands of ocher and gray create wheellike shapes and organic forms. The brooding purple walls of the corn crib contrast with its snow-covered roof, and repeated brush strokes of deep purple radiate out from the roof into the dark woods. The sense of vitality is enhanced by Dove's use of clearly visible brush strokes, which resemble pulsations of energy. He eliminated the separate forms through the use of indistinct contours that merge into one another and into the environment; the modest corn crib entirely fills the shallow landscape background of the canvas.

In April 1935 **Corn Crib** was exhibited in "Arthur G. Dove Exhibition of Paintings (1934–35)" at An American Place in New York. Twenty-three years later the Art Center purchased this painting from The Downtown Gallery, New York. In 1959 **Corn Crib** was included in a retrospective of the artist's work at the San Francisco Museum of Art. MJR

Purchased with funds from the Coffin Fine Arts Trust; Nathan Emory Coffin Collection of the Des Moines Art Center, 1981.41

Oil on canvas, 51 3/16 x 38 3/16 inches
(130 x 97 cm)

jean dubuffet

French, 1901–1985   **Le Villageois aux cheveux ras (The Villager with Close-Cropped Hair),** 1947

"People are more beautiful than they think they are. Long live their true faces." So proclaimed the headline on the front of the newspaper-format catalogue of Jean Dubuffet's exhibition titled "Portraits" at the Galerie René Drouin in Paris in October 1947. The presence of armed guards at the gallery was a precaution to prevent a recurrence of the chaos that had accompanied the artist's exhibition at the same gallery just seventeen months earlier: six paintings had been damaged by a crowd that considered the artist's works an affront to the grand tradition of French painting. However, emotions were kept in rein at "Portraits," although one of the individuals whose caricatured visage appeared in several of the pictures on view was so upset that he threatened to destroy them with his umbrella.

"The persons I find beautiful are not those who are usually found beautiful," Dubuffet wrote in the catalogue. He elaborated: "…usually, what people consider beautiful is a young lady with curly hair, nice regular small teeth, no pimples on her face, nice clean nails, no insects, etc., well, all that I say doesn't particularly interest me. If she has pimples, it doesn't bother me.…Funny noses, big mouths, teeth all crooked, hair in the ears – I'm not at all against these things." He went on to extol older

people, obesity, and grimaces, and stated that "people who have a star or a shrub or a map of a river basin across their faces" interested him much more than so-called classical beauty.

The artist was just beginning to formulate his philosophy on art and life which would culminate in a speech that he delivered in Chicago and called "Anti-Cultural Positions" (1951). In it he questioned most of Western civilization's long-held beliefs regarding scientific and aesthetic values defined initially by the ancient Greeks and elaborated upon by succeeding generations. Instead he praised values associated with "primitive" societies: instinct, feelings, passion, even madness, since he believed these attributes and conditions to be closer and truer to man's core. He coined the term "Art Brut" (raw art) to characterize the art of the insane and of children, i.e., those who create viscerally without the intervention of formal training. He even collected thousands of such works and donated them to the City of Lausanne, Switzerland, where they are now housed in a museum.

Between August 1946 and August 1947, Dubuffet completed one hundred and sixty-one portraits of twenty-two individuals which are illustrated in volume three of his catalogue raisonné which he titled **More Beautiful Than They Think (Portraits)**. Although **The Villager with Close-Cropped Hair** was finished in May, thus within the above time

frame, and although its highly specific facial features are obviously those of a particular person, the artist chose not to include the painting in either the exhibition or the **Portraits** volume. The twenty-two persons portrayed include his wife, his two art dealers, and three fellow artists, but the great majority of the works are of novelists, critics, poets, playwrights, and other literary luminaries in postwar Paris. **The Villager** differs from the other paintings and drawings of this type in one important respect: rather than a homogeneous or monochromatic space such as that in which the other figures reside, a village forms the background for the fierce protagonist who confronts the viewer head-on. And what a head it is, with its width greater than its height: with large, almond-shaped eyes and an arrow for a nose that points down to a thin-lipped, teeth-baring grimace; a stubble of hair peppers the upper periphery of the massive cranium. A yellow tracery of winding paths, orchards, gardens, towers, and other structures are all subjugated to the formidable individual who dominates the composition from top to bottom.

continued on page 104

Gift of Melva Bucksbaum in honor of the
Des Moines Art Center's 50th Anniversary;
Des Moines Art Center Permanent
Collections, 1998.1

Oil on canvas, 51 ¼ x 63 ¾ inches
(130.2 x 161.9 cm)

jean dubuffet

Paysage métapsychique (Metapsychical Landscape), 1952

Among those who knew Dubuffet, opinion is divided as to whether **The Villager** is a self-portrait. The strongest evidence supporting the view that it indeed is a self-portrait is a statement made in 1974 by the artist to a London dealer who had recently exhibited the work. Apparently Dubuffet unequivocally stated that he and the person depicted in the painting were one and the same, but because the artist enjoyed teasing, some uncertainty remains. What is certain, however, is that the painting is one of the artist's boldest images.

"Momentary places" is the designation given by Jean Dubuffet to a series of about thirty landscapes that occupied him from October 1952 through February 1953. Instead of rendering the illusion of space and depth that traditionally characterizes most paintings of this theme, in the Art Center's **Metapsychical Landscape** Dubuffet has, in effect, sliced away a section of earth and presented that to the viewer. There are no geological strata here, but rather a segment of matter in constant motion and teeming with inner energy. Organic elements wriggle their way upward through the ground, becoming a part of the high horizon line. The artist's title indicates that this landscape is not merely a physical one, but also one that transcends ordinary psychological phenomena.

By employing various experimental techniques – in particular using color-saturated turpentine over oily areas that were still fresh – Dubuffet was able to achieve what he referred to in his writings as "a whole play of spots and meanders and a breaking up of the surface into subtle designs interpenetrating each other."[1] Several days of drying would produce "those wrinkles and curlicues which one ordinarily tries to avoid," but which Dubuffet used for his own purposes. Even then he was not done, but would tear away some of the surface with a knife, "obtaining effects that resembled abraded skin." In **Metapsychical Landscape** the result suggests the appearance of a time when the world was in its primordial state in every way.

Probably more than any other artist of his generation, Dubuffet constantly sought and investigated new techniques, new effects, and new media. Eight months after this painting was completed, he was composing pictures made of butterfly wings.

Jean Dubuffet was born in Le Havre, France, in 1901. He studied art there and then moved to Paris as a teenager. He died in Paris in 1985. JD

SOWETO

TIAN

D·A·I·L·Y   P·A·I·N·T·I·N·G

IF YOUR
STORY IS
MORE
INTERESTING
THAN YOUR
OBJECT

THEN
YOUR STORY
IS YOUR
OBJECT

I MAKE
THESE PICTURE

IN LIFE IS NOT DONE
I KEEP

Mixed media on canvas, 115 x 173 x 9 inches
(292.1 x 439.4 x 22.9 cm)

Purchased with funds from the Coffin Fine
Arts Trust; Nathan Emory Coffin
Collection of the Des Moines Art Center,
1990.2

david dunlap

American, b. 1940   **D-a-i-l-y P-a-i-n-t-i-n-g,** 1987–89

For two decades David Dunlap has created monumental installations that use a range of objects, painting, and language to explore heroic stories and dreams. By superimposing painted words on a vibrant orange field, he plots out body parts, cities, states, and countries around the world. The intent is to meld regional and worldwide, far-reaching places with a greater understanding of ourselves. Influenced by Outsider Art, his work is fueled by personal convictions and by political content that often address international issues of human rights and social injustice with reference to historical incidents. The universal underlying theme, however, is Dunlap's affirmation of life.

Dunlap was born in Kansas City, Missouri, and received a Bachelor of Arts degree from Colorado College, Colorado Springs in 1962. He later earned Bachelor of Fine Arts and Master of Fine Arts degrees at Yale University, New Haven, Connecticut. He is currently a professor at the School of Art and Art History, University of Iowa, Iowa City.

The Art Center's **D-a-i-l-y P-a-i-n-t-i-n-g** (1987–89), a floor-to-ceiling installation, is a forceful and impassioned commentary about contemporary life: the roles it thrusts upon us, and the possibilities and issues we face. Originally using an orange-painted wall as the support, **D-a-i-l-y P-a-i-n-t-i-n-g** evolved into a painted canvas story of the artist's life on which are assembled drawings, paintings, notebooks, a notebook case, and a suit worn by Dunlap with a standard that he carried. This work was developed from Dunlap's award-winning installation in the Iowa Artists 1989 exhibition and was included in the artist's 1989–90 solo exhibition, both at the Art Center.

At the center of Dunlap's art are his notebooks – daily records combining his personal diaries with planning books. The pen, a conspicuous image in all his work, represents consciousness and stands erect like a figure. The notebooks and the cases reflect significant moments or ideas in Dunlap's life. He explained, "I include notebooks [in my work] because I want people to understand that my art-making comes from the activity of keeping a journal, from living a life."[1]

An extraordinary range of subject matter comprises **D-a-i-l-y P-a-i-n-t-i-n-g**. Displayed above eleven small drawings are four acrylic paintings that combine language with visual imagery. Across the top of the canvas is an orange-painted thread connecting the concurrent human rights struggles in Soweto Township (outside Johannesburg) and Tiananmen Square (Beijing). Facsimiles of notebooks #305 to #318 are contained within "Notebookcase #5" (titled and numbered by the artist), a part of the work. Inside the case is a poem given to Dunlap (by Gene Swan, then an Art Center guard) that binds our daily lives to art-making. Also, there is a logbook documenting the creation of **D-a-i-l-y P-a-i-n-t-i-n-g** and containing several possible configurations of the work. A specially designed suit, hat, and tie, completed in 1987, hang to the right of "Notebookcase #5." One of a series of wooden standards with painted emblems (i.e., ladder, lamp) mounted at the top rests next to the suit. Dunlap wore this suit and carried this standard in a series of multimedia performances focusing on US policy in Central America and South Africa. The attire symbolizes the official point of entry into a dynamic, conscious world (much as a business suit symbolizes entry into the commercial world) where life and art are interactive.
MJR

Purchased with funds from the Dr. and Mrs.
Peder T. Madsen Fund; Des Moines
Art Center Permanent Collections, 1971.12

Hand-colored etching and gouache,
9 ³/₄ x 14 inches (24.8 x 35.6 cm)

james ensor

Belgium, 1860–1949   **Entry of Christ into Brussels,** 1898

James Ensor, the son of mask and souvenir sellers, was born in 1860 in the seaside resort town of Ostend, Belgium. He studied art at the Brussels Academy, and although he exhibited with several artists' groups, and was a founding member of the avant-garde Les XX (Les Vingts), he remained outside the mainstream. Ensor's highly witty and satirical art, which often employed traditional Christian images, skeletons, and allusions to death, attacked bourgeois hypocrisy. He was also frequently self-mocking. His graphic oeuvre, executed largely between 1886 and 1904, totaled 142 etchings, drypoints, and lithographs, many hand-colored by the artist.

In 1888 Ensor completed an enormous canvas, prophetically titled **Entry of Christ into Brussels in 1889.** The setting is a broad avenue, lined with houses decorated with signs, banners, and flags. A banner stretching across the foreground is inscribed "Vive La Sociale." Despite the title of the work, the scene appears to be a Mardi Gras celebration cum political demonstration. The street is thronged with hundreds of figures, including gentlemen and ladies in everyday dress, politicians with sashes, masqueraders and clowns, a marching band and festival panoply. A figure of Death wearing a top hat occupies the lower left corner. People stand on balconies and wave from windows. Christ, mounted on an ass, is almost lost in the middle distance. Does Ensor's leap of imagination, transposing a

scene of Passion Week in Jerusalem to Carneval in Brussels, ask where is Christ when he is needed in the modern world? Or is this, as has been suggested, a self-portrait of the neglected artist?[1]

Ensor's image recalls Pieter Bruegel's paintings; views into upper-story rooms and odd scatological allusions are virtually quotations that pay homage to Bruegel. Ensor's placement of Christ lost in the unheeding crowd is reminiscent of the Christ in Bruegel's **Road to Calvary** (1564). Ensor's references to the sixteenth-century painter are not surprising, for in Belgium at the end of the nineteenth century the revival, appreciation, and legitimization of Flemish heritage emerged as a political as well as artistic movement. Another important early Flemish painter for Ensor was Hieronymous Bosch, whose hallucinatory paintings of Hell and Paradise provided inspiration for many of Ensor's more haunted images.

Ensor's monumental work was repeatedly rejected for exhibition, and remained in his home in Ostend for forty years. It was finally shown in 1929 in the inaugural exhibition of the Palais des Beaux-Arts, Brussels, and is now owned by the Getty Museum.

In 1898 Ensor made an etching titled **Entry of Christ into Brussels,** based on his painting. The print reverses the painting's composition and repeats many of its elements. The overall shape of the image is less elongated. The sense of deep space in the painting is replaced by a discontinuous space in the etching, with frontal flattening in the foreground, and an

extreme perspectival recession in the rear. Christ's presence is slightly more noticeable in the etching.

The minute line produced by the etching needle allowed Ensor to pack far more detail into the etched version of the subject. His scraggly, nervous, and impressionistic line ceaselessly delineates the vast scene. Members of the crowd are caricatured with horrific visages, grotesque noses, and Commedia dell'Arte masks. Open windows reveal rooms filled with figures. Words and phrases on banners, flags, and walls of houses include "Colmans Mustart," political slogans such as "Vive Jesus et les reformeurs," and "Mouvement Flamande," "Les XX," and "Salut Jesus Roi de Bruxelles."

The plate was etched in four states[2] and heightened with drypoint. Many impressions were variously hand-colored in watercolor and gouache by the artist. The Art Center's impression features a limited but strong palette of yellow, red, and blue, plus blue-green. The setting sun is a blaze of yellow, as is Christ's halo. Directly under the red-robed Jesus, a military officer is bedecked with medals. A man on the blue-green balcony wears parti-colored pants, one leg blue, one leg red, with a yellow diamond-shaped patch decorated with a leering face on his rear. Ensor's etching is a singular vision of Christ amidst uncaring, corrupt humanity, "a luminous presence swallowed in the legions of the mad."[3] AW

Purchased with funds from the Edmundson
Art Foundation, Inc.; Des Moines
Art Center Permanent Collections, 1988.2

Fluorescent light tubes and painted metal,
96 x 96 x 10 inches
(243.8 x 243.8 x 25.4 cm)

dan flavin

American, 1933–1996   **Untitled (For Ellen)**, 1975

Emerging as an important artist in the early 1960s, Dan Flavin used commercial light fixtures to create works of actual, not depicted, light that alter perceptions of space and color. The simplicity of the spare, geometric arrangements and straightforward ordinary materials places his work well within the Minimalist context of sculptors such as Donald Judd, Carl Andre, and Richard Serra. Like the Minimalists, Flavin insisted that his work be seen as a purely phenomenal, visual art, without metaphorical aspects. Yet the glowing emanations of his sculpture lend themselves to a range of subjective interpretations.

Like many of Flavin's works, the Art Center's **Untitled (For Ellen)** is a corner piece with tubes shining both toward and away from the viewer. Colors directed onto the wall planes converge at the corner, a space Flavin has made unavailable to the viewer – though very tempting and almost tactile. Other colors reach into the space of the room itself, surrounding the viewer and altering perceptions of the environment. Both walls retain the clarity of their different colors with little

"mixing" of separate hues despite their overlapping paths. At the same time, the areas beyond the planes of the wall are suffused with a radiant, indefinable, and rich illumination.

Flavin's first works dealing with light were a series of monochromatic paintings that incorporated light bulbs and were called "icons," though Flavin rejected any religious associations. His first pure light piece was **The Diagonal of Personal Ecstasy (The Diagonal of May 25, 1963)**, a single tube angled out from his studio wall. Fascinated by the light and its shadow, Flavin realized that "the actual space of a room could be disrupted ... and a section of wall ... visually disintegrated."[1] Subsequent works were arranged into restrained, geometric compositions that spread along a wall or fit into a corner, always taking into account the architectural environment which they inevitably transformed visually. Flavin's interest in using the corner, an area often neglected in our visual awareness, stemmed partly from his admiration for the Russian Constructivist Vladimir Tatlin, who was the first to create a nonobjective sculpture made of industrial materials and to suspend it in the corner, engaging space in a new, unsettling manner. Though he rejected the visionary, symbolic concepts in some of Tatlin's work, Flavin embraced his materialism, his interest in

untraditional spatial concepts, and his "attempt to combine artistry and engineering."[2]

Flavin was born in New York City and educated at the Cathedral College of the Immaculate Conception in Douglastown, New York. His family hoped for a religious vocation for the young man, but in 1953 he ended his formal education to serve in the US Air Force. Back in New York in 1956, he enrolled briefly at the Hans Hofmann School, then began educating himself in art at the New School for Social Research and Columbia University. He taught at the University of North Carolina, Greensboro (1967) and at the University of Bridgeport, Connecticut (1973). The Dan Flavin Art Institute for the permanent display of his work was established in Bridgehampton, New York by the Dia Art Foundation in 1983. LRD

Oil on canvas, 72 x 96 inches
(182.9 x 243.8 cm)

sam francis

American, 1923–1994 **Summer No. 2,** 1957

Sam Francis was born in San Mateo, California in 1923. He received his Bachelor and Master of Arts degrees from the University of California (1949 and 1950), then moved to Paris. Although he settled finally in Santa Monica, California in 1962, Francis always maintained a global vision, visiting and living in Japan as well as Europe. His early Paris paintings reflect the subdued grays of that city's atmosphere, but Francis is most associated with a characteristically clear, bright palette, perhaps influenced by the dazzling light of California.

Francis's work may be classed as fundamentally Abstract Expressionist, although he was never part of the New York School. Early paintings, such as the Art Center's **Summer No. 2**, are distinctly so. Grand in scale, gestural, and with an interlocking structure of figure and ground, color and white space, they recall the more brutal and reductive slashes of Franz Kline. But Francis's vision was a gentler and more contemplative one, a mixture of Eastern thought and calligraphy with the directness and boldness of Western culture. The blue of **Summer No. 2**, for example, is soft and rich, evocative of deep water or an infinite sky, but expanded and abstracted to be like a slice of space itself. The paint – and consequently the color – is applied in varying densities, thereby displaying an airiness and sense of space even within the most saturated areas. The paint is concentrated, almost coagulated, in a primary area that takes up approximately only one third of the canvas. In an almost organic way, its edges are soft and it subtly infiltrates the blank white areas, a quietly insistent but nonthreatening presence.

In addition to creating his large paintings, Francis was a prolific printmaker. Following his return to New York in 1958, he met Tatyana Grosman, and was persuaded to try his hand at lithography at Universal Limited Art Editions in West Islip, New York. Although that collaboration was brief and Francis's subsequent illness disrupted the connection, he did retain his interest in printmaking, going on to work with a number of print workshops and founding his own studio in 1970. He made around a thousand monotypes, as well as edition prints. TRN

Gift of Florence Carpenter; Des Moines Art
Center Permanent Collections, 1941.11

Oil on canvas, 37 ⁵/₈ x 55 ⁵/₈ inches
(95.6 x 141.3 cm)

frederick carl frieseke

American, 1874–1939   **The Hour of Tea,** before 1916

The influence of the French Impressionists was so great in the United States that American painters flocked not only to Paris but specifically to Giverny, the village north of Paris where Claude Monet began in 1883 to create the home and spectacular gardens that provided the motifs for much of his later paintings. A number of Americans came to search out Monet and experience the environment that nourished the French master. Frederick Carl Frieseke was among the second wave, who arrived around the turn of the century. He began spending summers in Giverny, and in 1906 purchased a home that had belonged to the American painter Theodore Robinson, which bordered Monet's land.

Frieseke was a midwesterner, born in Owosso, Michigan and educated initially at The School of The Art Institute of Chicago. He then moved on to the Art Students League in New York, and eventually to the Académie Julian in Paris. Although he was trained in academic painting by Benjamin Constant and Jean-Paul Laurens, his real master was the expatriate American painter James Abbott McNeill Whistler. Frieseke's earlier work shows clearly the influence of Whistler, although as his proximity and relationship to Giverny increased, Frieseke's work became more and more Impressionist.

The Art Center's **The Hour of Tea** has been associated with the institution from its incep-

tion; it is one of the original eighteen paintings that Florence Carpenter gave the center after the death of her husband, J. S. (Sanny) Carpenter, Des Moines's foremost early art collector and a civic leader. **The Hour of Tea** presents an arresting vision of a leisurely and elegant life on an idyllic afternoon. Dominating the canvas is a young woman reclining at her ease on a lawn chair and steadying her picture-frame hat so that she can peer out against the sun at the viewer. At her elbow is the tea tray, of which she is clearly in charge. She engages the viewer with a look of cool appraisal that carries curiosity but no real invitation. Indeed, assisted by the massed presence of the figures of the man and woman at her feet, who drink their tea in seeming oblivion to the intrusion of the viewer, the party seems complete and self-sufficient. In her regal pose and challenging gaze, the central figure in Frieseke's painting bears certain affinities with her forebears, ancestors from a different class or profession, such as Francisco Goya's **Clothed Maja** and **Naked Maja** or Edouard Manet's **Olympia**. TRN

paul gauguin

French, 1848–1903   **Reworked Study for Te Nave Nave Fenua (The Delightful Land),** 1892–94

Shortly after receiving this drawing in 1958, the Des Moines Art Center sent it to The Art Institute of Chicago for an important Gauguin exhibition. In the course of rematting it for the show, additional drawings on the verso of the sheet were revealed. The discovery was heralded in the press as a "major find … this is the first time a new Gauguin has been discovered in this fashion, and the first new work of the French painter to turn up in recent years."[1]

It was not until another important Gauguin exhibition at the Art Institute in 1988 that the two sides of the work were given separate and distinct titles. Previously titled **Standing Tahitian Nude (Eve)**, the image on the recto was retitled **Reworked Study for Te Nave Nave Fenua (The Delightful Land)**. The verso image was given the title **Crouching Seated Figure, and Head of a Woman**.

Paul Gauguin was born in Paris in 1848. He spent his youth in Orléans, with the exception of four years when he went to Peru to live with his father, a political exile. Gauguin entered the merchant marines at age seventeen. In 1871 he joined a brokerage firm, although he was also an amateur painter and a collector of Impressionist paintings. In 1883, at the encouragement of other artists, Gauguin left his job and family to devote himself entirely to painting. After spending considerable time in the town of Pont-Aven in Brittany, in 1891 Gauguin traveled to the South Pacific, living and working there almost exclusively until his death in 1903.

Although the Art Center's drawing was made shortly after Gauguin's arrival in the South Pacific, "it had its genesis around 1889 when Gauguin acquired photographs of the sculpted frieze from the Buddhist temple of Borobudur [Java] as part of his collection of images of details for his own subsequent works."[2] Gauguin requested the Tahitian woman who modeled for the drawing to strike a pose similar to that of the Javanese sculpture. Also in the work are smaller drawings of the details of the figure; to the right of the figure's bent elbow is another elbow, and in the upper right corner is another drawing of the hand.

Gauguin is best known for the works he made in the South Pacific Islands, and the Art Center's drawing holds an important place within that body of work. When Gauguin made this drawing in 1892, he only drew the figure with black charcoal. He took a pin and made small holes in the paper along the contour of the figure, whose pricked outline is especially visible from the verso. Gauguin then placed the drawing against a piece of canvas and redrew the image with charcoal, penetrating the holes and transferring the outline onto the canvas as the start of **Te Nave Nave Fenua (The Delightful Land)**, one of Gauguin's most important paintings (Ohara Museum, Kurashiki, Japan).

The subject of both the drawing and the painting is a variation on the theme of the Garden of Eden. In the Old Testament, Eve is tempted by a serpent to pluck an apple from the Tree of Knowledge. Because there are no snakes in the South Pacific, however, Gauguin substituted a lizard, which is to the left of the figure's head.

Two years after making this drawing and using it for the large painting, Gauguin reworked the image. In 1894 he added the color in pastel and drew the stream that runs behind the figure. DL

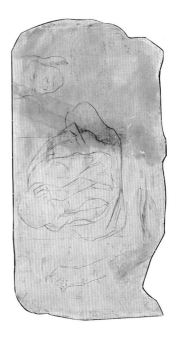

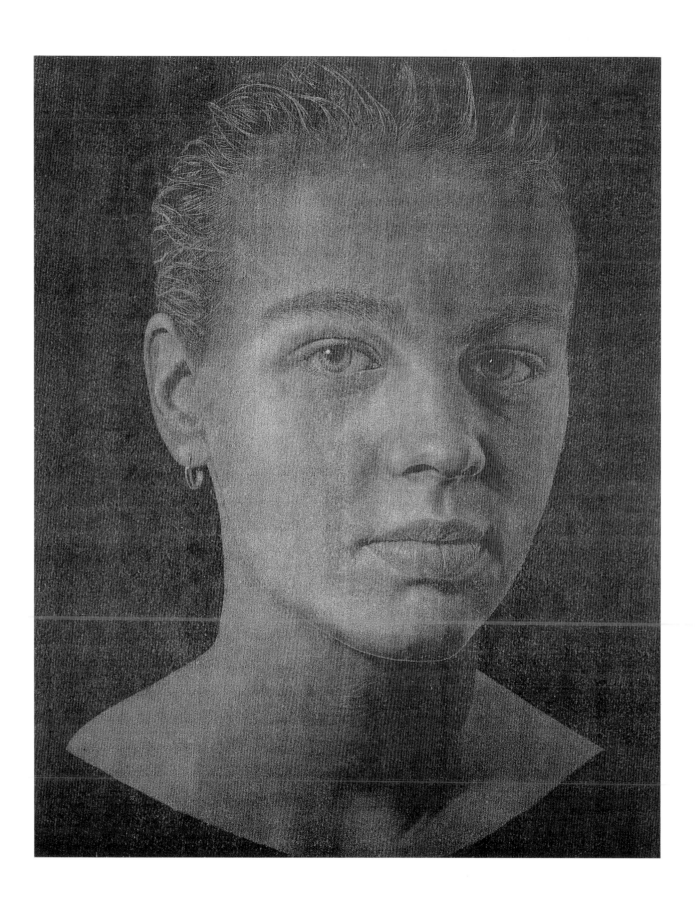

Purchased with funds from the Edmundson
Art Foundation, Inc.; Des Moines
Art Center Permanent Collections, 1992.30

Woodcut on Japanese paper,
107 x 83 inches (271.8 x 210.8 cm)

franz gertsch

Swiss, born 1930   **Natascha IV**, 1987–88

Natascha IV is a remarkably large work on paper, nearly eight feet high. To make the image the artist projected a slide onto a block of wood which he tinted blue. He used a tool to remove tiny pieces of wood, one after another, each removal creating a small hole. When the block is printed each piece of wood so removed appears as white against the blue tint, and also as white when the block is inked and printed, since the hole is too deep to hold ink.

To create this image the artist used only two elements: a single color of ink and the white areas from which the ink is absent. Extraordinary skill and vision are necessary to translate the projected photographic image into the almost otherworldly portrait that seems to materialize from the tiny units.

Once the wood block is prepared, it is inked by the artist, his wife, Maria, and his printer, Nik Hausmann. Inking is done by rubbing the back of the paper with the convex surface of a magnifying glass. **Natascha IV** required three blocks of lime wood, one each to generally emphasize drawing, highlights, and the outline of the head.

The paper is made from mulberry and linen fibers by a specialist in Japan, Iwano Heizoburo, who has been designated a "Living Treasure" by his country. **Natascha IV** exists in eighteen versions, each printed in a different monochromatic color. It took seven months to prepare the blocks and print the edition. The three earlier versions using **Natascha** as model are different images, and the prints are less than half the size.

Gertsch did not begin as a printmaker. He was born in 1930 in the Canton of Bern, where he resides today. He studied painting from 1947 to 1952. While he did make some woodcuts, he was primarily an abstract painter.

In 1969 Gertsch made the first of his large paintings which look very much like photographs. Throughout the next decade he based his paintings on photographs he took of family and acquaintances (Natascha is a friend of his children). These images are rooted in the particulars of the times. Styles of hair, makeup, and clothing are very specific, sometimes almost costumelike, and often reflective of what might be termed a counterculture or "hippy" appearance (stars and stripes, faded denim, and so forth).

In 1980 the fifty-year-old artist made a self-portrait that, in retrospect, signaled an evolutionary change. While this image, which is from the shoulders up, includes what the artist was wearing, the focus now shifts to the face. In the portraits beginning in 1982, whatever articles of clothing or jewelry do appear are relatively timeless, not pointedly reflective of a particular moment. This universality is furthered in the woodcuts to which Gertsch devoted himself exclusively from 1986 until 1996. Except perhaps to an expert, the clothing and jewelry in **Natascha** could just as well have been worn in antiquity as today. The near-absence of the particular combined with the sense of an image materializing as though from fundamental particles gives a supernatural aura to **Natascha IV**. This sense of the metaphysical is also characteristic of landscape woodcuts Gertsch made during this period. These images have a mystical quality found in landscapes in the Northern tradition by artists such as Albrecht Altdorfer or Caspar David Friedrich.

An exhibition of Gertsch's woodcuts (including **Natascha IV**) appeared at The Hirshhorn Museum and Sculpture Garden, Washington; The Museum of Modern Art, New York; and the San Jose Museum of Art, California in 1990. IMD

Bronze, 70 ¹/₂ x 37 x 17 ⁵/₈ inches
(177.2 x 93.9 x 44.7 cm)

alberto giacometti

Swiss, 1901–1966   **L'Homme au doigt (Man Pointing),** 1947

Alberto Giacometti's status as a Swiss citizen un-doubtedly played a key role in enabling the Paris-based sculptor to obtain an exit visa under the Nazi Occupation during World War II. He departed France on New Year's Eve 1941 – the last day that his visa was valid – and settled in Geneva where he remained until shortly after the end of the war some three-and-a-half years later.

That period spent in Switzerland became a watershed in the artist's career, even though his production was minuscule both in terms of the number of works he created and the scale of the works themselves. It was said – and it was very nearly true – that he was able to carry back to France his entire production of sculptures in a matchbox. The tiny sculptures were the seeds of what was to come.

Prior to the years in Geneva, Giacometti had been associated with the Surrealist move-ment, even though he was later denounced by the "pure" Surrealist intellectuals when he began to work from the model in the late 1930s. But after his wartime sojourn, the artist's development took a distinctly individu-alistic turn, one that he followed unwaveringly during the remaining two decades of his life.

The year 1947 marked this critical turn. Not only did a series of remarkable masterpieces such as **Tall Figure, Hand, The Nose, Head**

on a Rod, and **Man Pointing** emanate from the artist's primitive studio (no electricity, no running water), but, more importantly, it was the year in which the artist's signature style reached its full maturity after several modest and somewhat tentative attempts dur-ing the previous year. Elongated figures, craggy surfaces, and an appearance of emaci-ation are all characteristics of his postwar work. Writers such as Jean-Paul Sartre embraced this new look, claiming that it embodied Existentialism in a post-Holocaust age, but Giacometti would have none of this philoso-phizing about his art. He averred that his sole purpose in creating these attenuated forms was to capture the actual look of persons as he perceived them standing or moving in space.

Man Pointing, his largest three-dimensional work to that time and one that remains his most gestural, was completed in what must have been a frenzied burst of energy. Work-ing toward a deadline for a forthcoming New York exhibition, he began at midnight and finished it nine hours later. He had already completed the piece once, but then became dissatisfied with it, destroyed it, and began in plaster all over again. By the time workmen arrived to take the piece to the foundry to be cast in bronze, the plaster was still wet.

There is reason to believe, however, that Giacometti was able to execute only half of the sculptural composition that he had in mind that night, for he had actually conceived **Man Pointing** as one part of a two-figure com-position, and in 1951 he fulfilled his original concept by creating the second figure: a tall,

standing form in plaster that he placed within the long, arcing curve of **Man Pointing**'s left arm. He soon decided that the second figure was not successful and, always his own sever-est critic, he demolished it. From then on, **Man Pointing** would stand by itself.

There appears to be no record or definitive statement by the artist as to why he found the double-figure work unsatisfactory, and therefore one can only conjecture about the reasons behind his decision to permanently remove the second piece. Perhaps he had become accustomed to the solitary figure whose presence seemed to dominate his stu-dio – it looms in the background of several of his paintings and works on paper. Or per-haps he felt that the addition of the second element resulted in a sculpture that was merely anecdotal and transitory: a man pointing the way for his friend or a mentor instructing his protégé. By his eliminating the extra figure, the narrative aspect is largely eliminated. In-stead, **Man Pointing** becomes magisterial and commanding, a personage of dignity and authority. The specificity of the moment has been supplanted by something transcendental, something for the ages.

Alberto Giacometti was born in 1901 in the Swiss mountain village of Borgonovo near the Italian border. He died in 1966 in Chur, Switzerland, of heart failure brought on by chronic bronchitis. JD

Purchased with funds from the
Edmundson Art Foundation, Inc.; Des Moines
Art Center Permanent Collections, 1996.4

Metal, wood, and video, 91 x 94 x 60 inches
(231.1 x 238.8 x 152.4 cm)

jane gilmor

American, born 1947   **Windows,** 1995

Jane Gilmor is an Iowa native whose art addresses social issues. Born in Ames in 1947, Gilmor received her Bachelor of Science degree from Iowa State University in 1969. She holds three Master's degrees from the University of Iowa, in education, art, and - fine arts. Since 1974 Gilmor has been a professor of art at Mount Mercy College, Cedar Rapids, Iowa.

Since 1988 Gilmor has created sculptures and installations that combine metal reliefs of drawings and notes with found objects. The Art Center's **Windows,** which was made with the assistance of a grant from the Iowa Arts Council, is a collaborative example:

"**Windows** is the result of a collaboration between Jane Gilmor, artist Rick Edleman, and pediatric patients and their families from The University of Iowa Hospitals and Clinics of Iowa City, Iowa. During a year of weekly workshops children were invited to create drawings and writings on metal foil concerning their experiences, feelings, and fantasies while hospitalized. Videotaped images of some of the participating patients appear on the monitors in the small 'windows' of this structure. Inside viewers are invited to contribute their own stories, comments, or images in special guest books."[1]

The **Windows** project was intended to give seriously ill children and their families access to nontraditional art forms for personal expression and to encourage use of the imagination as both a survival tool and as a psychological "home away from home." It is the artist's belief that art can serve both as an intellectual critique of culture and as an avenue for making meaning of one's experiences, particularly when those experiences interrupt everyday life.

Many of Gilmor's works, such as **Windows,** have the feeling of a shrine. Gilmor has studied extensively roadside shrines in Greece and other places, as well as folk-art grottos such as the Grotto of Redemption in West Bend, Iowa. She emulates their feeling in her work, making her installations busy, crowded, and multilayered. Whole walls of notes overlap one another and found objects are placed on and in front of the notes. The metal drawings and notes are reminiscent of pressed-metal devotional icons, a type of folk art that Gilmor collects from all over the world. Also, Gilmor often includes various elements, such as the videotapes in **Windows,** to add different textures and sensory responses. DL

Purchased with funds from the Coffin Fine
Arts Trust; Nathan Emory Coffin
Collection of the Des Moines Art Center,
1953.15

Oil on canvas, 81 ½ x 49 inches
(207 x 124.5 cm)

francisco josé de goya y lucientes

Spanish, 1746–1828   **Don Manuel Garcia de la Prada,** c. 1811

This life-sized, full-length portrait of a Spanish aristocrat by one of Spain's most illustrious and venerable painters, Francisco Goya, was purchased in 1953 by the Des Moines Art Center with the express purpose of acquiring a "masterpiece." It was thought that a dazzling Old Master painting would impress the public and establish the fledgling museum as an institution with a serious purpose. Despite the undoubted quality of the painting, this plan was only partially successful, and the focus soon changed to the acquisition of mainly nineteenth- and twentieth-century works. Since that time, the emphasis has narrowed even further, to concentrate on Postmodern and even vanguard art, and the collections overall have expanded considerably.

Francisco Goya was born in 1746 in a small town near Saragossa. Although details of his childhood are sketchy, his father was a painter and his mother a descendant of minor Aragonese nobility. Goya was apprenticed to a local painter, then moved on to Madrid, where he met the academic court painter Francisco Bayeu, who helped form his early style and included him in a fresco commission in Saragossa. Goya spent a year in Italy. When he returned to Spain, he became involved in a number of fresco commissions. By 1786 he was officially connected with the Spanish court, and in 1799 was named first court painter. His tapestry cartoons and decorative frescoes, along with his innovative print series, were revolutionary. Goya was particularly moved by the horrors of war, and his paintings taking as subject matter the brutal tragedies enacted under the Napoleonic occupation of Spain are some of the most memorable and influential antiwar protests ever made.

A devastating illness in 1792 that left Goya deaf also marked the onset of the pessimism and power that infused the art of his later years. His great caustic and satirical print series, his startlingly unflattering portraits of the royal family, and the gripping so-called "Black Paintings" done toward the end of his life are the product of an idealism appalled at the ugliness of both the ordinary and the official reality that surrounded him.

In 1783 Goya painted a portrait of Charles III's chief minister, **Conde de Floridablanca**. From that time on, his reputation as a portrait painter was established, and he received numerous commissions from a number of influential patrons.[1] Despite the devastating and often frightening candor of his vision, Goya continued during the late 1790s and early 1800s to execute superb half- and full-length portraits of statesmen, men of letters, and Spanish noblewomen. The Art Center's painting of a Madrid magistrate, **Don Manuel Garcia de la Prada**, comes from this rich period of portraiture. Elegantly posed with his legs gracefully crossed and one hand resting on the back of a chair and the other caressing a small dog, Don Manuel seems fully at ease. He gazes out at the viewer with serene assurance, simultaneously accessible and formally reserved. Goya's portrayal is calm and sensitive, with no hint of the caricature that marks those individuals who did not merit his respect. TRN

Purchased with funds from Rose Lee and
Marvin Pomerantz, Harry Pomerantz,
and the National Endownment for the Arts;
Des Moines Art Center Permanent
Collections, 1992.11

Polystyrene, resin, wood, steel,
acrylic, lights, and motor, 14 x 11 x 14 feet
(4.27 x 3.3 x 4.27 m)

red grooms

American, b. 1937   **Agricultural Building,** 1991–92

Red Grooms's work stands at the crossroads of Pop Art, Neo-Expressionism, and mixed-media assemblage. Grooms is renowned as a painter, filmmaker, and a pioneer of "happenings." His work is characterized by wild fantasy and broad humor and is rooted in a precise observation of contemporary culture. Most of his characteristic works are individual constructions or environments in which he uses cutout figures and objects painted in brilliant colors.

Grooms was born in Nashville and currently resides in New York. He attended The School of The Art Institute of Chicago and the Hans Hoffman School of Fine Arts, Provincetown, Massachusetts. As Grooms recalled in a 1990 interview, "I was brought up a Baptist with that sort of 'pass the word' kind of communication, a 'witnessing' thing. Really, [the importance of] communication of some sort, actually a transcending kind of communication, I guess, was instilled in me. At the same time I always loved theatrical things. I guess those two things kind of wed in the work that I do."[1]

Agricultural Building is an animated sculptural environment depicting the Agricultural Building of the Iowa State Fair. The painted environment includes life-sized characters representing visitors to the fair and the popular butter cow that "talks." It is a large-scale work created from Grooms's 1990 visit to Des Moines and research on the Iowa State Fair. As he reminisced, "I kind of got my artistic start with the Tennessee State Fair. That was the first subject that I was very involved in. That was as a teenager. But that event did have a lot of excitement and inspiration for me."

In the Art Center's commission, Grooms paid homage to the fair by blending much of its atmosphere into form and substance, focusing on the prize-winning fruit and vegetable displays and decorative themes in the Agricultural Building. Sharp social commentary and witty playfulness are combined in characters ("Betty Sue," "Farmer Dave," "Duffy Lyons," and famous Iowans John Wayne and Herbert Hoover) who are rambunctious, self-absorbed, and bursting with life. These figural presences are important to the life of Grooms's work and are developed through his "sequence of personages" into a "sculptopictorama." His characters and architectural framework all receive a stylized, cartoonlike treatment. Visitors are encouraged to enter the sculpted pavilion to view the dramatic interior of champion fruits and vegetables, animated actions of characters, and a make-believe refrigerated studio with the butter cow. Grooms commented:

"I see the [**Agricultural Building**] as a chance to have symbolic values as well as regional. It should speak as 'all-American.' And I like this project because it is so American that I feel it would contrast well with a foreign country. I sort of like … something that will look peculiar if it's shown somewhere else." MJR

Oil on canvas, 68 x 88 inches
(172.7 x 223.5 cm)

philip guston

American, 1913–1980   **Friend – To M.F.,** 1978

During different periods of his life, Philip Guston worked in three distinctly different styles. The Art Center's 1978 painting **Friend – To M.F.** is a major work of his final period.

Born in Montreal in 1913, Guston moved to Los Angeles with his family at the age of six. While studying art in Los Angeles, Guston became good friends with Jackson Pollock, had his first one-artist show, in 1931, and developed a strong interest in the Mexican mural artists, particularly José Clemente Orozco and David Alfaro Siqueiros. In 1935 Guston moved to New York and joined the Works Progress Administration Federal Art Project as a mural painter. He resigned from the WPA/FAP in 1940, and joined the faculty of the University of Iowa in 1941, remaining in Iowa City until 1945.

Guston's Social Realist paintings from his first mature period (late 1930s through mid-1940s) often portray the dire circumstances of a generation pained by world events such as the Great Depression and World War II. In 1948 Guston was awarded the Prix de Rome by the American Academy in Rome. He made numerous trips to Italy to study Old Master painting, and he was especially fascinated with Piero della Francesca. Guston's own painting during the late 1940s became highly

abstract. During his second period, in the 1950s and 1960s, he was a leading member of the first group of US artists to achieve worldwide stature: the Abstract Expressionists. Guston had returned in 1950 to New York where he became acquainted with the Abstract Expressionists Willem de Kooning, Franz Kline, Barnett Newman, and Mark Rothko, in addition to Pollock, and was frequently included in shows with them.

The third and final period in Guston's work was seminal in the art world's acceptance once again of the representational image and the overt expression of emotion that came increasingly to the fore throughout the 1970s. In 1970 Guston made a dramatic shift in his work that stunned the art world: shaken by the tumultuous events in the United States during the second half of the 1960s, Guston came to feel that abstraction did not allow him fully to express his passions. He wrote of that time: "The war, what was happening to America, the brutality of the world. What kind of man am I, sitting at home, reading magazines, going into a frustrated fury about everything – and then going into my studio to adjust a red to a blue?"[1] Until his death in 1980, Guston continued to make paintings with recognizable images that were very personal. The huge head in profile with a bloodshot eye refers to the artist. The piles of shoes reference the fate of concentration-camp victims. The images of hooded figures reference the Ku Klux Klan.

Some of the artist's friends were disturbed by his return to recognizable images, especially since Guston had been one of the most internationally celebrated proponents of abstraction. One friend, the composer Morton Feldman, is the subject of the Art Center's **Friend – To M.F.** Despite the tension in their relationship, Feldman gave a eulogy at Guston's funeral. Guston's closeness to Feldman is suggested by the fact that the face in profile is akin to the artist's contemporaneous self-portraits in profile (perhaps recalling some of Piero della Francesca's portraits). And yet, photographs of the composer demonstrate that Guston captured aspects of "this mountain of a man" who frequently smoked. It has been suggested that the huge ear is appropriate for the likeness of a composer.[2] The puff of smoke issuing from the cigarette is a passage very much like Guston's Abstract Expresionist paintings, perhaps suggesting how that style went up in smoke. The Art Center's painting has been exhibited and reproduced numerous times. It appeared on the cover of a compact disc of Feldman's music, was featured in **The New York Times** in an article about the composer, and was lent to the Berlinische Galerie to accompany a concert featuring Feldman's four-and-one-half-hour composition **For Philip Guston**.
IMD

Purchased with funds from the Edmundson
Art Foundation, Inc. and partial gift of
Gagosian Gallery and the artist; Des Moines
Art Center Permanent Collections, 1993.10

Acrylic, Day-Glo acrylic, and
Roll-a-Tex on canvas, 95 1/2 x 87 5/8 inches
(242.6 x 222.6 cm)

peter halley

American, born 1953   **Fire in the Sky,** 1993

A native of New York, Peter Halley received his Bachelor of Fine Arts degree from Yale University in 1976 and his Master of Fine Arts from the University of New Orleans in 1978. He returned to New York in 1980 and quickly became a leading figure among the younger generation of artists intrigued by geometric abstract painting. In October 1992 the Des Moines Art Center organized the first one-person museum exhibition of Halley's paintings in the United States.

Halley does not view his paintings as exclusively abstract; his works make reference to the urban landscape. The artist uses the term "cell" to describe the large central square, such as the bright red area in the Art Center's **Fire in the Sky**, that occurs in most of his paintings since 1982. The texture in the cell comes from Roll-a-Tex, a commercial material simulating stucco. Halley's use of it is also somewhat self-referential, since it reminds the artist of the stubble of an unshaved beard.

Emerging from the cell are conduits that represent urban connectivity; the terms also allude to electrical circuitry, critical to contemporary urban existence. The artist has commented: "I was working alone at home, listening to the radio, turning on electric lights, being able to turn on the faucet, flush the toilet, talk on the telephone, turn on the air conditioner. I began to become obsessed with the idea that all of these natural things — air, light, noise, or speech were being piped in. I began to think of conduits."[1]

Fire in the Sky, like most of Halley's paintings, actually consists of two horizontally abutted canvases. The lower and smaller of the two represents below-ground and the large canvas above-ground. But Halley also sees the lower as the subconscious mind and the upper as the conscious mind. The conduits supply the connections, carrying feelings and thought between the conscious and the subconscious. The cell and conduits also convey psychological overtones regarding the isolation and alienation of the individual within the urban environment.

In addition to the textured sections, another important aspect of Halley's style is his use of Day-Glo paint, which reinforces the sense of an intense, "turned-on" environment. There are several areas of Day-Glo in **Fire in the Sky**, most notably the large orange-red conduit in the base that connects with the red cell.

Halley has a keen interest in science fiction, and the title of the Art Center's painting is taken from a science-fiction movie that had not yet been released at the time Halley made the painting. In addition to movies, names of rock bands and titles of songs are among the sources for the titles Halley gives to his paintings. While he does not recall making the association, **Fire in the Sky** is a line from "Smoke on the Water," a Deep Purple song. IMD

marsden hartley

American, 1877–1943   **Mont Saint Victoire**, 1927

Marsden Hartley worked in an atmosphere of tension between the new ideas of European Modernism and traditional concerns of American art. Although he was eager, as the Art Center's painting **Mont Saint Victoire** shows, to assimilate European styles such as Cubism, Fauvism, and Expressionism, he was just as eager to maintain a distinct American character. He developed into artistic maturity in the circle surrounding the art dealer/photographer Alfred Steiglitz and his 291 Gallery in New York during the second decade of the twentieth century. Steiglitz's crusade was to introduce European Modernism into an America that he regarded as deeply conservative and artistically backward. Hartley was one of the artists he championed in hopes of encouraging a greater sophistication.

Hartley was born in Lewiston, Maine, a state with which he would later identify strongly, explaining in 1937 that he wished to be known as "the painter from Maine." His early training was at the Cleveland School of Art (1898), and the Chase School (1899) and the National Academy of Design (1900–1904), both in New York. In 1909 he met Steiglitz, who gave him his first one-person exhibition

that year and who subsidized his first trip to Europe in 1912. In Paris, work by Cézanne, Matisse, Picasso, and other Cubists influenced him, as did the German Expressionist movement Der Blaue Reiter. Traveling in Germany, he met Kandinsky, Marc, Münter, and other Expressionists. His work from this period, such as **Portrait of a German Officer** (1914), shows not only the abstraction he learned from sources in both Paris and Munich, but also the strong color that characterizes the Art Center picture. Much of his subsequent career was spent moving restlessly between Europe and the United States, constantly working toward a balance between various influences and his own personal response. Hartley wrote essays and poems that reflect the often conflicting strains in his development.

Mont Saint Victoire dates from a European sojourn spent mainly in France. His 1926 move to Aix-en-Provence revived the influence of Cézanne and, as Cézanne had done, Hartley painted a series based on the nearby mountain, Saint Victoire. He even lived in a house that had served as one of Cézanne's studios, the Maison Maria, and which itself had been a subject in several paintings by the older master. As in Cézanne's "Mont Saint Victoire" series, Hartley used the landscape to achieve a strong, nearly architectonic spatial organization. Yet, the unnaturalistic color also reflects the earlier influence of German Expressionism as well

as the tones he had used in paintings from 1918 to 1922, especially those inspired by the Southwestern landscape of New Mexico. As if in homage to Cézanne, Hartley employed sharply directional strokes organized into clearly separated blocks of intense color. But instead of suggesting shifting planes in space rendered in the colors of nature, Hartley's painting is more dense, related less to observed nature than to the painter's own personal responses. Paintings from this period in Aix were exhibited in 1928 at The Arts Club in Chicago and then later at Steiglitz's new Intimate Gallery. Disappointed by the reception of these European paintings, Hartley returned to America, making only one more trip to Europe (1933–34) for the rest of his life. The abstracted, personal interpretation and the bold colors used in his **Mont Saint Victoire** can be detected in his later depictions of the Maine landscape, especially those of Mount Katahdin. Other works by Hartley in the Art Center collection represent his career from the 1920s on: **Still Life with Jugs** (c. 1922), **Still Life (Dahlias)** (1929), and **Maine Coast #2** (1940). LRD

Purchased with funds from the Coffin Fine
Arts Trust; Nathan Emory Coffin
Collection of the Des Moines Art Center,
1961.47

Oil on canvas, 32 x 25 inches
(81.3 x 63.5 cm)

childe hassam

American, 1859–1935 **Bridge in Snow (Brooklyn Bridge in Winter),** c. 1894

Born and educated in Boston, Frederick Childe Hassam learned art initially from a wood engraver and embarked on a career as a free-lance magazine illustrator while studying at night with a local artist and at the Boston Art Club and the Lowell Institute. Before leaving for his first trip to Europe in 1883, Hassam was familiar with the Barbizon School and had already attempted painting from nature. On his second trip, in 1886–89, he studied in Paris with the academic painters Gustave Boulanger and Jules Lefebvre at the Académie Julian, but was primarily influenced by the work of the French Impressionists. He exhibited in Paris at the Salon and even won medals at the Exposition Universelle in 1888 and 1889.

Back in the United States, Hassam settled in New York, spending his winters there and his summers in his native New England. He immediately founded the New York Water-color Club (1889) and joined the Pastel Society (1890). In 1898 he joined and exhib-ited with other American Impressionists who together were known as "The Ten." Hassam subsequently became one of the

leading exponents of American Impres-sionism, appropriating the French emphasis on staccato brushwork and a wide-ranging pure palette to render the moment in an atmospheric glimpse, while at the same time retaining some American conservative restraint. He was a prolific painter and his engaging art reflects a number of influences, perhaps most decisively the divergent approaches of the radiant palette of Monet and the more subdued tonalism of Whistler. Such mediation seems to be true in a number of Hassam's paintings, which appear to be anchored by a single dominant hue or color scheme treated as a motif.

The Des Moines Art Center's **Bridge in Snow (Brooklyn Bridge in Winter)** is char-acteristic of scenes Hassam painted in and around the City of New York upon his return to the United States. It demonstrates the objective observations of Monet, while at the same time exhibits a certain stylization in its strongly vertical format and the featured whiteness of the scene. Hassam's interest in people in the street, going about their busi-ness, and the abrupt and even plunging perspective, are strongly reminiscent of the early works of Gustave Caillebotte.

After about 1915 Hassam began to concen-trate on printmaking, beginning with etching and then turning to lithography, although he never ceased to paint as well. TRN

Gift of the Des Moines Association of
Fine Arts; Des Moines Art Center Permanent
Collections, 1927.1

Oil on canvas, 77 ¹/₈ x 37 ¹/₄ inches
(195.9 x 94.6 cm)

robert henri

American, 1865–1929   **Ballet Girl in White**, 1909

Robert Henri was born Robert Henry Cozad in Cincinnati, Ohio in 1865. His father was a "flamboyant figure, a sometime gambler who regularly invested his winnings in land speculations in the West."[1] Henri attended school in Cincinnati, but spent his summers working on his father's ranch in Nebraska, and joined his father in business in 1879. In 1882 Henri's father "in self defense shot and mortally wounded an armed adversary."[2] The family fled to Denver and then Atlantic City, New Jersey, changing their names along the way. Henri dropped his last name and changed his middle name from Henry to Henri.

As a child Henri illustrated his own story-books. In 1886 he enrolled in the Pennsylvania Academy of Fine Arts in Philadelphia, remaining two years before going to Paris to study at the Académie Julian. Both schools emphasized painting from a live model. After three years abroad, in 1892 Henri began teaching at the Philadelphia School of Design for Women. His studio became the main social setting for young artists, including William Glackens, George Luks, Everett Shinn, and John Sloan, all of whom were illustrators for the **Philadelphia Press**. Henri had his first one-artist exhibition at the Pennsylvania Academy in 1897, and three years later moved to New

York. Glackens, Luks, Shinn, and Sloan were either already there or would follow shortly. They were joined by Arthur B. Davies, Ernest Lawson, and Maurice Prendergast, whose work was stylistically similar to Henri's and who shared his artistic concerns. The group become known as "The Eight."

The year 1908 was important for Henri. A large exhibition of The Eight was a great triumph in New York; it toured the United States for two years. He remarried (he was widowed in 1905) and resigned his position at the New York School of Art, which he had joined in 1902, and opened his own school. Among his numerous notable students were Edward Hopper and George Bellows.

Throughout his career Henri balanced traveling in Europe with teaching and being an advocate for young artists in the United States. He began to spend time in Santa Fe in 1917, and in 1924 bought a home in Ireland where he spent his summers. Henri died in 1929. A memorial exhibition for him at The Metropolitan Museum of Art, New York in 1931 included the Art Center's painting, **Ballet Girl in White**.

Henri's main interest in his painting was people, and he was especially interested in dancers. "American dancers, notably Loie Fuller, Isidora Duncan and Ruth St. Denis, were all the rage on Europe's cultural stage in the years preceding World War I.... While Henri worshiped Duncan, and in 1919, painted an uncommissioned portrait of **Ruth St. Denis in Peacock**

Dance, it seems clear that **Ballet Girl in White** [the Art Center's work] represents a model striking a pose rather than a dancer of note.... We see a striking resemblance, in subject and treatment, with the identical size **Masquerade Dress: Portrait of Mrs. Robert Henri** of 1911 in the Metropolitan Museum of Art. It is tempting to speculate that the artist's beautiful wife stood for both pictures."[3]

In 1927 the Des Moines Association of Fine Arts organized an exhibition of works by Henri, Bellows, Luks, Glackens, Sloan, Eugene Speicher, and Leon Kroll. Two of the three paintings by Henri came from MacBeth Galleries, New York. However, for a third and larger work in the show, Henri suggested a painting from 1909 that he had kept. His letter of January 31, 1927, to the association states: "I have already decided on the two smaller canvases, and talking with Speicher he and I both thought (it being his suggestion) that the larger picture might be my **Ballet Girl in White** which is a full length figure and altho [sic] painted quite a while ago holds with anything I have done. I doubt it would be possible to get any triad of pictures that would be any better representation of me." The association purchased **Ballet Girl in White** directly from Henri during the course of the exhibition. DL

Four units, fiberglass on wire
mesh, and latex and cloth on wire,
overall, 90 $^7/_8$ x 147 $^5/_8$ x 42 $^1/_2$ inches
(230.8 x 375 x 108 cm)

eva hesse

American, born Germany, 1936–1970   **Untitled,** 1970

Eva Hesse pioneered a new approach to sculpture that incorporated soft, process-revealing forms, malleable materials, and untraditional references to the human, especially the female, body. Her work emerged in the 1960s as an alternative to the dominant style of Minimalism and as an early example of a Feminist language of form. Specifically, Hesse has been grouped with Process artists such as Lynda Benglis, Sam Gilliam, and Robert Morris (his work of c.1967–73). Although she was just coming into her artistic maturity at the time of her death from a brain tumor at the age of thirty-four, Hesse's work has been a major influence on subsequent art.

The Art Center's sculpture is one of the last Hesse was able to carry out. It is made up of four roughly rectangular shapes hung on the wall. Formed around a wire-mesh base, the translucent, yellowish fiberglass of irregular consistency looks pulled and manipulated. These wall elements have a hand-formed appearance that counters their overall geometric character, an ironic or witty quality that Hesse fostered in her work. Each has four sides that suggest the shallow boxes of

Donald Judd's Minimalist structures, but Hesse's are softer, without hard edges or precise joinings, and clearly made from a single piece of material worked by hand.

Emerging from the upper third of each "box" are two lumpy, eccentric, ropelike forms that fall randomly to the floor. To a considerable degree Hesse allowed the material to act on its own, to respond without her interference to natural forces such as gravity or deterioration. These soft strands of aluminum wire covered with gauze and latex are the antithesis of the industrially fabricated structures of Minimalism because the strips of gauze have obviously been hand-wound, slowly and laboriously, around the wire that emerges unadorned at the terminus of the line. Such a technique evokes women's traditional labor-intensive activities with fiber and cloth. In the late pieces, this winding also suggests bandaging, reflecting the surgeries that Hesse underwent to try to sustain her health.

Hesse's art returned an organic character to the sculpture of her time and, even more importantly, introduced a new means of referring to the body in an abstract, nonliteral way. The soft, light-catching tone of her materials and the shapes that evoke but do not imitate internal and external parts of the human body help to give her work immedi-

acy and warmth. She was also able to invest her art with personal metaphors and concerns about sexuality and vulnerability while retaining an intellectual, disciplined approach to form.

Eva Hesse came with her parents from Hamburg, Germany, to the United States in 1939. She studied at Cooper Union in New York (1954–57) and graduated with a Bachelor of Fine Arts degree from Yale University in 1959, having studied with Joseph Albers. Although her early work was in painting and drawing – and drawing remained an important activity – she concentrated on sculpture after 1964. During that year she lived in Germany where she encountered the work of Joseph Beuys and other German artists. Surrounded back in New York by Minimalist artists such as Sol LeWitt, Donald Judd, and Robert Smithson, Hesse struggled to define a new kind of form that would express her more internalized approach to art. In the last five years of her life, she constantly battled ill health to create a small but highly significant body of work. LRD

Purchased with funds from the Edmundson
Art Foundation, Inc.; Des Moines Art
Center Permanent Collections, 1992.32

Electronic light emitting diode (LED) sign,
6 ¹/₂ x 121 ¹/₂ x 4 inches
(16.5 x 308.6 x 10.1 cm)

jenny holzer

American, born 1950   **Selections from Truisms,** 1983–84

More than any other visual artist in recent decades, Jenny Holzer is associated with making art that depends upon words. This tradition of incorporating words into visual art began early in this century with Cubism, and played a role in the works of artists as diverse as the Belgian Surrealist René Magritte; the American painter Stuart Davis, best known for his abstractions; and the American Jasper Johns, for example in his painting **Tennyson** (1958) in the collection of the Des Moines Art Center.

After receiving her Bachelor of Fine Arts degree from Ohio University, Holzer attended graduate school at the Rhode Island School of Design, where in 1975 she began incorporating words into her abstract paintings. At the same time she became interested in art for the general public.

Holzer's words take the form of statements or narratives. Beginning in 1977 and into 1979, she made her now famous "Truisms": "mock clichés" which she said were "like the Great Ideas of the Western World in a nutshell."[1] Most of these took the form of posters printed with forty to sixty truisms. [There are 253 "Truisms".] This format allowed her to make "the big issues in culture intelligible as public art."[2] The "Truisms" are variously sincere, ironic, humorous, or disturbing.

In subsequent years Holzer developed other series of statements, some of which are more like narratives than clichés. Also unlike clichés, they became more frequently disturbing and personal, even adopting the first person pronoun. Some of these series are the Inflammatory "Essays" (1979–82), "Laments" (1988–89), and "Lustmord" (1993–94).

In 1982 Holzer began to use electronic signs, which became an essential visual element in her work and also underscored its "public-art" nature. Holzer stated: " ...I thought the signs were the official voice of everything from advertising to public service announcements."[3] Often using "Truisms," the early public signs were located in Times Square in New York, Candlestick Park in San Francisco, and Caesar's Palace in Las Vegas, among other sites. The "Truisms" scroll across the electronic sign under the control of a computer module programmed by the artist.

Holzer also made smaller signs, such as the **Selections from Truisms** in the collection of the Des Moines Art Center. The Art Center's sign is characteristic of the work Holzer was making in 1986, which was the year of her first major museum exhibition. This show was organized by the Des Moines Art Center, with a catalogue by the Interim Director Joan Simon, and traveled to museums in Aspen, Colorado; Cambridge, Massachusetts; Chicago; and San Francisco.

Holzer is a socially and politically engaged artist, and the content of her words is vital to her. At the same time, her visual sensibility is critical to making the content engaging. That visual sensibility has found further expression in remarkable site-specific installations that make use of reflections on polished floors, horizontal signs, a completely darkened environment, and objects such as stone benches or sarcophagi inscribed with her words and installed independently or combined with electronic signs.

Holzer was born in Ohio and lived there until she was a sophomore in high school. Following her graduate studies she moved to New York City in 1977, and currently resides in upstate New York. She has had numerous one-person shows internationally and has participated in many important group exhibitions, The Solomon R. Guggenheim Museum in New York mounted a major retrospective of her work in 1989, and in 1990 she represented the United States at the Venice Biennale, for which she won the Leone d'Oro prize for the Best Pavilion. IMD

Purchased with funds from the Edmundson
Art Foundation, Inc.; Des Moines Art
Center Permanent Collections, 1958.2

Oil on canvas, 28 1/8 x 36 inches
(71.4 x 91.4 cm)

edward hopper

American, 1882–1967   **Automat,** 1927

"A young woman contemplating her life over a cup of coffee," is how Gail Levin described Edward Hopper's painting **Automat**, in the catalogue of the landmark 1980 exhibition "Edward Hopper: The Art and the Artist."[1] But this description overlooks the work's enigmatic nature and air of mystery.

Hopper is repeatedly described as having been as introverted and private as the people in his paintings. He was born in Nyack, New York in 1882, and grew up in a house that overlooked the Hudson River. Shy and bookish as a child, he had reached a height of six feet by the time he was twelve. He was fascinated by boats and built his own when he was fifteen. Two years later he entered the Correspondence School of Illustrating, New York, to pursue his other interest – drawing. In 1900 he entered the New York School of Art, commuting from Nyack for six years to study illustration and painting with William Merritt Chase, Robert Henri, and Kenneth Hayes Miller. His fellow students included Rockwell Kent and George Bellows.

After short-term employment as an illustrator at an advertising agency, in the fall of 1906 Hopper went for ten months to Paris. Instead of engaging in the bohemian life, he lived with a family arranged through the

Baptist Church. Hopper quickly came under the spell of the Impressionists and began emulating their light and practice of painting out-of-doors. He returned to Paris for short periods in 1909 and 1910.

Early on, Hopper experienced very little success. He commuted to New York three days a week for commercial design and illustration work, and gave art lessons in Nyack. In 1913 he sold a painting at the Armory Show and five years later won a prize for a poster design. In 1920 he had a show at the prestigious Whitney Studio Club, but none of his works sold.

In 1923 his career began to pick up. The Brooklyn Museum included six watercolors in an exhibition and purchased one of them for the collection. One year later his first one-artist gallery show sold out. Able finally to give up illustration and support himself from his art, Hopper also got married in 1924. His wife, Jo, was a former fellow student with Robert Henri; she is the woman in most of Hopper's subsequent paintings.

From 1924 on Hopper's career was a great success. In 1934 Hopper purchased a home and studio in South Truro, Massachusetts, where he and Jo subsequently spent their summers. When Hopper and Jo died, in 1967 and 1968 respectively, Hopper's estate of more than 2,000 works of art was bequeathed to the Whitney Museum of American Art, which had been particularly supportive of him. "Hopper guarded his privacy throughout his career and remained

extremely thrifty.... He would eat in the shabbiest restaraunts and diners, wear clothes until they were threadbare and buy second-hand cars that he drove until they gave up the ghost."[2]

Hopper painted many figures, such as the woman in **Automat**, who reflect his sense of thrift and isolation. In an automat diner during the 1920s and 1930s, a person could easily be alone, without interacting even with a server. Although the overall composition of **Automat** is fairly minimal, the deeply introspective woman is intriguing because of her bare hand and legs. Does she wear only one glove because she is in such a hurry that she does not take the time to remove the other glove, or is it the cold that causes her to keep on her coat and one glove? The smallness of the radiator and the figure's distance from it emphasizes the sense of cold. As alone as the woman seems within the oasis of the automat, the deep darkness outside the window seems even more lonely.

Hopper and his wife traveled a great deal, and "in so doing, he became interested in the psychology and environment of travelers – in hotels, motels, trains, highways and filling stations. These became the haunting themes of many of his paintings."[3] The woman in **Automat** could certainly be one of the lonely travelers Hopper observed. DL

Purchased with funds from the Janss
Foundation and the Coffin Fine Arts Trust;
Nathan Emory Coffin Collection of
the Des Moines Art Center, 1972.30

Enamel on acrylic with spotlights,
54 inches diameter (137.2 cm)

robert irwin

American, born 1928   **Untitled,** 1968–69

Robert Irwin's untitled discs epitomize the 1960s avant-garde impulse to investigate radically new aesthetic and perceptual realms through the employment of unconventional media and techniques. A native of Long Beach, California, Irwin studied at the Otis Art Institute, Jepson Institute, and Chouinard Art Institute in Los Angeles between 1948 and 1953. By the late 1950s he was exhibiting at the Ferus Gallery in Los Angeles and painting in a gestural Abstract Expressionist style. In the 1960s Irwin, like many other artists of his generation, renounced expressive gesturalism and began to reduce his artistic means. In the early 1960s he painted nearly square, monochromatic canvases in a muted hue, traversed by a few narrow, horizontal lines that stopped short of the picture's edges. In his dot paintings of 1964–67, Irwin stretched each canvas over a convexly bowed, nearly square framework, and covered its surface with thousands of evenly spaced red and green dots, densely clustered in the center and tapering off towards the edges with the gradual elimination of the green. Viewed

from a distance, an Irwin dot painting appears to glow and vibrate; a misty greenish square seems to advance slightly from its center while the edges fade imperceptibly into a halo of pink.

Irwin's growing concern with visual perception and the relationship between the center and edge of the painting led him to adopt the convex disc format in 1966. The first series of discs were fabricated of aluminum and sprayed with pale laquer, nacreous at the center and faintly shaded in red and green along the periphery. Each disc was projected from the wall on an eighteen-inch metal tube and illuminated from above and below by a quartet of equally spaced Sylvania floodlights, creating a clover-leaf pattern of interlaced shadows. Viewed from the front, the disc seemed to dematerialize, while the shadows assumed an unexpected palpability. "Visually," commented Irwin, "it was very ambiguous which was more real, the object or its shadow ... the real beauty of those things [was] that they achieved a balance between space occupied and unoccupied in which both became intensely occupied at the level of perceptual energy."[1]

The Art Center's untitled work belongs to Irwin's second series of discs (1968–69), which were cast in acrylic resin and supported by plexiglass rather than metal tubes. The acrylic discs are spray-painted, but their

mid-sections are bisected by a three-inch horizontal band, which appears transparent, but is in fact painted with opaque gray in the center that fades to actual transparency at the edges. The confusion between illusionistic and real space visible through the horizontal axis of the disc increases the perceptual uncertainty of the viewing experience. Disc, shadows, and wall ultimately merge into a single aesthetic continuum, transcending the traditional separation between the art object and its surroundings.

Irwin has stated that "the discs resolved that one simple question – how to paint a painting that doesn't begin or end at the edge – by more or less transcending painting.... After the discs, there was no reason for me to go on being a painter."[2] In 1970 Irwin gave up his studio and sold his tools and art supplies. Since then he has concentrated on the manipulation of light and space in interiors and in the creation of site-specific works in urban and natural landscapes. DC

Oil on canvas over oil-on-wood
landscape by unknown artist,
16 x 20 inches (40.6 x 50.8 cm)

jess (burgess collins)

American, born 1923　　**"A Panic That Can Still Come Upon Me": Salvages II,** 1963–72

Jess (Burgess Collins) was born in Long Beach, California in 1923. Although he made collages as a child, in college he majored in chemistry. In 1943 Jess was drafted into the US Army Corps of Engineers and trained in the Chemical Warfare Service. In his free time, however, Jess explored painting and drawing in addition to collage. In 1946 he reentered the California Institute of Technology, Pasadena, receiving a Bachelor of Science degree in chemistry in 1948.

Shortly after graduating, while employed as a control chemist in Richland, Washington, Jess was transformed by a dream concerning the world and its destruction by 1975. "I decided that if that was going to be the case, I wanted to do something that was truly meaningful to me."[1] He moved to Berkeley and enrolled in the graduate art program at the University of California, but switched immediately to the California School of Fine Arts, San Francisco, where he studied for a short time with such notable painters as Clyfford Still and David Park. While at Berkeley, however, he attended a reading by the Beat poet Robert Duncan; the two formed a lifelong relationship, living together from 1951 until Duncan died in 1988.

In 1950 Jess began working on several different series, including nonobjective paintings, romantic paintings, and "Paste Ups" (collages). "Salvages," a series based on the reworking of his older paintings or the manipulation of anonymous found paintings, includes the Art

Center's **"A Panic That Can Still Come Upon Me": Salvages II**.

In 1960 Jess accompanied Duncan to his family home where Duncan was to select some things for his inheritance. Jess found, and was given, an anonymous landscape painting. Reworked over a period of nine years, this landscape evolved into the Art Center's work. Jess described the encounter: "I saw on the wall [of Duncan's home] this tiny nameless forest landscape, pleasant, unassuming, bland. Only the painting of the central tree caught me up. The next waiting subject of 'Salvages II' was not my doing, but an anonymous other's work."[2]

While Jess maintained for this work a forest image, only the central tree from the original painting remains uncovered. Its smooth, flat surface contrasts with Jess' thick impasto. As well, the original palette was very dark, whereas Jess reworked it with bright pastels. The contrast between the central original tree and the newer areas of the work is quite pronounced.

Populating Jess' forest are several images of men and animals. At the left a herd of horses gallops across the top of the composition while a single horse rears below; a squirrel pauses on a branch with his tail raised alertly; a bull fighter engages a bull with his cape; a seated man plays the banjo; two other men look furtively into a bush; and a nude man with legs spread provocatively lies back on the grass while engaging the viewer's eye. At the

right side of the painting, a horned, half-man/half-goat creature stares at the viewer with open mouth. No apparent visual connection or encompassing narrative unites these images. The overall feeling of the work is that of disparate events within a fantasy landscape, collaged together irrespective of time, space, and meaning.

On the back of the painting are eleven found photographic images of the figures Jess painted on the front, forming a collage that outlines the painting. The images "one by one arrive by chance encounter, either by sifting thru my stored image bank or just by happening to cross my path at any moment."[3] A quotation on a piece of cardboard from Duncan's essay "The Truth and Life of Myth; An Essay in Essential Autobiography" also forms part of this collage: "In the world of saying and telling in which I first came into words, there is a primary trouble, a panic that can still come upon me where the word no longer protects, transforming the threat of an overwhelming knowledge into the power of an imagined reality, or abstracting from a shaking experience terms for rationalization, but exposes me the more."

Jess feels the "words to be a true part of the work, not merely a tag for remembrance. The 'Salvages II' quotation applies in my spirit as much for paint and images as it does for conceptions and words."[4] TAC

Purchased with funds from the Coffin Fine
Arts Trust; Nathan Emory Coffin
Collection of the Des Moines Art Center,
1971.4

Encaustic and canvas collage on canvas,
73 1/2 x 48 1/4 inches (186.7 x 122 cm)

jasper johns

American, born 1930   **Tennyson,** 1958

Perhaps the leading American painter of his generation, Jasper Johns was born in Augusta, Georgia and grew up in South Carolina before briefly attending the University of South Carolina, Columbia in 1947–48. He served in the military, studied at a commercial art school, and worked in a book-store and as a window designer as he began his career in New York in the early 1950s.

Johns's work has always focused on the relationship between knowledge, language, and perception, and the ways in which these traditionally separate spheres of human understanding overlap. In the process he has questioned our assumptions about the visual world by introducing language into painting, thereby integrating intellectual references into a principally visual medium.

In his early work Johns depicted a variety of seemingly self-evident objects: alphabets, flags, maps, numerals, and targets. In lavishing exhaustive painterly attention on "things the mind already knows," in the artist's phrase, he caused us to doubt the depth of our knowledge and perception, and implicitly to question the nature of what is appropriate subject matter.

Among Johns's most intriguing subjects in the 1950s were language, literature, and books. In one work of the period, **Book** (1957), Johns simply painted the pages of an open book in gray encaustic. The following year he made the Art Center's **Tennyson**; a large vertical painting dominated by dense gray brushwork over a surface of encaustic and canvas collage. That is, Johns painted a length of canvas and then folded it down against itself, with the folded element mounted in the center. Plainly visible beneath the fold at the right is a partially hidden passage of red paint, a veiled reference to inaccessible content within the book. He divided the area above the fold into two lateral zones, and stenciled the name "Tennyson" in large Roman letters along the bottom. The painting's title and the actual appearance of the name on the canvas refer to Alfred, Lord Tennyson (1809–1892), a celebrated English Victorian poet.

Although the reason for Johns's invocation of Tennyson is unknown, he has often inscribed writers into his work in a similar fashion. Examples include the paintings **In Memory of My Feelings – Frank O'Hara** (1961), **Periscope (Hart Crane)** (1963), and **Celine** (1978). It should be noted that Johns made at least three works on paper titled **Tennyson**, one in the collection of the artist (1958), one in the collection of The Hirshhorn Museum and Sculpture Garden in Washington, DC (1959), and one made several years later and now in the Ganz Collection (1967). NB

Purchased with funds from the Coffin Fine
Arts Trust; Nathan Emory Coffin
Collection of the Des Moines Art Center,
1987.7

Twenty-one units, stainless steel, each,
4 x 27 x 23 inches (10.2 x 559.4 x 274.3 cm);
overall, 4 x 230 x 108 inches
(10.2 x 599.4 x 274.3 cm)

donald judd

American, 1928–1994   **Untitled,** 1976–77

Untitled (1976–77), a major Minimalist sculpture by Donald Judd, is a work that deals with the plane of the floor and geometric configurations that explore variations on a basic unit. It is made of twenty-one stainless-steel squares identical in their external measurements, but each with different internal divisions. These divisions deal with the measurement of their depth and the variation of planes and angles that can be explored within the internal space of each unit. Each unit is placed directly on the ground without a base and spaced evenly one from the other in a grid formation. In the 1960s Judd was one of the first artists to make sculpture directly on the floor, taking away the aspect of presentation inherent in a base, and making the work a real presence equal with the floor and the walls. Each unit is coexistent with the others, the combination of all creating the total work, but each unit is a self-sufficient form.

As one of the major artists of the Minimalist movement, Judd was as well known for his articulation of the principles of this approach to art as he was for his work itself. He used industrial materials in their pure form to make elemental structures that are both self-contained objects as well as objects that have a relationship to the space they are within. The work is intended to be self-contained in its content as well, not carrying an associative, symbolic, or narrative content, but concerning itself solely with physical, spatial, and intellectual properties.

In its reduced abstract form, Judd's work is an expression of complex thought, and the idea of the absolute. It is the answer to a problem, the synthesis of an idea. Yet each work contains within it both a sense of completion and the promise of other solutions, so his work is never intellectually static. Like a thought or a story that can be expressed through the use of nouns to carry meaning without the embellishment of adjectives to make description, Judd's materials speak for themselves. Through direct form and material and the purity and integrity of his craftsmanship, the richness inherent in the sculpture, in both body and surface, is expressed. In making sculpture both clean and complicated through a study of materials and their physical proeprties, and in relation to themselves and to surrounding space, Judd's work touches on some of the most basic questions about physical being and the power of the intellect to order one's existence. The work is involved with an essential order as object and in relation to space and architecture.

Untitled is a study of form, both internal and external, its intricacies, proportions, and combinations. Form and content are one.

Through this work one becomes more aware of the plane of the floor, the walls, the space above in the room, how one stands, what the air feels like in the room, how much there is of it, the volume of emptiness as tangible as the sculpture that defines and measures it.

Born in Missouri, Judd studied at the Art Students League in New York and made his living initially as an art critic. While he began his work as an artist making paintings, he started making three-dimensional objects in the early 1960s. He began using metal in addition to wood because of the greater precision inherent in this medium, and continued throughout his work to use industrial materials unadorned and straightforward but immensely beautiful in their spare quality and the richness of the material itself. He made a body of work dealing with primary forms and materials, exploring the nature and complexity of geometric objects and their relation to space. Throughout his immensely productive career, Judd continued to make sculpture and work on paper as well as architecture and furniture. Toward the end of his life, he lived in Texas, New York, and Switzerland. JB

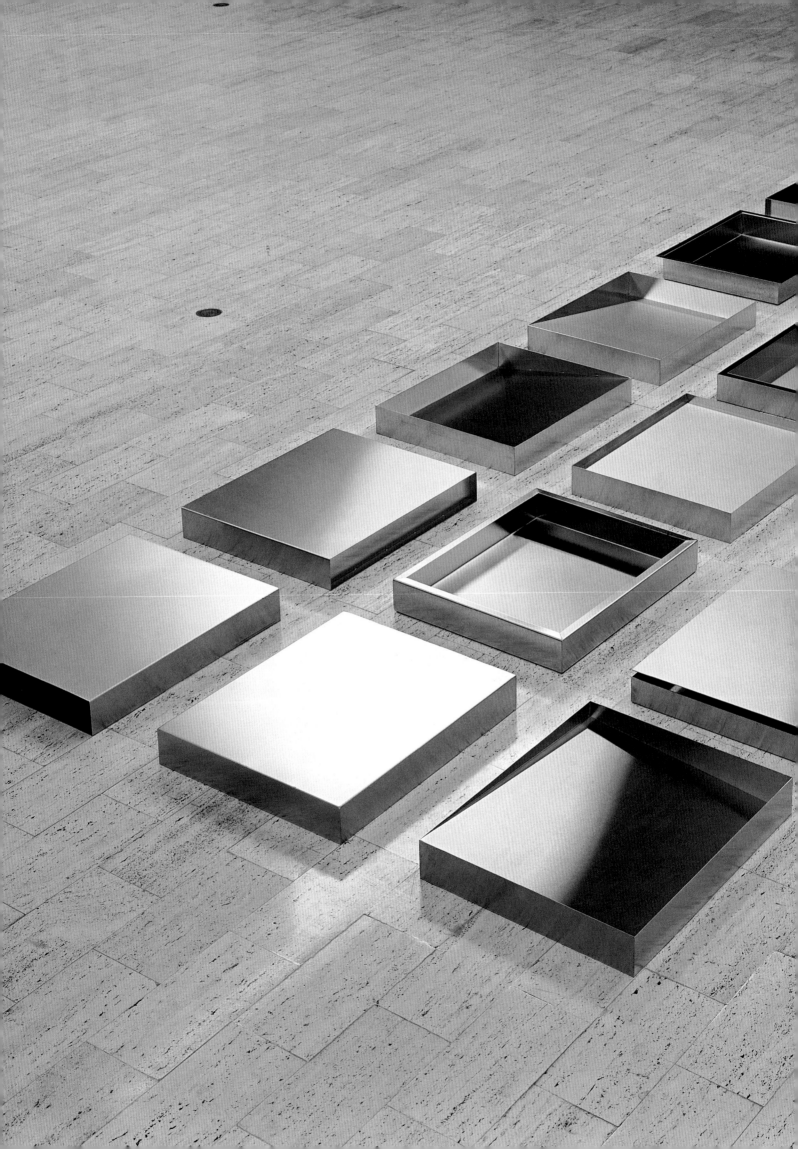

Oil on canvas, 90 x 65 inches
(228.7 x 165.1 cm)

ellsworth kelly

American, born 1923   **Yellow Blue,** 1963

Ellsworth Kelly pioneered hard-edge abstraction in the mid-1950s, painting large canvases whose precision-contoured forms, flat colors, and immaculate surfaces stood in opposition to the then-dominant gestural style of Abstract Expressionism. Born in Newburgh, New York, Kelly studied art at the Pratt Institute in Brooklyn (1941–42) before serving in the Army (1943–45). In 1946–48 he studied drawing and painting at the Boston Museum School and painted figurative works in an expressionist vein. In 1948 Kelly moved to France, and studied at the Ecole des Beaux-Arts in Paris until 1950.

In France, Kelly began drawing objects and shapes observed in the landscape – chimneys and roadside markers, windows and walls, shadows and reflections – which served as the basis for collages, reliefs, and paintings that distill their subjects into essential geometric forms and patterns. Stimulated by a visit to the studio of Jean Arp, Kelly also started to experiment with the effects of chance, cutting up drawings and recombining their pieces to form random compositions. In the early 1950s he also produced checkerboard paintings of bright

colors arranged according to the laws of chance, and paintings resembling large color charts composed of separate panels of pure color placed side by side.

In 1954 Kelly returned to New York and began to paint the elegant, hard-edged abstractions that secured his reputation. He typically would translate some commonplace aspect of the urban environment – the form of a shadow, the arc of a suspension cable – into one or two simple shapes, painted in a single, flat color against a ground of another color. He worked mostly in black and white during the mid-1950s, and then reintroduced red, yellow, blue, and green into his palette near the end of the decade. In the late 1950s Kelly also started making planar metal sculptures that can be understood as three-dimensional versions of his paintings.

Although by the early 1960s Kelly had come to depend less upon the observed environment for visual stimulation, his pictorial forms continued to suggest origins in the real world. In the Art Center's **Yellow Blue**, for example, an intensely yellow, ovoid shape slants upward from the lower left into a field of vivid blue. With prolonged viewing the truncated yellow shape, at first understood as completely flat and nonreferential, begins to appear volumetric and takes on representational connotations, evoking, for example, an egg, a wooden spoon, or a pool of light.

Just as the deceptively simple yellow shape becomes increasingly interesting the longer one contemplates it, so too does the relationship between the yellow and blue areas of the painting. The yellow seems at first to divide the blue field completely, but closer examination reveals a thin vein of blue remaining at the right edge that contains the yellow. An irresolvable tension arises between the bright yellow, inflating like a balloon, and the deep blue, which wraps itself around the yellow and checks its expansion. This powerful play of visual forces is rendered almost physical by the painting's imposing scale, which engages not only the eye but also the body.

As he often does, Kelly executed in different media and color combinations a number of works closely related in composition to **Yellow Blue**. Among these are the aluminum relief sculpture **Blue Over Blue** (1963); the paintings **Blue Green** (1961), **Red Orange Blue** (1963), and **Red Blue** (1964); the screenprint **Red/Blue (Untitled)** (1964); and two drawings and a collage, each entitled **Study for "Red Blue"** (1963).[1] DC

Purchased with funds from the Coffin Fine
Arts Trust; Nathan Emory Coffin
Collection of the Des Moines Art Center,
1988.12

Oil, acrylic, emulsion, and ash on canvas,
with lead objects and ballet shoes on
treated lead, 153 ¹/₂ x 220 ¹/₂ x 10 inches
(390 x 560 x 25.4 cm)

anselm kiefer

Germany, b. 1945   **Untitled,** 1987–88

Anselm Kiefer is part of the resurgence of European art that gained prominence in the 1970s. German artists in particular came forward with passion and frankness, confronting their heritage in a revived expressionistic style and vigorous new imagery. Kiefer's contribution has been especially significant for the revival of history painting, a type of art generally avoided by Modernism and made problematic by the horrors of twentieth-century politics and warfare.

The Art Center's work is typical of Kiefer's massive, mixed-media paintings that blend abstract form with realism and actual objects. The subject matter is German history, the acknowledgment of past crimes, and the role of the artist (or the cultivated, civilized mind) in the evolution of a more humane world. Kiefer's work has often been thought of as redemptive in its acceptance of culpability and meditation on the causes and preventions of inhumanity. **Untitled** is divided into two sections, one clearly a landscape, the other suggestive of a darkened sky. The painting overall is sober, even grim, in its shades of gray and brown. The rough surface has the look typical in Kiefer's work of a damaged, savaged object. There are layers of paint (sometimes mixed with ash) and of metal sheets that are corroded, bent, torn, and split apart. Other areas appear to have been burned. The entire painting possesses a strong sense of its own history, an object worked over in a long process of

artistic struggle. The most distinctive painted form is a set of railroad tracks that disappear around diverging curves. The "landscape" they traverse is barren, as if it is the trampled and devastated ground left after a battle. The rails have usually been interpreted as a reference to the trains that transported so many people to places where they were dreadfully harmed or killed. It is common for Kiefer to write words of symbolic significance in his works and this painting contains several. **Abend**, German for "evening," is handwritten at the base of the tracks. It may indicate the twilight before the descent of darkness for an entire society or it may relate to German transcendental landscapes in which the setting sun symbolizes the end of life and the beginning of the soul's journey into eternity. Directly above this word is written **Land**, which has the same meaning in English as in German. It may refer to the literal land of Germany, soaked with the blood of so many victims. Joined to the word below, the term **Abendland** translates generally as the Occident, or the Western world. On the right side of the painting the letters "Eu" may refer to Europe, and are also the chemical symbol for Europium, a rare earth metal. Perhaps Kiefer's intention here was to recall the engulfing of all of Europe in the conflagration of World War II. Or he may have had in mind the fate of Western civilization and its struggle against Nazism, often characterized as a struggle to save Western civilization from what Winston Churchill called "a new Dark Age."

The idea of rescue or redemption is suggested most strongly by the ladder and the ballet shoes in the upper half of the painting. The contorted metal ladder connecting the two halves is generally interpreted as symbolizing the aspiration of the human soul to rise toward an intellectual and spiritual plane of peace and compassion. It begins where the railroad tracks end, suggesting the hope of escaping the worst in human impulses, both culturally and as individuals. The ballet shoes refer to artists, especially as they represent what is finest in the human soul. Taking up Joseph Beuys's concept of the artist as a shaman, Kiefer uses highly symbolic means to carry a powerful message about humanity and the consequence of history. Through the painting's extensive use of lead, for example, a metal alchemists sought to transform into gold, Kiefer again refers to the refinement of destructive human inclinations through art.

Kiefer was born in Donaueschingen in 1945. He received a degree in law from Freiburg University, then studied with Joseph Beuys at the Staatliche Kunstakademie in Düsseldorf. He began exhibiting in 1969 with a photographic series documenting European sites associated with German history. Books and sculpture have also been important media for Kiefer. Along with Georg Baselitz, Kiefer represented Germany at the Venice Biennale in 1980. LRD

paul klee

Swiss, 1879–1940   **Anchorage (Anlege Platz)**, 1928

Paul Klee's inventive, witty, and highly imaginative personal style marks him as one of the great artists of the twentieth century, but prevents him from being categorized as belonging to one particular school or movement. Although there are affinities to the work of the Surrealists and the German Expressionists, any work by Klee is first and foremost a work by Klee, rather than a depiction of a specific subject or an example of an art-historical period. An accomplished violist as well, Klee frequently used equivalents for musical structure in his visual compositions, creating themes and variations, rhythms and repetitions, Bach-like fugues.

Klee divided his time between Germany and Switzerland, where he was born, near Bern. He moved to Munich in 1898 and studied art at a private school and at the Akademie. He is most identified institutionally with the Bauhaus in Germany, where he taught from 1920 to 1931. Subsequently he taught for

two years at the Düsseldorfer Akademie, but was dismissed in 1933 when the Nazis came to power. He returned to his native Switzerland where he spent the remainder of his life, working while battling a skin disease that claimed his life in 1940 at the outbreak of the war.

Klee's famous observation about his method – "taking a line for a walk" – is evident in the strongly graphic structure of the Des Moines Art Center's painting on paper **Anchorage**. As is generally true throughout his oeuvre, the painting is quite small and deceptively simple. Here Klee has abstracted a scene of boats at anchor by reducing the linear forms to geometric shapes not much more complicated than newspaper vessels made by a child. Indeed, as early as 1902, the twenty-three-year-old artist wrote in his diary: "To have to begin by what is smallest is as difficult as it is essential. I would like to be like a newborn child, knowing nothing whatever about Europe, ignorant of poets and fashions, in fact an almost primitive being. Then, I would like to do something very humble, to elaborate on my own a tiny formal motif which my pencil could manage without any

trace of technique. One favourable moment is enough. The little thing is there on the paper, easily and concisely fixed. It is done. It was a tiny act, but a real one, and by the repetition of such small but original acts a work will one day be born on which I can truly build."[1]

The considerable pictorial sophistication of **Anchorage** proves that Klee achieved his goal. The simple, triangular shapes are locked tightly to an open, right-angled grid that suggests the greater rigidity and stability of a pier, thereby freeing the boats to seem afloat in a more fluid world. The entire composition hugs the center of the panel, an island of human activity in a space that seems vast despite the painting's modest size. It suggests that mankind occupies only a fraction of the universe, but within his domain he builds and creates order. TRN

Gift of Elizabeth Bates and John Cowles;
Des Moines Art Center Permament
Collections, 1963.3

Oil on canvas, 44 ³/₄ x 60 inches
(113.7 x152.4 cm)

oskar kokoschka

Austrian, 1886–1980   **Portrait of Mr. and Mrs. John Cowles**, 1949

Although portraiture formed the basis of Oskar Kokoschka's career, he created only four double portraits.[1] The Des Moines Art Center is privileged to have one of them in its collection.

Kokoschka grew up in Vienna. While he was studying at the School of Applied Arts in Vienna to become a secondary-school art teacher, his painted portraits of family members were noticed by a professor, who took him into his tutelage as a painting major and teaching assistant. He was assigned the life drawing classes and instead of having the models pose rigidly, he asked them to move about. A sense of movement has always been prevalent in Kokoschka's portraits.

By 1907 Kokoschka had been invited to join the Wiener Werkstätte, a prestigious design workshop that included the artists Gustav Klimt and Egon Schiele. Klimt considered Kokoschka "the greatest talent of the younger generation."[2] By 1910 Kokoschka had left the Werkstätte, moved to Berlin, and was concentrating on portraiture. He began to socialize with avant-garde artists and intellectuals, several of whom he painted. His uncompromising vision gave his subjects mottled complexions and dour, nervous, wide-eyed expressions. He paid particular attention to his sitters' hands, which often appear to be twitching. But although Kokoschka was busy, he was struggling to make ends meet.[3]

A dark period of Kokoschka's personal life began in 1912 when he fell madly in love with Alma Mahler (widow of composer Gustav Mahler). Their three-year, mismatched love affair was devastating for Kokoschka. In 1914 Mahler aborted his child, embarked upon an affair with the architect Walter Gropius, and convinced Kokoschka to join the cavalry at the start of World War I. In 1915 he was shot in the head, and fell from his horse and was bayonetted in the lungs by a Russian soldier while still conscious. He was hospitalized for both physical and emotional damage.

Kokoschka's professional life had taken a turn for the better, however. He secured a professorship in painting at the Dresden Academy of Fine Arts in 1919 and began a series of landscapes. In 1923 his success enabled him to resign his position to travel and paint. Returning to Dresden in 1927, he resumed portraiture, now with greater richness of color and fullness of volume.

When Hitler staged the 1937 Degenerate Art exhibition in Munich, which included Kokoschka's work, the artist fled first to Prague and then to London, accompanied by Olda Palkovska, whom he married in 1941. In 1953 he moved to Villeneuve, Switzerland, and opened an art academy in Salzburg, Austria. He traveled the world teaching, lecturing, and showing his work.

In 1949 the Minneapolis newspaper publisher and art collector John Cowles commissioned Kokoschka to paint a portrait of his wife,

Elizabeth, for their twenty-fifth wedding anniversary; the commission changed to a double portrait before Kokoschka arrived. **Portrait of Mr. and Mrs. John Cowles** is very thoroughly documented in letters to Olda, who did not accompany Kokoschka to Minneapolis. He speaks of repainting the work three times, and while he states that "the Cowles are very close to each other," in his painting he put distance between them.[4]

Executed with Kokoschka's signature bright colors and rapid, expressionistic strokes, each sitter occupies a different space, established by a green curtain on the left that encloses John but leaves out Elizabeth, who is enveloped by red patterned upholstery. Elizabeth's hand extends into John's side of the painting, and while she is looking at him, he looks out to the viewers. At the bottom of the painting the figures are more connected, with John's legs overlapping Elizabeth's. While not totally separated, the two do not seem totally comfortable with one another. Kokoschka seems to have captured what John Cowles, Jr. meant when he stated that "his parents were 'complicated people' with 'long years of stress in their marriage.'"[5]

Kokoschka returned to Minneapolis in 1952 and 1957 to teach at The Minneapolis Institute of Arts and complete more portrait commissions. None of subsequent works has the intrigue of the Art Center's painting. DL

Purchased with funds from Roy
Halston Frowick; Des Moines Art Center
Permanent Collections, 1991.46

Vacuum cleaners in plexiglass with
fluorescent lights, 124 ¹/₂ x 28 x 28 inches
(316.2 x 71.1 x 71.1 cm)

jeff koons

American, born 1955   **The New Shelton Wet/Dry Triple Decker**, 1981

Throughout the 1980s, in several series of works that look strikingly different but embody related themes, Jeff Koons established himself as one of the most provocative artists of his generation. He was born in York, Pennsylvania in 1955. He studied at the Maryland College of Art in Baltimore and at The School of The Art Institute of Chicago, where he received his Bachelor of Fine Arts degree in 1976. He moved in 1977 to New York, where he currently resides. One-person exhibitions of his work have been organized by the Museum of Contemporary Art, Chicago (1988) and the San Francisco Museum of Modern Art (1992).

At The New Museum of Contemporary Art in New York in 1980, Koons presented work from a series called "The New." There were three sculptures consisting of factory-fresh vacuum cleaners stacked within plexiglass cases and very brightly illuminated with fluorescent lights. From this series of thirty-five works conceived from 1980 to 1982, the Art Center's **The New Shelton Wet/Dry Triple Decker** was described by Koons as his "grand piece."[1] The Art Center's work was made in 1981, although approximately two-thirds of the series were not executed until the second half of the 1980s when Koons had sufficient financial means to fabricate the encasements for the remainder.

Koons referred to the vacuum cleaners in **The New Shelton Wet/Dry Triple Decker** as "breathing machines," since air and liquid pass through them. Each machine is androidlike – indeed, reminiscent of the humanized robot R2D2 in the movie **Star Wars** (1977). Of the Art Center's work with its three objects of different sizes, Koons said there is a "papa, mama, and baby" family relationship.

Life cycles and issues of life and death are central metaphors in Koons's work. Newness, youth, and life pass despite attempts to arrest change, such as encasing the vacuums to preserve newness. The encased vacuum cleaners suggest the womb or incubator, but paradoxically one may be reminded of a casket. The fluorescent lights – reminiscent of Dan Flavin's appropriation of the same industrial material for his Minimal sculptures – assist this duality. While they are on, the sculpture is "alive"; when the plug is pulled, it is lifeless.

Koons's very first series, the "Inflatables" (1979), are brought to life by breathing air into them; but the air seeps out and, without rejuvenation, the objects become flaccid and lifeless. The "Equilibrium Tanks" (1985) contain basketballs floating in water – like embryos in amniotic fluid. But the air and fluid both need periodic rejuvenation. The **Jim Beam – J. B. Turner Train** (1986) consists of stainless-steel casts of decorative encasements for bottles of bourbon, with

real bottles of liquor placed within. If one "uses" the bourbon, the spirits will be gone and so will the sculpture as conceived by the artist. Some works in the series "Made in Heaven" (1989–92) show the artist and his then-wife, Cicciolina (Ilona Staller), copulating; they and their child will eventually grow old. In 1992 the artist made a spectacular flower topiary, over thirty-seven feet tall, of a puppy. The metal frame is permanent and even contains an internal watering system, but the flowers die seasonally.

In addition to personal issues of life and death, "The New" also has important sociological dimensions pertaining to consumerism, which was prominent in the 1980s, the decade in which the term "yuppie" came into wide usage. As the title itself indicates, the works in this series present the new, specifically a consumer item. The incorporation (or appropriation) of manufactured objects, such as the wet/dry vacuums, was central to Koons's work from the late 1970s through the mid-1980s. By placing the vacuums within plexiglass, Koons attempted to preserve their factory-freshness, and the way in which they are lit further glorifies them as commodities. "The New" can be seen as an emblem for the generation that gave birth to t-shirts with the emblazoned motto, "Born to shop." IMD

ăb'străct[1], a. Separated from matter, practice, or particular examples, not con‐ crete; ideal, not practical; abstruse; (with *the*, as noun) the ideal or theoretical way of regarding things (*in the* ~). Hence ~LY[2] adv., ~NESS n. [ME, f. L *abstractus* p.p. of ABS(*trahere* draw)]

Gift of Mr. and Mrs. Paul Waldman,
New York; Des Moines Art Center Permanent
Collections, 1977.36

Photostat mounted on board, 48 x 48
inches (121.9 x 121.9 cm)
Pencil and collage on board (documentation),
5 ³/₄ x 4 ³/₄ inches (14.6 x 12.1 cm)

joseph kosuth

American, born 1945   **Definition: Abstract (Art As Idea As Idea),** 1967

One of the leaders of a language-based movement that came to be called Conceptual Art, Joseph Kosuth was educated in Toledo and Cleveland, Ohio. In New York by 1965, Kosuth dismissed the possibility of painting either in a figurative or a representational manner in favor of work with language. Influenced by Marcel Duchamp and Ad Reinhardt, as well as the philosopher Ludwig Wittgenstein, Kosuth believed that the use of language would substantially redirect art away from appearances, and even aesthetics, and toward ideas. Kosuth shared this commitment with Robert Barry, Douglas Huebler, and Lawrence Weiner, colleagues who together would form the nexus of this new movement. While Kosuth's own work helped define Conceptual Art, he has also been equally important as a theorist, writer, and commentator, and he has been a regular and influential contributor to the dialogue concerning art since the mid-1960s.

From the outset Kosuth addressed the nature of what might be considered legitimate content in art. In one landmark work, **One and Three Chairs** (1965; The Museum of Modern Art, New York), Kosuth presented a chair in three distinct ways: in a photograph, as a photostat dictionary definition, and in the center an actual chair. In so doing he called into question traditional processes of representation and understanding, and

replaced them with a language-based substitute. In another early work, **Five Words in Blue Neon** (1965; Herbert Collection, Ghent, Belgium), Kosuth literally mounted "five words in blue neon" on a wall, effectively conjoining the work, its title, and its description.

The Des Moines Art Center's **Definition: Abstract (Art As Idea As Idea)** (1967) is one in a series of works in which Kosuth further explored the idea of representation. In the "Art As Idea As Idea" series, Kosuth took as his subject words with an understood meaning in the dialogue surrounding art. He appropriated a dictionary definition of each term and mounted a photostat reproduction of those words on a wall. The artist was doubtless attracted to the term because abstraction has been a prevailing mode of art-making in this century, but also because the definition he found (" ... separated from matter, practice or particular examples, not concrete; ideal, not practical ...the ideal or theoretical way of regarding things ... ") corresponded precisely to his own concept of and approach to art. NB

The Des Moines Art Center's Louise Noun
Collection of Art by Women, 1992.2
Collage and oil on paper,
30 x 22 1/2 inches (76.2 x 56.5 cm)

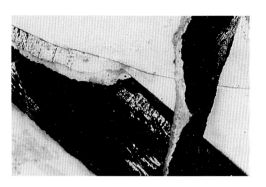

lee krasner

American, 1908–1984   **Black and White Collage,** 1953

Lee Krasner's **Black and White Collage** is part of the Des Moines Art Center's Louise Noun Collection of Art by Women. Louise Rosenfield Noun is a Des Moines scholar and philanthropist who has been an active patron and asset to the Art Center since it was founded. In fact, Noun – the chronicler of the history of the Art Center in this present book – was enrolled by her mother as a member of the Des Moines Association of Fine Arts when it first opened in 1917. Although a collector for many years, in the late 1960s Noun decided to focus on art by women. She has generously donated many of her outstanding works to the Art Center, including this important collage by Lee Krasner.

Krasner was born in Brooklyn, New York in 1908. From 1926 to 1949 she studied art at several prominent New York schools, including the Women's Art School of Cooper Union, the Art Students League, the National Academy of Design, and with Hans Hofmann. Also during these years, from 1934 to 1942, Krasner was a mural painter with various divisions of the Works Progress Administration and related organizations. During the late 1940s and in the 1950s, Krasner was an important participant in the development of Abstract Expressionism,

although she was repeatedly overlooked in favor of Jackson Pollock, whom she had married in 1945.

"There is no question that the identity she accepted when she married made it immeasurably harder for Krasner to attain personal artistic success; she herself was fully aware of this. 'I was not the average woman married to the average painter,' she conceded to a newspaper reporter in 1973. 'I was married to Jackson Pollock. The context is bigger and even if I was not personally dominated by Pollock, the whole art world was.' Wryly articulating the paradox which defined her situation, Krasner told another interviewer, 'Unfortunately, it was fortunate to know Jackson Pollock.'"[1] Krasner was repeatedly referred to in the press as Mrs. Pollock.

Krasner's first retrospective was organized by the Whitechapel Art Gallery, London, in 1965, but it was not until 1975 that a retrospective toured the United States, organized by the Corcoran Gallery of Art, Washington. Another large-scale touring retrospective was organized by the Museum of Fine Arts, Houston in 1983. Krasner died in 1984 during the course of the exhibition.

Among the Abstract Expressionists, Krasner was uniquely innovative in her use of collage. While she had worked with collage as early as 1939, it was a 1949 exhibition of cut-paper collages by Henri Matisse that particularly influenced her to begin a thorough

exploration of the medium two years later. The Art Center's collage is an important example of Krasner's work in this medium, and in a way it was a loose collaboration with Pollock.

"According to the original owner, ... [this work] was a Christmas gift from Krasner and Pollock in 1954. When they gave it to her, they told her that the pieces of drawn paper which Krasner collaged, were from works by Pollock which he had torn up. Discards of Pollock's become increasingly important elements in Krasner's large compositions... done in the last two years before his death [in 1956]."[2]

For **Black and White Collage**, Krasner tore scraps of paper that Pollock had painted, arranged them on a backing, and added her own strokes of black paint. The appropriated and new portions of the work are very unified; it is not possible to tell which marks are Pollock's and which are Krasner's. By tearing rather than cutting the paper, Krasner imbued the work with a roughness and force. The strong diagonals of the collage elements are a successful, but unusual deviation from the verticality of most of her collages. This shift adds energy and movement, making the composition one of the most outstanding of Krasner's collages. DL

Purchased with funds from the Edmundson
Art Foundation, Inc.; Des Moines Art
Center Permanent Collections, 1954.24

Oil on canvas, 65 3/8 x 40 1/8 inches
(166.1 x 101.9 cm)

yasuo kuniyoshi

American, born Japan, 1889–1953   **Amazing Juggler,** 1952

Yasuo Kuniyoshi was at the height of his powers when he painted the Art Center's **Amazing Juggler** in the year before his death from cancer at the age of sixty-four. Gaudily dressed in a multicolored costume, with a pointy hat and grinning, sword-nosed mask, Kuniyoshi's performer impressively juggles four balls in the air while balancing on a bicycle. In the background an acrobatic clown tumbles through space and a female performer rides on the trunk of an elephant. At the upper right we glimpse the blue sky and the structure of poles and cables that supports the circus tent. The warm colors in the center of the picture – reds, golds, pinks, and purples – create a festive atmosphere appropriate to the playful subject. But the harsh, even grotesque, figuration; the dry, scumbled paint handling; and a strangely dissonant quality in the palette also impart a vaguely disturbing, even anxious, cast at odds with the ostensible gaiety. This anxious quality seems concentrated in the figure of the juggler, whose ambiguous mask may easily be interpreted as communicating pain rather than pleasure. In the masked juggler we may see a stand-in for Kuniyoshi himself, continuing to perform his astonishing feats

of artistry even as suffered through the painful illness that would soon end his life.

Born in Okayama, Japan, Kuniyoshi came to the United States in 1906. He studied at the Los Angeles School of Art and Design (1907–1910) and then moved to New York, where he studied at the National Academy of Design (1910), the Henri School, the Independent School of Art (1914–1916), and the Art Students League (1916–20). Until the mid-1920s, Kuniyoshi supported himself primarily as an art photographer. In 1925 he spent ten months in France and Italy, and in 1928 he toured England and Spain and studied lithography in Paris. After a brief trip to Japan in 1931, Kuniyoshi embarked on a successful teaching career at the Art Students League (1933–53) and at the New School for Social Research (1936–53). He also served in the American Artists Congress (1937–40), was elected the first president of the Artists Equity Association (1947–50), and in 1948 became the first living artist to be honored with a retrospective at the Whitney Museum of American Art. But despite his professional success, the Japanese-born Kuniyoshi was prohibited by law from ever becoming an American citizen, and only his vigorous opposition to Japanese militarism saved him from being interned as an enemy alien during World War II.

Over the course of his career, Kuniyoshi's art went through three distinct phases. Between 1921 and 1927 he painted fantasy scenes in a self-consciously primitive manner, partly inspired by American folk art. His palette was dominated by earth tones and reds. From 1927 to the early 1940s, Kuniyoshi painted directly from the model, and worked in a more sensuous and fluent manner, retaining his earth tones but adding cooler colors. In the mid-1940s Kuniyoshi's compositions grew more complex and his palette more colorful, incorporating iridescent yellow, orange, green, lavender, and blue. He once again drew on his imagination for his iconography, and created complex and disturbing images that demonstrated his concern for the state of the world in the wake of World War II. Kuniyoshi's subjects now included quasi-Surrealistic still lifes, desolate landscapes haunted by forlorn figures, and, perhaps most memorably, masked and costumed performers, such as the **Amazing Juggler**. Despite their carnivalesque themes, these late paintings have, in the artist's words, "implications of very sad things."[1] DC

Purchased with funds from the Coffin Fine
Arts Trust; Nathan Emory Coffin
Collection of the Des Moines Art Center,
1994.12

Charcoal on multiple sheets of
paper hinged to rag board, 70 x 40 inches
(177.8 x 101.6 cm)

alfred leslie

American, born 1927   **Jane Elford #3**, 1968

Alfred Leslie was born in New York in 1927. He served in the US Coast Guard at the end of the Second World War, and then returned to study at New York University, followed by the Art Students League and Pratt Institute.

Leslie began his career in the late 1950s as a so-called "second-generation Abstract Expressionist" dedicated to the groundbreaking aesthetic developed in the work of artists such as Willem de Kooning, Franz Kline, and Jackson Pollock. The Art Center's collection includes an abstract painting of this type by Leslie, **Small Iron Picture** (1961).

In 1962 Leslie surprised the art world by turning to figuration. He said: "…I had not set a course to become a realist artist or a figurative painter. But there was a point at which I realized that if my work was to develop and evolve, and if I was to mature as an artist, these figurative ideas could not be ignored, even though following them could seem to imply that I would be turning my

back on the twentieth century, turning my back on my abstract achievement."[1]

Leslie concentrated on larger-than-life-sized frontal figures, mostly nudes, painted in **grisaille** (black, white, and gray). It is relevant that Leslie had been a photographer and filmmaker for many years, using a black and white format almost exclusively.

Although numerous visitors to Leslie's studio had seen these works and they had been recorded in photographs and on film, only one of them was exhibited before the studio was destroyed on October 17, 1966 by one of the worst fires in the history of New York; the building, at 940 Broadway, was leveled, and twelve fire fighters were killed. Only three out of Leslie's fifty to sixty **grisaille** paintings survived, and only six of his numerous drawings.

Leslie reestablished a studio and began painting again in **grisaille**, but discontinued after completing only four paintings. In the painting **Jane Elford**, completed in 1968, Leslie introduced a small amount of color for the first time. The Art Center's is one of two large-scale, black charcoal drawings on multiple sheets of white paper completed in

relation to the painting. A smaller drawing of Elford's head is in the collection of The Metropolitan Museum of Art, New York.

In this thoroughly elaborated drawing, Leslie approached each third of the figure (from top to bottom) frontally. The absence of any downward or upward perspective accounts for much of the monumentality and directness of the figure, as well as an intensity similar to that of Leslie's frontal paintings. The work is drawn with an immediacy and boldness that hark back to Leslie's work as an Abstract Expressionist. Further adding to the intensity are the clenched hands.

Leslie remains active and respected as one of the most important figurative painters in the United States to emerge in the second half of the twentieth century. IMD

Alfred Leslie   169

Purchased with funds from the Edmundson
Art Foundation, Inc.; Des Moines Art
Center Permanent Collections, 1989.1

Ink wash, 25 feet 11 inches x 24 feet
8 ½ inches (7.79 x 7.60 m)

sol lewitt

American, born 1927   **Wall Drawing #601, Forms Derived from the Cube (25 Variations),** 1989

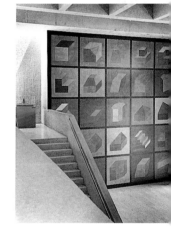

Sol LeWitt's wall drawing **Forms Derived from the Cube (25 Variations)** was made specifically for its location in the Des Moines Art Center and executed directly on the surface of the wall. LeWitt's great contribution in his wall drawings was to extend the reach of drawing from the paper to the wall, thereby opening up drawing to the architectural scale of a room and a building. Particular designs are derived both from LeWitt's ongoing vocabulary of forms and the given characteristics of the site at hand.

The wall drawings, first created in 1968, have been carried out in the context of a prolific body of work that encompasses sculpture, books, works on paper, and graphic design. The drawings expand traditional restrictions of the medium to address the interior surface and architecture of a room. The drawing is one with the wall, making the architecture visible, yet enhanced and transformed. By doing away with the frame of the portable drawing, LeWitt makes the architecture of a given space the drawing's support and frame. Most recently the artist has further expanded his visual vocabulary by making sited wall paintings.

LeWitt is described as a Conceptual artist, meaning that the idea of the work is of primary importance; the idea in his work is carried out by others according to his instructions and a particular system developed for each work. His work is a rational system expressed in a visual way. As audible music results from the instructions of a musical score, the complex and expansive visual beauty of LeWitt's wall drawings is derived from a set of written instructions given to others to carry out. Each manifestation includes the variation of the individual draftsman as well as the conditions of a given space, and fills a room with color and light, like sound in a concert hall. In LeWitt's words, "Each person draws a line differently and each person understands work differently. Neither lines nor words are ideas, they are the means by which ideas are conveyed."[1] Colored lines, basic forms in repetition, extension, and combination with others, make something simple, complex; something elusive, defined; and something delicate, powerful.

While using a simple geometry of form, the Art Center's wall drawing employs many coats of colored ink to create a beautiful, velvety surface rich in color and light. The work enhances the stern gray concrete of the I. M. Pei building and is enriched by the play of light that fills the room from the large plate-glass window adjoining the wall that bears the drawing. JB

Oil and magna on canvas,
129 x 204 ¼ inches (327.7 x 518.8 cm)

roy lichtenstein

American, 1923–1997   **The Great Pyramids,** 1969

There are few instances of antiquity at the Des Moines Art Center, but Roy Lichtenstein's painting **The Great Pyramids**, provides one of them.

Lichtenstein was born in New York in 1923. During high school he attended the Parsons School of Design and the Art Students League. In 1940 Lichtenstein entered Ohio State University, Columbus, majoring in fine arts. He served in the US Army from 1943 to 1946, but spent the end of his tour of duty studying history and French at the Cité Universitaire in Paris.

Lichtenstein completed his Bachelor of Fine Arts degree at Ohio State in 1946, joined the graduate program, and became an under-graduate instructor. His early paintings were highly abstracted, but in 1948 he began to incorporate into them stories and historical subjects, such as Beauty and the Beast and Washington Crossing the Delaware.

In 1949 Lichtenstein received his Master of Fine Arts degree and was included in his first group exhibition in New York. In 1951 he was denied tenure at Ohio State, but had his first one-artist exhibition in New York. He moved to Cleveland, but left in 1957 to teach at the State University of New York, Oswego. At this time Lichtenstein was using elements of Abstract Expressionism in his painting style, but also incorporating cartoon characters such as Mickey Mouse. In 1960 he joined Douglass College, Rutgers University, New Brunswick, New Jersey.

In 1961 Lichtenstein's career in Pop Art became firmly established. He created a series of paintings of everyday objects, cartoons, comic strips, and advertisements. Especially interesting are the comic-strip paintings, with a dialogue bubble and a simulation of the Benday dots found in newspaper illustrations. The paint no longer has any reference to gestural Abstract Expressionist brushwork, but is flat, with crisp edges outlining and separating images.

In 1964 Lichtenstein began a series of landscape paintings, replacing the earlier themes of war, especially air battles, and women. The series culminated in 1969 with the Art Center's painting, **The Great Pyramids**. In these works: "He presents the basic elements of a landscape – its shape, its volumes, its light and shade, its reflections – but gives us a shorthand version of it. To deprive the landscapes of much of their reality, he has rendered some of them in black and white ... or used primary colors to depict earth, sky, and water. He has bent nature to his design, a design that includes heavy black outlines that do not exist in the landscape. He has changed organic forms into geometric ones and has created a highly structured image from a less orderly reality."[1]

Lichtenstein included only two monuments within the landscape series, the Greek Temple of Apollo and the Egyptian Great Pyramids of Gizeh. The Art Center's painting is the most impressive of these works. The pyramids are rendered in black and white only, with yellow used for the earth. Also, although the pyramids are geometric forms, the stone has weathered over the centuries to appear softer and more organic than Lichtenstein's hard-edged images of them. They were originally covered with a pristine, shiny, and smooth white coating of limestone. Lichtenstein reductive style seems almost to have restored the pyramids to their previous glory. DL

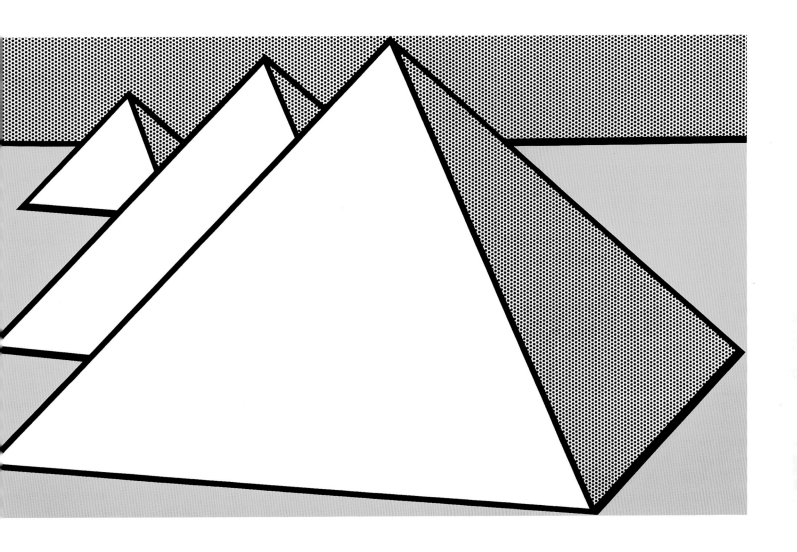

Purchased with funds from Gardner Cowles;
Des Moines Art Center Permanent
Collections, 1972.2

Acrylic on canvas, 98 x 132 inches
(248.9 X 335.3 cm)

morris louis

American, 1912–1962   **Untitled 1–89,** 1959

A master of stained-canvas, color-field painting, Morris Louis produced some of the most original and impressive abstract paintings of the later 1950s and early 1960s. Born Morris Louis Bernstein in Baltimore, the artist studied at the Maryland Institute of Fine and Applied Arts in 1927–32. In 1936 he moved to New York and two years later changed his name to Morris Louis. In 1936 Louis participated in the experimental workshop of the Mexican muralist David Alfaro Siqueiros and in 1939 he was employed for several months by the WPA Federal Art Project. Louis returned to Maryland in the early 1940s and made abstract paintings and collages under the influence of Jackson Pollock and Robert Motherwell.

Louis moved to Washington, DC in 1952 and began teaching at the Washington Workshop Center of the Arts. There he struck up a friendship with a fellow teacher, Kenneth Noland, who was twelve years his junior. In April 1953 Noland took Louis to New York and introduced him to the in fluential art critic Clement Greenberg. The three men visited the studio of Helen Frankenthaler, where they saw her recently completed painting **Mountains and Sea** (1952). Inspired by Pollock's 1951–52 technique of pouring black enamel directly onto unprimed cotton duck, Frankenthaler had stained her canvas with thinned washes of oil paint, creating open areas of color that lay within the canvas weave.

Louis immediately recognized Frankenthaler as "the bridge between Pollock and what was possible," and began to follow her example of staining colors directly into the canvas.[1] To make a series of pictures in 1954, Louis tacked unprimed canvas onto a large stretcher and poured successive layers of paint over the surface, tilting the stretcher to control the streams of pigment. Rather than oil, Louis employed Magna, an oil-miscible acyrlic resin paint that could be thinned to the transparent consistency of watercolor and was quick-drying, allowing several layers of color to be applied in a single painting session without muddying the hues or concealing the canvas weave. The resulting fanlike patterns of subtly blended, close-valued colors led these paintings to be called "Veils."[2]

After again working in a more conventional Abstract Expressionist style between late 1954 and 1957, Louis created a second series of over 100 "Veils" in 1958–59. The Art Center's **Untitled 1–89** was probably one of the later pictures produced in this series. While the colors of many of the "Veils" appear to descend, those in **Untitled 1–89** seem to rise, spreading upward in a broad, mushroomlike shape cropped off at the top and barely contained along the lateral edges by thin strips of empty canvas. The generally unified tonality is subtly articulated by flamelike shapes of yellow and green that flare up from the image's base, kindling pyric metaphors. The "wall of gaseous yellow expands like a giant flame," art historian Robert Rosenblum observed of the Des Moines painting, while curator John Elderfield commented that "the picture evokes the first fires of creation or some molten core of natural energy."[3]

While such metaphorical readings have their appeal, they are ultimately unnecessary for the purely aesthetic appreciation of **Untitled 1–89**. The veil of disembodied color, spreading across nearly eighty-eight square feet of canvas, creates an enormous chromatic field that physically engages the spectator. Subtly blended colors and gentle shifts of hue and value create diaphanous effects of extraordinary beauty and resonance. DC

Purchased with funds from the Coffin Fine
Arts Trust; Nathan Emory Coffin
Collection of the Des Moines Art Center,
1962.21

Oil on canvas, 30 1/8 x 24 3/16 inches
(76.5 x 61.4 cm)

stanton macdonald-wright

American, 1890–1973 **Abstraction on Spectrum (Organization 5)**, c. 1914–1917

"I strive to divest my art of all anecdote and illustration," wrote Stanton MacDonald-Wright, "and to purify it to the point where the emotions of the spectator will be wholly aesthetic, as when listening to good music."[1] Much like a musical composition, **Abstraction on Spectrum (Organization 5)** features a dominant "theme" of bright circles cascading down a central column, with arcs and wedges set in counterpoint along either side. The colors are harmoniously arranged in "chords," and the motifs are arranged "rhythmically" so that they appear to develop through time rather than existing strictly in space. A veritable symphony of color and form, MacDonald-Wright's painting demonstrates that "color is just as capable as music of providing us with the highest ecstasies and delights."[2]

This was the central assertion of Synchromism, the only avant-garde movement initiated by American artists before World War I. Morgan Russell and Stanton MacDonald-Wright exhibited together as the Synchromists in June 1913 in Munich, in October 1913 in Paris, and in March 1914 in New

York. In the manifestoes that accompanied these exhibitions, the Synchromists boldly claimed to have achieved the first real advance in modern painting since Impressionism, and asserted the superiority of their art to that of the Cubists, the Futurists, and especially the Orphists, whose color abstractions bore some resemblance to their own.

MacDonald-Wright was born in Charlottesville, Virginia, and moved with his family to Santa Monica, California in 1900. He studied at the Art Students League in Los Angeles in 1904–1905 and in 1907 sailed for Paris, where he studied briefly at the Académie Colarossi, the Académie Julian, and the Ecole des Beaux-Arts. By 1911 MacDonald-Wright had met Morgan Russell, with whom he shared an interest in nineteenth-century scientific color theories. The two friends developed that interest under the tutelage of Ernest Percyval Tudor-Hart, with whom they studied in 1911–1913. Tudor-Hart's practice of drawing mathematical analogies between music and color encouraged Russell in 1912 to invent the term "Synchromy" (from the Greek, "with color"), with its obvious musical connotations.

Russell and MacDonald-Wright's earliest Synchromies were semiabstract depictions of still lifes or human figures – the latter often derived from Michelangelo sculptures – rendered in intersecting planes of bright,

saturated color. Rejecting traditional perspective and chiaroscuro modeling, the Synchromists created pictorial space through changes in color temperature, using warm colors to suggest projection and cool colors to suggest recession. Russell painted the first nonobjective Synchromies in the fall of 1913, and the next year MacDonald-Wright followed, although by 1916 he had returned to figurative subjects.

Among the many nonobjective canvases MacDonald-Wright painted in Europe in 1914 was one entitled **Organization 5**, now unlocated but known from its black-and-white reproduction in the catalogue of the 1916 Forum Exhibition of Modern American Painters.[3] The Art Center's **Abstraction on Spectrum (Organization 5)** is virtually identical in composition to that 1914 Synchromy, but was apparently painted three years later in New York.[4] Its original owner was the photographer and art dealer Alfred Stieglitz, who in 1917 gave MacDonald-Wright his first solo exhibition. DC

Purchased with funds from the Edmundson
Art Foundation, Inc.; Des Moines
Art Center Permanent Collections, 1933.18

Acrylic and pencil on canvas,
72 inches in diameter (182.9 cm)

robert mangold

American, born 1937   **Circle Painting No. 5,** 1973

Born in 1937, Robert Mangold grew up in New York State, halfway between Buffalo and Niagara Falls. His abilities as an artist were encouraged while he still was in junior high school. In 1956 he enrolled in the Cleveland Institute of Art with the intention of focusing on magazine illustration. Gradually he became interested in painting and sculpture, but it was not until the winter of 1958–59 that he saw major exhibitions of abstract art. Mangold found himself compelled by the directness of abstract painting and the absence of the need to get caught up in the subject: "I wasn't sure if I liked it, but I knew I was in the presence of something important."[1]

In his third year at the Cleveland Institute (1959), Mangold was awarded a Yale University summer art fellowship. He subsequently transferred to Yale where in 1961 he received his Bachelor of Fine Arts degree. His classmates included Nancy Graves, Brice Marden, Richard Serra, and Sylvia Plimack, whom he married in 1961. In 1962 Mangold worked as a guard and then in the library of The Museum of Modern Art, New York. He received his Master of Fine Arts degree from Yale University in 1963.

Mangold's first mature paintings date from 1964. These abstract geometric paintings on plywood, evenly sprayed with oil paint, linked Mangold to Minimal artists such as Dan Flavin, Donald Judd, and Frank Stella. In 1969 Mangold began using canvas instead of plywood and applied the paint – now acrylic – with a roller. He relates that up until the early 1970s, his art was "a kind of visual exercise book"[2] and the colors were "interchangeable." But subsequently his choice of colors became very thoughtful: "I wanted to think about each color that was used and why I was using that particular color," also acknowledging that painting was "emotional."[3] He later clarified: "Sometimes you want the painting to look very bright and gay, and sometimes you want it to be very somber."[4]

The Art Center's painting is one of seven large – six feet in diameter – circle paintings the artist made in 1973. He also made nine smaller ones of varying sizes that year. Of the several large paintings, in addition to Des Moines's, four are in the collection of The Solomon R. Guggenheim Museum in New York. Each has a different color and different geometric image. The purple field in the Art Center's painting is relatively rare in Mangold's work.

Preliminary to each of these paintings were numerous drawings in which the artist

searched for a model that was satisfactory, especially in regard to the "distortion" characteristic of the works in this series. On close examination of many of his paintings in the 1970s, seemingly symmetrical works are found to be "distorted." What appears to be a circle actually is distended slightly and therefore not a true circle. The apparent square in the Art Center's painting is actually open on two sides. This calculation is balanced by the intuitive choice of color with its emotional overtones. Unified balance is fundamental to Mangold's work. The artist said that he has "tried to make the three components of the work (shape, surface and interior structure) come forth as a unity, one thing of no more importance than any other. These three elements of the work exist with a kind of competing presence, so that you cannot consider any of them separately...."[5] For more than thirty years, Mangold has persistently explored different formats, all of which are expressions of his essential interest in the union of reason and intuition and in the formal pictorial elements (line, color, surface) that he developed decades ago. IMD

Three panels, beeswax and oil
on canvas, each, 60 ¹/₂ x 35 inches,
(153.7 x 88.9 cm); overall, 60 ¹/₂ x
105 inches (153.7 x 266.7 cm)

brice marden

American, born 1938   **Range,** 1970

Brice Marden was born in 1938 in Bronxville, New York, half an hour outside of Manhattan. His interest in art was early and intense; on occasion he cut his high-school classes to hitchhike into Manhattan to visit art museums. He obtained his Bachelor of Fine Arts degree in 1961 from the School of Fine and Applied Arts at Boston University, where most of his studio courses were devoted to the human figure.

In 1963 Marden received his Master of Fine Arts degree from Yale University, where fellow students included Chuck Close, Robert Mangold, and Richard Serra. In 1963 Marden moved to New York, where he has since lived with his wife, the painter Helen Harrington Marden.

Many artists in the 1960s made work that appeared to varying degrees reductive, impersonal, mechanical, systems-based – reflective of surging post-World War II industrialism. Marden's work shares the appearance of being reductive, but at the same time he intends his paintings to be intuitive and personally expressive rather than driven by a system. In his graduate thesis at Yale, he wrote: "The paintings are made in a highly subjective state within Spartan limitations.…I believe these are highly emotional paintings not to be admired for any technical or intellectual reason but to be felt."[1]

From 1968 to 1980 Marden made multipanel paintings with oil paint into which he mixed wax. The resulting surface is very fragile and seemingly translucent. Through 1973 most of these paintings were grounded in the gray tonalities to which Marden dedicated himself while completing his master's degree. There are only eighteen or so major works from this important six-year period, and the Art Center's **Range** is among the larger; it has been reproduced in monographs of the artist and in publications about twentieth-century art. Other museums with major Marden paintings of this period include The Museum of Modern Art, The Solomon R. Guggenheim Museum, and the Whitney Museum of American Art, all in New York; the Museum of Contemporary Art in Chicago; the Walker Art Center in Minneapolis; and the Museum of Contemporary Art in Los Angeles.

Marden says his paintings begin "with some vague color idea; a memory of a space, a color presence, a color I think I have seen."[2] According to the artist, **Range** suggests in its colors, openness, and title, the Western landscape; as a teenager Marden thought of being in rodeos. "Range" also implies the range of color in the three panels, a spectrum broader than in most of his work up until that time and foreshadowing the wider range of colors Marden gradually introduced. While the colors in each of the three panels in **Range** is distinctly different, the degree of darkness in each is carefully adjusted to create a uniform tone.

In addition to the color choices, Marden's paintings are personal through the way in which they are made. He uses brushes and palette knives to apply the colors, laboring to produce a handmade surface with a sheen and subtle markings as individual as skin. The bottom edge intentionally remains unfinished as a way of underscoring the handmade process.

Two major shifts occurred in Marden's work during the 1980s: in 1981 he abandoned the use of wax because he became tired of its vulnerability, and in 1985 he introduced a kind of calligraphic drawing suggestive of Asian sources. Basic to all his work, however, is Marden's conviction about the intuitive nature of his art: "I consider my work a hedge between the romantic and the formal."[3] IMD

Purchased with funds from the Coffin Fine
Arts Trust, partial gift of Mildred and Arnold
Glimcher; Nathan Emory Coffin Collection
of the Des Moines Art Center, 1992.12

Acrylic, pencil, and Shiva gesso on canvas,
72 x 72 inches (182.9 x 182.9 cm)

agnes martin

American, born Canada, 1912   **Untitled #3,** 1974

Nature has played an important role in the development of Agnes Martin's art. In fact, many of her early paintings and drawings carry such titles as **Wheat**, **Tideline**, **Earth**, and **Desert Rain**. She has also spoken about her childhood memories of the vast open spaces and the soft, shining color of her father's wheat field as being influential on her art. While Martin denies that her later works, such as the Art Center's painting, are abstracted from actual observed scenery, she does say: "I paint aesthetic analogies of belonging and sharing with everything. The wind in the grass, the glistening waves following each other, the flight of birds, all speak of happiness. The clear blue sky illustrates a different kind of happiness and the soft dark night a different kind. There are an infinite number of different kinds of happiness."[1]

Agnes Martin was born in Maklin, Saskatchewan, Canada in 1912. She grew up in Vancouver and moved to the United States in 1932. In 1942 Martin received her Bachelor of Science degree from Teacher's College, Columbia University, New York. In 1946 she began to study at the University of New Mexico, and started teaching there one year later. From 1947 to 1953 Martin taught in New Mexico, Washington, Oregon, and Delaware. She became a US citizen in 1950 and settled in New York in 1957, the beginning of a productive ten-year period. Her studio was in the same downtown Manhattan building at Coenties Slip as those of artists Ellsworth Kelly, Robert Indiana, James Rosenquist, and Jack Youngerman.

By 1967 Martin had established a reputation for monochromatic (usually gray) paintings based on a grid system. From 1965 on she adhered to a 72-by-72-inch format for her paintings. She has stated: "My formats are square, but the grids are never absolutely square, they are rectangles a little bit off the square, making a sort of contradiction, a dissonance, though I didn't set out to do it that way. When I cover the square surface with rectangles, it lightens the weight of the square."[2]

Martin's paintings have often been grouped with works by other Minimal artists such as Donald Judd and Sol LeWitt, but whereas their works are often made of industrial materials and arranged in a systematic pattern, Martin's lines and color always retain the imperfections of their hand application. Her work has a personal, spiritual affect that reflects her concern with beauty, truth, perfection, and happiness. She has written:

"When I think of art I think of beauty. Beauty is the mystery of life. It is not in the eye it is in the mind. In our minds there is awareness of perfection. We respond to beauty with emotion. Beauty speaks a message to us."[3]

Martin had begun to show her work in New York galleries and museums as early as 1958, but despite considerable success, she stopped painting in 1967 and moved to New Mexico, where she continues to live and work. She built her adobe house with her own hands, and, though she made no paintings for seven years, she thought about painting a great deal.

In 1974 Martin made and exhibited a seminal group of ten paintings in which for the first time color – blue and pink – was as important as form. The color was often applied in a way that made it seem more like light or air than pigment. The Art Center's painting is the third in this important series. Within pencil-drawn rectangles are delicate washes of pinks and blues, set off by the white border. DL

Gift of Elizabeth Bates and John Cowles;
Des Moines Art Center Permanent
Collections, 1959.40

Oil on canvas, 38 x 23 ³/₄ inches
(96.5 x 60.3 cm)

henri matisse

French, 1869–1954   Dame à la robe blanche (Woman in White), 1946

Henri Matisse, along with Picasso, ushered in many of the fundamental concepts of the prevailing style of the twentieth century. One of his distinctions was his use of abstraction, simplified line, and pure color to produce recognizable imagery that was life-affirming and joyous. Early in his career, he stated the goal for his art: "What I dream of is an art of balance, of purity and serenity devoid of troubling or depressing subject matter, an art which might be…like an appeasing influence, like a mental soother, something like a good armchair in which to rest from physical fatigue."[1] While this description of his work is undoubtedly accurate, it does not acknowledge the discipline and careful calculation that produced the warm-spirited, spontaneous look of his painting.

The Art Center's **Woman in White** dates from Matisse's last group of major paintings. The painting is typical of Matisse's imagery, especially after his move to Nice in the South of France near the end of World War I: the theme of a woman seated in a color-filled interior was a dominant and enduring one. Matisse's decision to remain in France during the Nazi Occupation was regarded as heroic. The war, however, had little impact on his imagery. His primary challenge during this time was the deterioration of his health, leaving him frequently bed-ridden and unable to sit or stand to paint. By the end of the war, however, he was improved and eager, at over seventy-five years of age, to show his vitality in a series of large, vibrant paintings that includes the Art Center's 1946 work.

Woman in White is from a series of paintings done at Vence, where Matisse lived from 1943 to 1949. Most closely related to the Art Center canvas is **L'Asie (Asia)**, also from 1946. In both paintings a three-quarter length female figure is positioned in the foreground against an ornamented background. Looking nearly full-face out of the canvas, the women wear striped garments whose folds create angles while each holds a long strand of large blue and white beads. The facial features are similar and may be based on those of Matisse's nurse, who later became Sister Jacques of the Dominican nuns at Vence. The Des Moines painting shows a large, confidently drawn, calm and contemplative figure in a reduced but vivid palette of red, violet, blue, black, and white on white, along with a broad area of glowing brownish-orange flesh. The design motif of heart and lozenge shapes is repeated in rhythmic variations throughout the canvas. The Art Center also owns a 1944 pen and ink drawing, **Head of a Girl**, whose costume and hairstyle relate to **Woman in White**.

The painting might also be placed in the context of Matisse's cutouts or découpages, which had been his primary form of expression since the onset of his ill health in the early 1940s. Also in the Art Center collection is one of Matisse's most distinguished accomplishments in this medium, **Jazz**, published in 1947. The broad, clear shapes, the simplified but buoyant line, and the use of only a few intense colors all suggest an interplay between this late painting and Matisse's technique of "cutting into color." Also in that year Matisse again expressed his belief in depicting only the essentials in a work of art, taking as his theme his 1947 statement that "Exactitude is not truth." With its emphasis on interior rhythms, economy of line, and freely brushed shapes in bold color juxtapositions, **Woman in White** might be a good example of the approach he elucidated the year after it was painted: "There is an inherent truth which must be disengaged from the outward appearance of the object to be represented. This is the only truth that matters."[2]

Henri Matisse was born in Picardy at Bohain-en-Vermandois in 1869. He studied and practiced law from 1887 to 1891 but abandoned his law career to begin a serious study of art. In Paris he studied with William Bouguereau at the Académie Julian, but in 1892 he left the academic painter to work with Gustave Moreau, whom he considered his most important teacher. He gained his initial fame as one of the Fauve painters exhibiting in the Salon d'Automne of 1905.
LRD

Purchased with funds from the Edmundson
Art Foundation, Inc.; Des Moines
Art Center Permanent Collections, 1993.19

Fourteen panels, acrylic on panel and
oil on panel, each, 80 x 12 inches
(203.2 x 30.5 cm); overall, 80 x 168 inches
(203.2 x 426.7 cm)

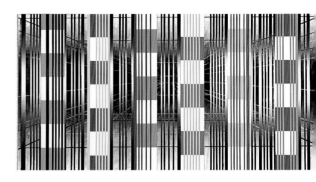

will mentor

American, born 1958   **A History of Agribusiness,** 1992

Will Mentor is a relative newcomer to Iowa, yet his most important series of paintings is deeply representative of the region. Born in Longmeadow, Massachusetts in 1958, Mentor received his Bachelor of Fine Arts degree from the Rhode Island School of Design in 1981. After graduating, Mentor moved to New York where, among other jobs, he worked for the painter Elizabeth Murray.

In 1984, before Mentor's first New York gallery show, he moved to Fairfield, Iowa. A long-time practitioner of Transcendental Meditation, Mentor had previously become affiliated with the community of intellectuals and artists surrounding Maharishi International University in Fairfield. Throughout his career Mentor has been engaged by two very diverse places – New York and Fairfield.

Mentor's first years of showing in New York were tremendously successful, from both a critical and market viewpoint, landing him a place, at the young age of twenty-eight, in the third edition of H.H. Arnason's **The History of Modern Art** (1986). Mentor has continued to have one-person exhibitions every year since 1984, as well as inclusion in many group shows. He works concurrently on numerous series of paintings and works on paper, incorporating widely diverse themes, such as Mozart's **Don Giovanni**, the Civil War, and spirituality. In 1987 he

began the paintings for which he is best known and that are the most Iowa-related: commentaries on the business of farming, the largest industry in Iowa. The Art Center's **A History of Agribusiness** is the apex of this series.

Constructed against a dark, deeply spatial area of one-point perspective, the immediate foregrounds of these paintings are flattened by the vertical striations of Universal Product Code bars. Because Mentor's work emerged in the East Village in New York during a period of great activity, marked by a pluralism of styles, his bar-code paintings were labeled "Neo-Geo" because of their geometric abstraction.

In the early bar-code paintings, Mentor often connected two canvases with plexiglass cases containing corn. On one side the bar codes remained essentially black, although lightening to gray and white in areas where Mentor depicted reflected light, and the others would be painted in the colors of manufacturers of corn-based products, such as Karo corn syrup, Mazola corn oil, or Doritos corn chips. A 1988 art review sums up the early bar-code works: "The thought here is that the rampant commodification fostered by our consumer society ... has affected nature's bounty (corn) and the land itself (the space grid and the labeled-colored grid, echoing the gridded appearance of farmland as seen from the air) by creating an overproducing and possibly out-of control economy (the millions of stockpiled bushels of excess corn and other foodstuffs)."[1]

Mentor's more recent bar-code paintings have focused not on corn products, but rather on the production of corn itself. The colors most frequently included are the yellow and green of John Deere, the leading manufacturer of farm equipment. **A History of Agribusiness** consists of fourteen abutted panels alternating between black bar codes and bar codes incorporating the colors of John Deere, Ford (another producer of farming equipment), and Garst Seed Company, an Iowa-based leading manufacturer of seed corn.

The deep perspective background of these more recent paintings now refers to the straight rows of plowed fields of corn, a beautiful but completely unnatural phenomenon. Also, corn is now so highly hybridized that it rarely, if ever, grows wild and essentially has become an unnatural plant. With the production of corn being integral to Iowa's and the Midwest's history and economy, these paintings are very regionally informed.

By choosing the term "agribusiness" for the title, Mentor acknowledged a shift in Iowa's life style: agrarian life has largely diminished as agri"culture" is steadily being replaced by large-scale, high-tech agri "business."

In 1996 the Art Center presented the first one-person museum exhibition of Mentor's work. DL

Purchased with funds from the Edmundson
Art Foundation, Inc.; Des Moines
Art Center Permanent Collections, 1992.9

Monitor lizard and neon, approximately
35 feet high (10.67 m)

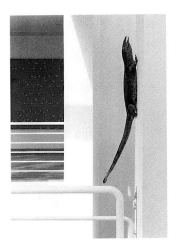

mario merz

Italian, born 1925   **Untitled,** 1989

At the core of Mario Merz's work are dualities such as the natural and manmade world, an opposition suggested in the Art Center's untitled sculpture with its combination of a taxidermied monitor lizard and neon numbers. The sculpture is one of several in which the artist combined these two elements in vertical and hoizontal arrangements (a horizontal example is in the collection of The Solomon R. Guggenheim Museum, New York).

Merz was born in Milan in 1925. When he was a child his family moved to Turin. The artist's father designed engines for Fiat, and his mother was a music teacher. Merz attended a scientifically oriented high school and then entered medical school. He joined an anti-Fascist group called "Justice and Liberty," and was arrested in 1945 and sent to prison for distributing anti-Fascist literature. In prison he did a great deal of drawing, continuing an interest in art and poetry he had developed some years earlier.

After the war, to avoid being forced into a career decision by his parents, Merz went to Paris. He earned money by driving a truck,

and spent much of his free time in museums, where he was influenced especially by the works of Jean Dubuffet, Jean Fautrier, and Jackson Pollock. Merz returned to Italy and dedicated himself to art, first as a painter and then, increasingly, as a sculptor.

Merz began to use neon in 1966. In the Art Center's **Untitled**, the neon numbers are in a particular mathematical sequence known as the Fibonacci progression, first put forward in 1202 by Leonardo of Pisa, also known as Fibonacci. The sequence involves taking the numeral one, and then one again, and adding them together to get two; taking two and adding that to the previous number, one, to get the next number which is three; three and the previous number, two, provide the next number which is five, and so on. This mathematical system can be seen in nature, from genetic theory (e.g., the proliferation of rabbits) to spiral arrangements in some growth patterns (e.g., pine cones and seashells). Most important here is the meaning this theory holds for Merz, who wrote: "The Fibonacci numbers expand in an accelerated manner, they inspired my idea that it was possible to represent with new faculties all the examples that occur in the world of expanding materials viewed also as vital living lives...living materials that exhibit rapid and controllable expansion."[1] Merz

sees numbers as not alien to humankind. "Numbers are a relative extension of the body through the five fingers."[2]

The monitor lizard at the top of **Untitled** is related to the Fibonacci numbers because the pattern on some reptile skins reflects the sequence. But the lizard also serves as a contrast. While Fibonacci numbers evolve quite rapidly from one to over 10,000, as in the Art Center's work, reptiles are among the world's creatures that have evolved the least from prehistory. Thus, the duality of rapidity and slowness is juxtaposed, and the lizard expresses another layer of the duality of the natural and manmade worlds. In referring to the reptiles and rhinoceri that are frequent symbols in his work, Merz has expressed a personal view of their duality: "It's both a robot and an animal at the same time."[3]

Since 1968 Merz has been a prominent leader of the Italian group Arte Povera, so called for their use of nontraditional "poor" art materials often taken from everyday life. In addition to making sculptures representative of this movement, Merz continues to paint and draw. IMD

Purchased with funds from Florence Call
Cowles; Des Moines Art Center
Permanent Collections, 1949.151

Bronze, 138 1/2 inches high (351.8 cm)

carl milles

Swedish, 1875–1955   **Man and Pegasus**, 1949

In the late 1930s, when Eliel Saarinen and Carl Milles were on the faculty of the Cranbrook Academy of Art in Bloomfield Hills, Michigan, Saarinen created a proposal for a Smithsonian Gallery of Art in Washington, DC. Included in the proposal was Milles's **Man and Pegasus**, to be installed in a reflecting pool. Although this museum was never executed, the design was adapted in part for the Des Moines Art Center; **Man and Pegasus** was installed at the Art Center in 1949.

Carl Milles was born in Örby, Sweden in 1887. After being apprenticed as a wood-worker, Milles moved to Paris in 1897 and began to study as a sculptor. Three years later his work was seen by Auguste Rodin, who hired Milles to work in his studio. In 1901 a major commission turned Milles's career around; he quickly became highly regarded, and his life shifted from one of poverty to one of great commercial success. He moved to Sweden in 1908 and became a professor of sculpture in Stockholm in 1922. During a trip to the United States in 1929,

Milles visited Cranbrook and met Saarinen. In 1931 he joined the faculty in a position arranged by Saarinen.

Man and Pegasus was made in an edition of six. Milles installed one cast at his home and sculpture park in Sweden after his retire-ment in 1950. The other versions are in an office plaza in Dallas; the Hakone Open-Air Museum in Japan; the Middleheim Sculpture Park in Antwerp; and in Djakarta, India.

For most of its history, Milles's sculpture has been referred to in Des Moines as "Pegasus and Bellerophon." As soon as it was installed in 1949, Helen Boswell, an art historian and the wife of then-Art Center Director Richard Howard, wrote an article in which she discussed the Greek myth: "Pegasus, the winged horse, first sprang from Medusa when her head came off. Bellerophon cap-tured him ... and used the horse to excellent advantage in fierce combat. But when the enterprising rider started to soar to heaven, Zeus sent a hornet to sting the horse and Bellerophon tumbled to earth, while Pegasus soared upward and took his place among the stars.... "[1] The sculpture supposedly depicted the moment when Bellerophon attempted to fly on his own, before falling to earth.

But while Milles was definitely inspired by the Bellerophon myth in creating his sculp-ture, he chose to depict a more positive image. He stated: "Greek and other artists always depicted Pegasus with the rider on his back, while I visualize ... [Bellerophon] flying independently ... both animal and man having expressions of longing for some-thing, we don't know what."[2] The man depicted in the sculpture is not falling, or failing, but departing from the horse and beginning to soar upwards on his own. The separation between the man and Pegasus is emphasized by the sideways shift in the horse's body as it banks to turn downward to earth. Milles chose to further distance his sculpture from the Greek myth by giving it the more universal title **Man and Pegasus**. This sculpture is now considered such an image of positive rather than negative ambi-tion (as in the myth), that Stockholm in its bid to host the 2004 Olympic Games, has proposed the image of **Man and Pegasus** as part of the logo. This work, which has achieved an almost hallmark status in Des Moines, is a symbol of hope and accomplish-ment recognized by persons of diverse cul-tures and backgrounds. DL

Purchased with funds from the Coffin Fine
Arts Trust; Nathan Emory Coffin
Collection of the Des Moines Art Center,
1966.2

Oil on paper, mounted on board,
40 ¹/₂ x 29 ¹/₂ inches (102.9 x 74.9 cm)

joan miró

Spanish, 1893–1983   **Femmes, Oiseau, Etoiles (Women, Bird, Stars)**, 1942

Although Joan Miró moved to Paris in 1920 and there evolved his mature style under the influence of the Surrealist poets and writers, he remained, as did his colleague Picasso, fully Spanish at heart. Miró was from Barcelona, the intellectual and spiritual heart of Catalonia, a fiercely independent and culturally sophisticated region of Spain. He studied at the Barcelona School of Fine Arts and then at the Academia Galí. Although he participated in the French avant-garde, adopting the brilliant palette of the Fauves and employing some of the fragmented forms of Cubism, Miró also drew upon Catalan folk art in the development of his personal style. His brand of abstraction is distinctly fanciful and frequently playful, characterized by flat, usually organic, forms disporting themselves against a plain, undifferentiated background. The compositions evoke affinities with theater, since Miró's entities often seem to be enacting a symbolic narrative within the artificial and featureless space of an empty stage. In addition to the players, there are subsidiary elements, "props," such as a moon or stars, all floating freely in the same fantastic universe. Graphic elements help to structure the space and establish connections within the compositions, directly tethering forms or suggesting relationships or movement.

The Des Moines Art Center's **Women, Bird, Stars** from 1942 is one of a number of Miró works based on this triad and related themes. It was painted in Spain, where Miró returned in 1940, settling once again in Barcelona and then living on the island of Majorca. Miró created a personal cosmology in which simple, primitive entities convene lyrically and spiritually in a visionary space that remains outside the boundaries of descriptive reality. Whether such convocation comes together in the mind or on some supernatural plane is never clarified. The forms themselves are reduced to basic, defining characteristics, such as gender or hieratic status.

The simple poetry of the Art Center's composition is characteristic of Miró's paintings of the early 1940s. Here one cheerful female figure is represented by a simple, elongated triangular form surmounted by a childlike drawing of a face and holding the string of what seems to be an enormous red balloon. To the right on the empty and minimal ground plane stands a second, cockeyed female figure, recognizable chiefly by her clear yellow face and the repetition of formal motifs such as the happy-go-lucky blue polkadots circumscribed by a black outline and culminating in a pointed black "tail." Both figures stand on two legs terminating in a shorthand translation of feet into toylike black balls that resemble wheels and add a suggestion of whimsical, mechanical mobility. Clearly Miró was interested here in the formal similarities of elements rather than the differences. At the upper right is a graphic bird form that serves the function of a beauty mark – gently steering the eye to the important elements of this painting on paper. Modest and discrete "stars" – rendered as schematic line drawings in "holes" of blank paper left in the paint are sprinkled around the sky.

Miró worked in numerous media: a full range of explorations on paper with drawing, printmaking, watercolor, pastel, and collage; sculpture in ceramic as well as traditional materials; and painting on copper and Masonite in addition to canvas. TRN

Commissioned by the Des Moines Art Center with funds from the
National Endowment for the Arts, Melva and Martin Bucksbaum,
Carolyn and Matthew Bucksbaum, City of Des Moines, Des Moines
Founders Garden Club, Herbert Lewis Kruse Blunck Architecture,
George Milligan Memorial, Judy Milligan McCarthy, The Nathan
Cummings Foundation, Norwest Banks N. A., Louise Noun, The
Andy Warhol Foundation for the Visual Arts, The Science Center of
Iowa, and McAninch Corporation, 1996.20

Wood, steel, cement, and granite,
6 1/2 acres (26.3 hectares)

mary miss

American, born 1944   **Greenwood Pond: Double Site,** 1989–96

Greenwood Pond: Double Site (1989–96)
is a major outdoor work by Mary Miss, a
leader in the field of public art. Her large-scale
work challenges the traditional notion of
sculpture as "object" and brings the public
into an experience and direct interaction
with structures integrated into a particular
site. Miss received her Bachelor of Arts
degree in 1966 from the University of California, Santa Barbara, and her Master of
Fine Arts in 1968 from the Rinehardt School
of Sculpture, Maryland Art Institute,
Baltimore. She lives and works in New York.

Miss' work has focused on the role of the
artist in the public domain. Her work is
developed from the specifics of a particular
project and site. In addition, much of
Miss' art is influenced by such issues as her
fascination with the spatial experience
of theater and film. The artist often uses the
term "layering" in her speech and notes,
a term that recalls the subliminal, stratified
aspect of her imagery, and suggests the
overlapping of forms and ideas. In **Double
Site**, spaces are literally layered – horizontally, vertically, or within the depths of such
individual elements as wooden and screen
lookouts, multileveled bridge/stage, canti-
levered walkway, pavilion, and pathways.
"I would never say that my aim was to create
an imaginary world, but I am interested in
questioning the boundaries – physical, spatial, or emotional – that we take for granted.

The effect of **Double Site** on people moving
through the various access points is very physical and pinpoints the spectator as the
connector. In the gradually unfolding space,
the spectator can walk, explore, and climb
around the water's edge or go below the surface of the ground to sit at eye level with
the surface of the pond. As a passive comp-
lement to these activities, Miss defined spaces
for refuge that invite the viewer to stop and
contemplate the project. Miss said in an
interview about **Double Site**: "My interest
is not to collage together these disparate
parts, but to keep putting them, one on top of
the next. I would be hard put to extricate
one at a time and say what that one meant."[1]

By integrating elements into a site, Miss
alters the site without physically imposing a
monumental piece of sculpture. Shifting
viewpoints, multifaceted situations, and ever-
changing audience perceptions are all
factors that inform the project. This approach
explains the interest Miss has in emphasizing the viewer's involvement with a place. It
is not about sign reading – it is about relying
on one's senses.

Miss initially came to Des Moines in 1989
on an invitation to choose a site and develop
a design proposal for a large-scale, site-
specific project. After a nearly two-year hia-
tus, she returned to collect information
about Iowa and the components of this project. In 1990 the City of Des Moines and the
Art Center became the chief partners in supporting the **Double Site** project. In 1991 they

were joined on specific issues and pragmatic
concerns by the Des Moines Founders
Garden Club, The Science Center of Iowa,
Iowa Natural Heritage Foundation, and
the Polk County Conservation Board. These
government, community, and cultural
groups became part of Mary Miss' inclusive
process, and collaborated on the common
goal of preserving and re-creating prairie and
wetland ecosystems. Her work-in-progress
was a living and working milieu in which each
train of discourse, critical analysis, and practice, fed and enriched the others.

Greenwood Pond: Double Site is the first
urban wetland project in the State of Iowa and
also the first in the nation. It moves away
from the notion of sculpture as "object" and
toward art understood and realized through
its relationship with nature and outdoor
space. In the sculptor's words: "Tracing the
various paths through and around Greenwood
Pond your experience as the viewer becomes the vehicle to lace together the various layers of the place – city park, classroom,
artwork, wetland, meeting place. You are
the link between the built and the natural,
the site's past and its future uses." MJR

Oil on canvas, 26 x 32 ¹/₂ inches
(64.1 x 81.9 cm)

claude monet

French, 1840–1926   **Rocher du Lion, Rochers à Belle-Ile (Lion Rock),** 1886

Claude Monet's name is practically synonymous with Impressionism. Throughout an extraordinarily long and prolific career (1859–1926), Monet demonstrated a continually fresh vision and a capacity for embracing challenges, whether imposed from the outside art world or psychologically from within. Because of his fascination with the problem of representing the natural world as filtered through variations in point of view or light changing according to weather or time of day, Monet frequently worked a single theme exhaustively, even when he was not specifically making a study of a particular motif.

After the early 1880s, Monet was almost exclusively a landscape painter. The year 1886, in which the Des Moines Art Center's **Lion Rock** was painted, marks the Fifth (and last) International Exhibition of the Impressionists at the Georges Petit Gallery in Paris, and thereby the end of the period of classical Impressionism (1874–86). Having decided to spend some time painting on the northern coast of France in Brittany, in mid-September Monet left the French mainland for the island of Belle-Ile-en-Mer on what was planned to be a two-week stay. He finally returned to his home in Giverny only at the end of November, having remained two months longer than he intended in order to paint numerous versions of the distinctive rocks and stormy seas surrounding the island.

Lion Rock, showing the rock formation that derives its name from its resemblance to the form of a recumbent lion, is one of the brooding canvases from this sojourn. When the painting entered the Des Moines Art Center, it did so under the title **Cliffs at Etretat**, another locale also on the Brittany Coast where Monet also made a number of paintings in the autumn of 1886. It was this distinctive rock that ultimately allowed for the correct identification of the site.[1] As is true for other works in this series, Monet used a rich, but uncharacteristically somber, palette, dominated by deep greens and purples. The flecks of white and conspicuously rough, bold brush strokes seem to underscore the choppiness of the sea as the waters swirl around the rocks.

In his Romantic treatise **La Mer** (1860), writer Jules Michelet remarked that France was indeed fortunate to be "in the enviable position of having two seas," the Mediterranean and the Atlantic.[2] In these paintings of the Brittany Coast, Monet was certainly inspired by the power of the Atlantic, rather than the picturesque calm of the Riviera. His paintings just one year earlier at Etretat in Normandy still have something of the sunny warmth of a gentle clime. **Lion Rock**, however, and the other paintings done in the fall of 1886, represent Monet responding to the threat as well as the beauty of the sea. He felt it incumbent upon him to render the "sinister, tragic aspect" of the site – a challenge because he was aware of his own inclination "to soft tender colors."[3] TRN

Bronze, 64 inches high (162.2 cm)
Edition 3/7

henry moore

British, 1898–1986   **Seated Woman (Thin Neck)**, 1961

The farm on which Henry Moore lived from 1939 onward dates back to the seventeenth century. The farmhouse had once been the home and shop of a butcher, and the garden was littered with small fragments of bone. Moore was so fascinated with bones – as well as other natural forms – that he kept skulls of an elephant and a rhinoceros in his studio. He would collect bone fragments from his garden and physically make them part of the small, plaster maquettes that were the first manifestations of his sculptural ideas. A sharp, flat fragment inspired the Art Center's sculpture **Seated Woman (Thin Neck)**.

Moore was born in 1898 in Castleford, England. In grade school he studied drawing, sculpture, and ceramics. In 1917 Moore enlisted in the army and was sent to the French front. That December he suffered gas inhalation and came back to England for hospitalization, returning to France just before the Armistice ended World War I.

In September 1919 Moore entered the Leeds College of Art on a veteran's grant. Two years later he won a scholarship to the Royal College of Art in London, where three years later he became an instructor of sculpture. In 1928 he received his first one-artist show as well as his first public commission, a relief sculpture for an underground station in London. He joined the Chelsea School of Art as head of sculpture in 1929.

When the Chelsea School was evacuated in 1939 because of World War II, Moore became an official War Artist, a position he held for four years. His chief responsibility was to record in drawings the bombing of London. One evening in a bomb shelter, Moore became fascinated with the richness and variety of body positions he found among the people taking refuge there. He began drawing the people, and the War Artists Advisory Committee hired him to continue the project in earnest. What became known as the **Shelter Sketchbook** provided Moore with a wealth of figure studies that inspired his sculptures throughout his career. **Seated Woman (Thin Neck)** is undoubtedly based on a person Moore drew in the underground shelter.

In 1945 Moore received his first honorary degree, from the University of Leeds. In 1948 he won the International Prize for Sculpture at the Venice Biennale. In 1951 he had a major retrospective at London's Tate Gallery, and four years later he was made a Companion of Honor by Queen Elizabeth II. He was awarded many similar honors internationally. In 1977 Moore established a foundation to support younger artists. After his death in 1986, a memorial service was held at Westminster Abbey in London.

Moore's characteristic working method matured around 1945, when he could afford to cast his sculptures in bronze. When Moore had an idea for a sculpture, he first made a plaster maquette about six to twelve inches in size; if he liked it, he then cast it in bronze. If

Moore felt a maquette would be successful on a large scale, he next made a working model, generally about three feet in size. If he felt the work could advance to an even larger scale, he created what he called a "monumental." Only some of the maquettes would ever reach that stage. Furthermore, often there would be many years separating the development of a sculpture, so while **Seated Woman (Thin Neck)** is dated 1961, Moore likely began working with this form many years earlier.

In **Seated Woman (Thin Neck)**, Moore emphasized the body part that was most important to him: the head. He stated: "Actually, for me the head is the most important part of a piece of sculpture. It gives to the rest a scale, it gives to the rest a certain human poise and meaning, and it's because I think the head is so important that I often reduce it in size to make the rest more monumental."[1] Here, in one of Moore's most frontal sculptures, there is a dramatic difference in the treatment of the figure's head and the remainder of the form. While the head and neck are attenuated and tilt upward, the bulk of the form is heavy, rounded, and solidly rooted on its base, providing an intriguing contrast.

continued on page 200

Gift of The Principal Financial Group;
Des Moines Art Center
Permanent Collections, 1998.26

Bronze, from an edition of 3,
73 x 53 x 99 inches
(185.4 x 134.6 x 251.5 cm)

henry moore

Three Way Piece No. 1: Points, 1964–65

Moore frequently divided his sculptural forms into two or three parts in order to enhance the viewer's experience of them. However, in **Three Way Piece No. 1: Points**, a significant fiftieth-anniversary gift to the Des Moines Art Center from The Principal Financial Group, Moore maintained a single, basically rounded form and created an undulation within it that results in three very distinct views. The title reflects Moore's express desire to make a new kind of sculpture, less dependent on gravity, which could be seen in at least three positions and be effective in all of them. Moore changed the texture and patina of the bronze in various areas to enhance the bulging quality of the out-thrust areas. The imposing, substantial form rests on three delicate points, perfectly positioned and balanced in regard to the bulk they support.

Moore's only regret concerning the sculpture was that he made it too large and heavy to be turned over by one person.

The other two casts of **Three Way Piece No. 1: Points** are located at the Law School Garden at Columbia University, New York, and in Fairmount Park, Philadelphia. **DL**

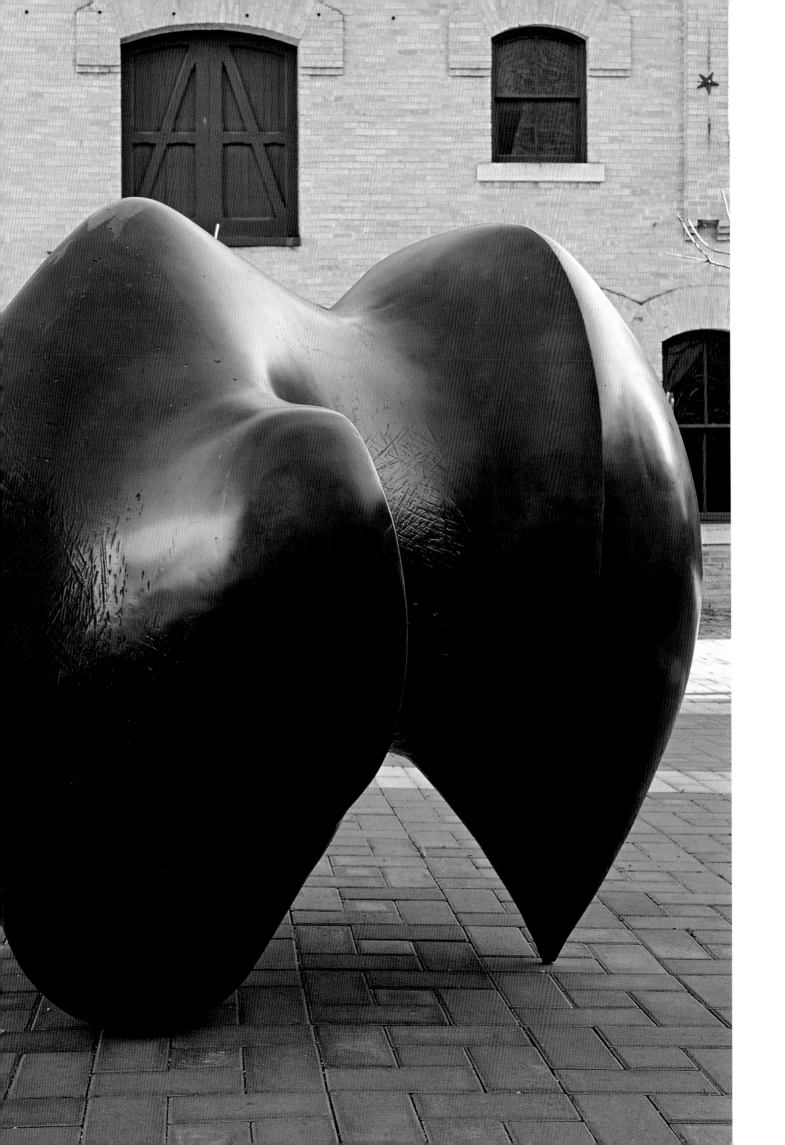

Purchased with funds from the
Des Moines Association of Fine Arts and
the Edith King and William W. Pearson
Bequest by exchange; Des Moines Art Center
Permanent Collections, 1982.5

Hand-colored lithograph on paper,
18 11/16 x 24 11/16 inches (47.6 x 62.8 cm)

edvard munch

Norwegian, 1863–1944   **Vampyr (Vampire),** 1895

Edvard Munch is often considered the paradigm of the Symbolist artist, the proto-Expressionist whose images of tortured love-hate sexual fantasies are the essence of fin-de-siècle art. His friends and contemporaries, writers and art historians of the avant-garde, helped to create the artistic persona that has come down to our times. Munch's name has become synonymous with misogyny and a sense of isolation.

Munch was born in Norway, lost his mother when he was five and was raised by his father and his mother's sister in Oslo. He grew up a sickly child. As a young man he spent some time in Paris before moving in 1892 to Berlin, where he became involved with avant-garde artistic and literary circles. His sexual relationships and morbid anxieties provided much of the inspiration for his art. He returned to Oslo in 1910.

Although Munch made this lithograph in 1895, he had previously made a painted version of the same image, which depicts a woman who bends her head to the neck of a man whose featureless head rests against her breast. Munch first exhibited the painting, originally titled **Love and Pain**, in

December 1893. Susceptible to the process of his own mythologizing by his admirers, he retitled the painting in 1894, two months after the publication of Stanislaw Przybyszewski's (1868–1927) often-quoted description of the painting:

"A man broken in spirit; on his neck, the face of a biting vampire. There is something terribly silent, passionless about this picture; an air of doom measureless in its fateful resignation. The man spins around and around in infinite depths, without a will, powerless. But he cannot rid himself of that vampire nor of the pain, and the woman will always sit there, will bite eternally with the tongues of a thousand vipers, with a thousand venomous teeth."[1]

"It's just a woman kissing a man on the neck," Munch tried to recant years later.

The writer Adolf Paul claimed to be one of the models for this image: "One day I went up to (Munch). He was painting at the time.... His model was one with fire-red hair which streamed over her shoulders like spilled blood. 'Kneel down in front of her, he shouted at me. Put your head in her lap!' I obeyed. She bent over me, pressed her lips to my neck, her red hair fell over me. Munch painted, and in a short time he had his **Vampire** finished."[2]

Whether this depicts a parasitical or tender relationship, there are ample parallels for the former in Munch's work from the mid- to late 1890s. For example, he created many images dealing with the theme of the female sexual predator, the **Femme Fatale**, expressed by woman's flowing hair, including **Madonna**, **Lust**, and **In a Man's Brain** (all from 1895), and **Attraction** (1896).

Munch's printmaking and painting activity were closely linked. He made over 500 prints, experimented with new approaches to color woodcut, etching and drypoint, and lithography. Many of his works were printed with variant inkings. The Des Moines Art Center's impression of the lithographic version of **Vampire** is a beautiful early proof with hand-coloring, printed on a warm gray paper. Saturated red, and pink and blue-green washes illuminate the dense blacks that Munch drew with lithographic crayon and tusche. In 1902 the print was reissued using the same lithographic stone together with three jigsawed woodcut blocks to print color areas. AW

Purchased with funds from the Ellen Pray
Perry Maytag Madsen Sculpture
Acquisition Fund; Des Moines Art Center
Permanent Collections, 1997.7

Bronze, 71 x 24 x 22 inches
(180.3 x 61 x 55.9 cm)

juan muñoz

Spanish, born 1953   **Piggyback (Left)**, 1996

Most of Juan Muñoz's art is figurative and narrative: he makes sculptures, installations, drawings, and prints, and also has produced poetic prose narratives. While the sense of a story line is as strong and palpable as in a haunting dream, Muñoz's exact meaning is elusive. He has described himself as a storyteller, and stated: "I build metaphors in the guise of sculptures because I do not know any other way to explain to myself what it is that troubles me."[1]

Muñoz was born in Madrid in 1953 and lives there today. Although he studied art in London and New York, a connection is apparent between much of his work and traditional Spanish art and culture. For example, among his early sculptures are balconies, a Spanish image celebrated in Goya's **Majas on a Balcony** (1810). Muñoz's work often exhibits an element of fantasy as well, such as infuses Goya's "Los Caprichos" and also characterizes works by other twentieth-century Spanish artists such as Miró and Picasso. Muñoz has made sculptures of dummies, which have a precedent in

Goya's **The Mannequin** (1791), and of dwarfs which recall paintings like Velásquez's **Las Meninas** (1656). Common to all these works are narrative images that are highly evocative.

Most of Muñoz's sculptures in this decade have been dedicated to the human figure. The figures are slightly but discernibly smaller than life-sized. He works in plaster, resin, and bronze. Sometimes his figurative work made for interior spaces takes the form of installations with a single figure and dramatically patterned floor. In 1977 in New York, the Dia Center for the Arts mounted an installation of figures in rooms and spaces so extensive that it created the impression of a small village. Outdoor work has taken the form of a group of bronze figures that seem engaged in some communication among themselves. Indeed, Muñoz has made a series of such works entitled "Conversation Pieces."

The Art Center's **Piggyback (Left)** shows one male figure piggybacked atop another. Characteristically, this work is suggestive of meaning but open-ended. It seems more evocative of one person helping (carrying) another, rather than, as in the story of Sinbad

the Sailor, for example, the person on top controlling the other against his will. Another interpretation is that both faces are of the same person and the work is a metaphor for the "baggage" – psychological and physical – each of us carries.

Piggyback (Left) is a unique bronze cast. There exists a very similar version, **Piggyback (Right)**, with slight differences such as how far the legs hang down and how close the elbows are to the body. In 1997 the artist made three additional versions in which one of the faces in each pair of figures has Asian features.

Muñoz had his first one-person show in Madrid, followed by numerous solo shows at museums internationally. They include Bordeaux, Boston, Chicago, Dublin, Geneva, Krefeld, New York, and Washington, among others. IMD

Purchased with funds from the Coffin Fine
Arts Trust; Nathan Emory Coffin
Collection of the Des Moines Art Center,
1990.12

Oil on canvas on
wood, 80 1/4 x 72 1/8 x 23 inches
(203.8 x 183.2 x 58.4 cm)

elizabeth murray

American, born 1940   **Sad Sack,** 1989

Elizabeth Murray was born in Chicago in 1940. She received her Bachelor of Fine Arts degree from The School of The Art Institute of Chicago in 1962 and a Master of Fine Arts degree from Mills College, Oakland, California in 1964. Murray first began to show her paintings in 1975 in New York, where she now lives and works. She became associated at that time with a group of younger "New Image" artists, who strove to reintroduce figurative images into abstraction. Also included in this group were Susan Rothenberg and Joel Shapiro.

At the beginning of her career, Murray worked with conventional rectangular canvases. As her work developed, however, she began to shape her canvases and then to overlap them, striving to achieve a three-dimensional painting. The Art Center's **Sad Sack** fully realizes this interest.

After making a full-scale preparatory drawing and a small clay model of the work, Murray made an armature out of soft plywood that was built up in layers and then sanded to achieve the rounded form. Canvas was stretched around and onto the armature and the construction was painted. As with all of Murray's works, evidence of the painting's assemblage – such as the joining of the plywood and the staples securing the canvas to the armature – is apparent to the viewer.

Images of containers, such as a cup, are recurrent in Murray's work, and the full three-dimensionality of **Sad Sack** emphasizes that idea. In **Sad Sack**, both the cup and the teapot are alluded to by the outward curving form that may be read as either a broken-off handle or a spout. The overall green weaving pattern that envelopes it refers to a basket. **Sad Sack**'s form also evokes the vessels of the body, such as the heart, stomach, head, or womb. The last image is particularly significant: the blue weaving through the basket pattern represents sperm, and the artist feels that the work has a relationship to the end of her own child-bearing years.[1]

In regard to all of the vessel images, it is important to note that **Sad Sack** is hollow and empty. The contrast between the strength of the overall form and its apparent droopy emptiness make it seem, to Murray, very soulful. Having always been interested in film, entertainment, and cartoons, Murray found in the attitude of the painting a reference to the doleful cartoon character "Sad Sack." DL

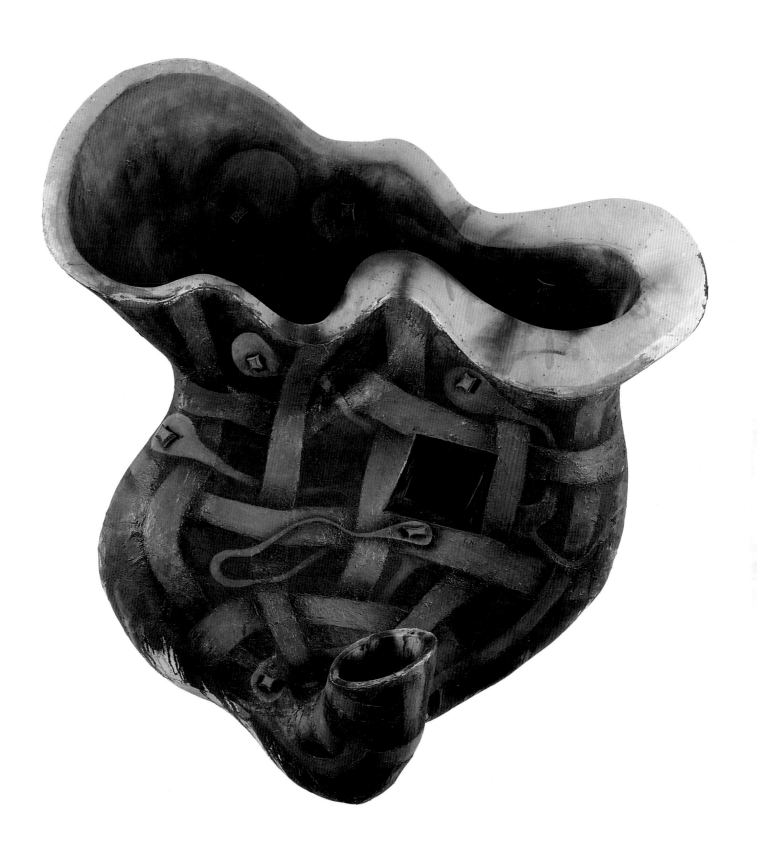

Commissioned with funds from the National
Endowment for the Arts and Anonymous
Donors; Des Moines Art Center Permanent
Collections, 1990.18

Bronze, 144 x 84 x 48 inches
(365.8 x 213.4 x 121.9 cm)

bruce nauman

American, born 1941   **Animal Pyramid,** 1990

The work of Bruce Nauman is not easily categorized. It is problematic for Nauman's art to be grasped in "schools" of thought as each work is individual and labels too frequently gloss over the intricacies of difference and the specificity of thought. Nauman has worked in many different styles, forms, and materials since the late 1960s, making sculpture involving language, the body as subject matter, constructed space involving the interaction of the viewer, video, and traditional sculptural objects using nontraditional materials and subject matter. Nauman's work has to do with an interpretation of his own life and the world around him, as well as an investigation of what art can be. The work is highly subjective and illustrates both a process of thinking and the process of its own making on the part of the artist and the viewer. There is never only one interpretation; the work is multilayered.

Bruce Nauman's commissioned work **Animal Pyramid,** made for an exterior space adjacent to the Art Center, is a twelve-foot-high cast-bronze sculpture consisting of seventeen separate animal forms: five caribou, eight deer, and four foxes. Nauman commented that this piece "needs to be seen in relation, not just to the park, but to [the] architectural setting...the formal parts of the building, the squareness and then the curves, must have something to do with how I thought about the pyramid."[1] Like much of Nauman's work, **Animal Pyramid** has multiple references and interpretations and contains both humor and a sense of the absurd as well as serious commentary on the human condition. The dark patinated bronze forms are cast from taxidermy models which bring to the work the issue of animal slaughter and a commentary on the hunting and display of animals. While this sculpture refers to the tradition of outdoor sculpture, with its use of animal forms and cast bronze, it simultaneously parodies the form, subverting the convention by adding social critique and a sense of the absurd, couched in the high theater of a most unlikely "animal act." JB

Purchased with funds from the Coffin Fine
Arts Trust; Nathan Emory Coffin
Collection of the Des Moines Art Center,
1974.79

Acrylic on canvas, 70 ³/₄ x 69 ¹/₂ inches
(179.7 x 176.5 cm)

kenneth noland

American, born 1924   **Whirl,** 1960

Kenneth Noland gained recognition in the early 1960s as a leading practitioner of color-field painting, the dominant mode of abstract painting in the United States in the wake of Abstract Expressionism. Born and raised in Asheville, North Carolina, Noland served in the Air Force during World War II, then studied art in 1946–48 at Black Mountain College, near his hometown. There he took classes with the geometric abstractionists Josef Albers and Ilya Bolotowsky, who instilled in him an abiding interest in strong color relationships and clear compositional structures. Noland also was attracted to the whimsical late work of Paul Klee. In 1948–49 Noland lived in Paris, where he studied with the Cubist sculptor Ossip Zadkine and painted in a colorful, Klee-inspired manner. He also saw works by Henri Matisse that furthered his appreciation of the sensuous power of color.

In 1949 Noland moved to Washington, DC and began teaching, first at the Institute of Contemporary Art (1949–51), and later at Catholic University (1951–60) and the Washington Workshop Center of the Arts (1952–56). Returning to Black Mountain College in the summer of 1950, he met the

critic Clement Greenberg and the artist Helen Frankenthaler, who introduced him to recent developments in Abstract Expressionist painting. That interest was reinforced by a friendship with Morris Louis, Noland's fellow instructor at the Workshop Center, whose paintings of the early 1950s were strongly influenced by Jackson Pollock. In April 1953 Noland and Louis traveled to New York, where Greenberg took them to see Frankenthaler's recently completed painting **Mountains and Sea** (1952), which she had made by staining oil paint directly into the raw canvas. Excited by the technique's possibilities, Noland and Louis adopted the method themselves, using Magna, a quick-drying synthetic paint.

Like Pollock and Frankenthaler, Noland frequently painted on unprimed canvas spread across the floor. This allowed him to approach his work from every side and encouraged him to develop the centrally oriented, symmetrical composition of nested circles that emerged as his signature format in 1958. Noland began each of these pictures by staining a crisp circle into the center of a nearly square canvas and then surrounding it with concentric rings. This deceptively simple arrangement freed the artist to concentrate on such variables as the width, number, spacing, texture, edge definition, and, most importantly, color of the circular areas. At the same time, the staining technique allowed him to liberate his color from

all physical associations and achieve an absolute unity of hue and surface.

With its central circle of saturated orange surrounded by bands of white, green, black, and aqua blue, the Art Center's **Whirl** exemplifies Noland's refreshingly intuitive approach to the selection and juxtaposition of colors. Equally engaging is the contrast between **Whirl**'s hard-edged inner rings and rough-edged outer band, which seems to spin rapidly in a counter-clockwise direction. A similar contrast in another of Noland's circle paintings moved one early viewer to say: "It draws you into the center like a target and then throws you out to the edge like a pinwheel."[1]

By 1961 Noland had eliminated all the rough edges from his paintings and with them the potential for such metaphorical readings. He continued to explore the purely aesthetic possibilities of bright, flat colors arranged into geometrically ordered compositions.
DC

Purchased with funds from the Coffin Fine
Arts Trust; Nathan Emory Coffin
Collection of the Des Moines Art Center,
1984.3

Oil on canvas, 37 1/8 x 31 3/8 inches
(94.3 x 79.7 cm)

georgia o'keeffe

American, 1887–1986   **From the Lake No. 1,** 1924

Georgia O'Keeffe was born in Sun Prairie, Wisconsin in 1887. As a young woman she studied art at The School of The Art Institute of Chicago; the Art Students League, New York; the University of Virginia, Richmond; and Columbia University, New York. Subsequently she taught art at numerous sites in the United States, including Texas and South Carolina. In 1918 O'Keeffe sent drawings to a friend in New York who showed them to the photographer and gallery owner Alfred Stieglitz. Stieglitz began to exhibit O'Keeffe's paintings and shortly thereafter she moved to New York. The two married in 1924.

Although based in Manhattan, O'Keeffe spent much of her time in locations conducive to experiencing a natural landscape. Among her favorite sites was Lake George, in upstate New York, which she frequented with Stieglitz. However, she was also drawn to the open stretches of the Southwest, which she generally visited without Stieglitz. Upon his death in 1946, O'Keeffe moved to Abiqui, New Mexico, where she lived for the remainder of her life.

O'Keeffe's realistically painted flowers and bones are her most widely recognized works; her abstractions, such as the Art Center's painting, are less well known. **From the Lake No. 1** was painted in 1924, and although the painting is highly abstracted, it contains many specific visual references to the site. The lake is surrounded by wooded hills of a rich green and brown; the water is a deep blue-green with highlights of white and yellow as waves reflect the sky and sun; the blue-gray sky is filled with big, billowy clouds. O'Keeffe's use of observed natural elements as the basis for her abstraction is important throughout her work. The undulating shapes and strokes in **From the Lake No. 1** mimic musical rhythms.

The Art Center's painting is a transitional work within the artist's oeuvre, with some details that recall earlier paintings and other details that are found frequently in later works. George Irwin, who owned the painting from 1965 to 1984, described its transitional nature: "It is not a 'one idea' work as many of hers are, in my opinion. It shows 'where she has been' in the yellow and white form previously used in calla lilies paintings and anticipates the sensuous and highly controlled curving forms in blue and green in the Jack-in-the-Pulpit paintings of 1930 and the mysterious egg-shaped form of the blue cloud and gray sky, found in the pelvis [bone] paintings of 1944/45. However, the painting is more than a skilled representation of elements, as I feel that the complex composition represents O'Keeffe at the height of her talents in technique, along with emotional and spiritual expression."[1]

Toward the end of her career, O'Keeffe painted abstract paintings almost exclusively. Very late in her life, when she had lost her eyesight, she continued to make art, molding clay into rounded and sensuous abstract forms. DL

Purchased with funds from the Coffin Fine
Arts Trust; Nathan Emory Coffin
Collection of the Des Moines Art Center,
1972.92

Naugahyde, wood, chain,
plastic, and wire, 144 x 77 x 59 inches
(365.8 x 195.5 x 149.8 cm)

claes oldenburg

American, born Sweden, 1929   **Three-Way Plug, Scale A (Soft), Prototype in Blue,** 1971

"I am for an art that is political-erotical-mystical, that does something other than sit on its ass in a museum." So begins Claes Oldenburg's 1961 manifesto in which he proclaimed his unconventional and frequently irreverent views about the nature and function of art. At the time that it was written, Oldenburg was creating brightly colored plaster sculptures of mundane objects: food, clothing, and everyday household items. His art was the antithesis to the dominant spirit and concept of the Abstract Expressionist painters – the sublime and the transcendental. Oldenburg's only concession to that older generation of artists (Pollock, de Kooning, et al.) was in his use of certain devices, especially the improvisational application of paint and the accidental drips that lent an air of spontaneity and a look of being unfinished.

Perhaps Oldenburg's most daring innovation came the following year with the first appearance of his soft sculptures. For centuries sculpture had been made of rigid materials – marble, wood, plaster, metal, stone – and the object was meant to be in a fixed position at all times. But in the first half of the twentieth century, that precept was changed dramatically. Alexander Calder's mobiles, with their variously moving elements, were followed by Joseph Cornell's box constructions that could be manipulated so that the objects inside would shift into different positions. A new era had arrived.

Oldenburg's employment of canvas, leather, vinyl, cloth, and other pliable materials further enlarged the vocabulary of sculpture; their form changed according to how they were installed. **Three-Way Plug, Scale A (Soft), Prototype in Blue** is a prime example of this genre. It most resembles a conventional sculpture when its twelve-foot length is fully suspended from the ceiling. But the moment that the piece is lowered so that the two prongs touch the floor, the plug assumes a quite obviously anthropomorphic character with a Brobdingnagian "head/body" punctuated by two "eyes" and a "nose," all atop two spindly "legs." Depending on its installation, the sculpture can appear to be walking on wobbly legs like some giant infant, or it can recline on its side or sit with its legs splayed apart. However, its grand scale, glossy surface, aggressive bright blue color, and the outrageous subject itself defy anyone to accuse it of "sit[ting] on its ass in a museum," in Oldenburg's pithy view of the innocuous passivity of many works of art.

The subject of a plug first appeared in the artist's repertoire in a drawing of 1965 and was repeated later that year in a sculpture made of cardboard. The subject recurred frequently in various materials and sizes in the ensuing years. The Des Moines plug had its genesis on New Year's Day 1971, when the artist came to the Art Center and spent most of the afternoon there sketching and taking notes. Observing that the viewer tended to look upward toward

the light source in the clerestory windows of the newly opened indoor sculpture court and to the dramatic play of architectural elements overhead, he solved this "problem" with a large, colorful form that would arrest the viewer's eyes in mid-air and bring the gaze downward toward the other sculptures. Though it was not a commission, the scale and color of the Des Moines work were determined to a large extent by the Art Center's architecture.

In 1975, four years after he created the "Blue Plug," the artist completed a related work for the Walker Art Center in Minneapolis (**Three-Way Plug, Scale A, Brown**). The two sculptures share the same theme and scale, but because the color of the Walker's piece is a more ordinary brown with a somewhat duller finish, the effect is of a sober, less amiable, and perhaps less radical sculpture.

The artist was born in 1929 in Stockholm, and soon thereafter came with his parents to the United States where his father was subsequently appointed Swedish consul in Chicago. After studying at Yale University and at The School of The Art Institute of Chicago, Oldenburg settled in New York. JD

Purchased with funds from the Edmundson
Art Foundation, Inc.; Des Moines
Art Center Permanent Collections,
1996.26.a-.g

Motor-driven marionettes, audio tape, external
speakers, wood, cloth, felt, cast resin, and cam-
operated motor-driven mechanism for suspension
Seven marionettes, each 31 inches high
(78.7 cm)

dennis oppenheim

American, born 1938　　**Theme for a Major Hit**, 1974–96

Dennis Oppenheim was born in 1938 and received his Bachelor of Fine Arts degree from the California College of Arts and Crafts in Oakland in 1965. After further study at Stanford University, he moved to New York in 1966 and his work soon became central to a variety of nontraditional art-making approaches. In 1967 Oppenheim made one of the first Earthworks, and the following year he was included in the exhibition "Earthworks" at Dwan Gallery, New York, with Michael Heizer, Robert Morris, and Robert Smithson. That year he also contributed a performance work to a show called "Plastics West Coast," and in 1969 he made his first film.

Some of Oppenheim's Earthworks required significant physical use of his body and thus there was a natural transition by 1970 to the making of Body Art, in which Oppenheim was once again a leader. Earthworks and Body Art include a conceptual component to provide structure: for example, an action taking place within a demarcated time frame or upon a plotted section of land (maps often were components of Earthworks). Thus, Oppenheim also contributed significantly to the unfolding of Conceptual Art. In recent years Oppenheim's production has focused increasingly on sculpture, from studio pieces to very large outdoor installations, often with a kinetic element.

Oppenheim also has taught extensively. By the end of 1970, he had held teaching positions at the California College of Arts and Crafts, Yale University, and the Aspen Center for Contemporary Art in Colorado.

The most important Oppenheim work in the Art Center's collection, **Theme for a Major Hit**, is a version of the artist's first use of marionettes. In 1974 Oppenheim made a single, twenty-four-inch-high motor-driven marionette with a cast-fiberglass head produced for the artist as a portrait. The formally dressed marionette moved to a soundtrack with music over which is the constantly repeated phrase: "It ain't what you make, it's what makes you do it."

Later that year the artist made ten additional figures, which were exhibited in Basel, Switzerland, and then stored by a dealer who subsequently went out of business. Fifteen years later, to Oppenheim's surprise, the figures were made available to him. In the meantime, he had made ten or twelve more, which were exhibited in varying numbers, but never all together. The Art Center's version of **Theme for a Major Hit**, which consists of seven marionettes, is comprised of figures from both groups. Six other museums in the United States and Europe have single marionettes, but the Art Center is the only one with a group of these dancing figures.

Oppenheim regards the figures in **Theme for a Major Hit** as surrogates of himself. This work therefore is a continuation of his

Body Art works, many of which have a dark side, usually in the form of self-inflicted pain or danger. While neither threat is overt in this work, the sight of figures being jerked repeatedly by forces beyond their control is a disturbing element. **Theme for a Major Hit** also looks forward to the artist's later motorized works.

Many of Oppenheim's Earthart and Body Art works are documented on photopanels, which are works of art in themselves. The Art Center's **Wishing the Mountains Madness** (1977) is an example of Earthart wherein 550 wood stars four feet in diameter and "painted in different colors but mostly silver, were randomly scattered from trucks in three different areas."[1] It was the artist's attempt to insert some "madness" into a region that he found disturbingly bucolic. **Tooth and Nail** (1970) is from a Body Art film in which the artist made an analogy between the artistic practice of "welding or fusion of two similar members"[2] and the process of applying nail polish to teeth and fingernails. The Art Center also owns six videotapes which document thirty-seven of Oppenheim's films, including **Tooth and Nail**. IMD

Purchased with funds from the Edmundson
Art Foundation, Inc.; Des Moines
Art Center Permanent Collections, 1996.29

Wood, plexiglass, ceramic, water, and
video equipment (Citizen 30 PC projector,
Samsung VP2504 VCR, videotape,
tripod), 53 x 11 x 11 inches (134.6 x 27.9
x 27.9 cm) plus video equipment

tony oursler

American, born 1957　　**Pressure Blue/Green,** 1996

Tony Oursler was born in New York in 1957. He received his Bachelor of Fine Arts degree in 1979 from the California Institute of the Arts, Valencia. He lives and works in Los Angeles, where he has been making videos for twenty years. He also makes sculptures and installations that often include videos. Although he had been using dolls as props since his early videos, Oursler began exploring this usage in a more focused way in 1988. He researched how someone who was not an artist "might make a figure if they had to, for instance: a farmer and a scarecrow; a kid on Halloween, a dummy; an angry crowd, an effigy."[1] Thus stimulated, he began to make doll-like figures. However, he was not satisfied with the faces, because when he drew on them the figures lost "their magical effect."[2] Consequently, he left the faces blank.

In 1992 Oursler learned of a new liquid crystal (LCD) video projector that offered the solution he had been seeking: it allowed him to project a videotape of a talking face onto the face of the figure. The nature of the projector requires somewhat dark space.

Oursler scripts the patter and videotapes the script being performed, usually by a professional actor who sometimes improvises and thereby collaborates. The uncannily engaging result has to do with more than the illusion of a talking face on a motionless dummy. More important in connecting with viewers are the nature of the words being spoken and how the spoken content is wedded to the way the figure is positioned. The acting of the performer, under Oursler's direction, also is important.

Some of Oursler's figures approach life-size, but most are only a few feet tall. Many are in a position of being trapped, and the patter – sometimes directed at the viewer – often indicates awareness of this plight. Some figures are trapped beneath furniture (a sofa, a mattress) or speak from a partially closed suitcase. The faces may also appear without bodies, talking from within giant medicine capsules, a jar, or – as in the Art Center's **Pressure Blue/Green** – from within a tank of water.

Disembodiment and fragmentation have occurred increasingly in Oursler's work. There have been lips in a jar, faces in capsules, heads under water, and more recently (1996), suspended eyeballs so large (eighteen inches in diameter) that one can see reflected in them images of what they were viewing at

the time the video was being shot. There is a dark side to these images of disembodiment and entrapment. Oursler said that the figures always give the impression of "a stranger in the wrong place."[3] Moreover, in the tradition of scarecrows meant to frighten, the figures are somewhat macabre: Oursler recounted how he was repeatedly frightened by a life-sized figure he placed in a chair at his desk. Simultaneously, like dolls and puppets, the works entertain. They also follow in the tradition of tales wherein such figures come alive – from Pinocchio to E.T., from Hoffman's fairy tales (the basis of Tchaikovsky's **Nutcracker**) to the Chucky horror films (**Child's Play**).

The Art Center's work is one of four examples of heads immersed in water. The illusion is of a submerged head, holding its breath, and therefore able to produce only gurgling murmurs. The head is a ceramic form which the artist designed and then had manufactured. Within this small series the Art Center's work is unique, since it carries the face and voice of the artist himself. IMD

Oil on canvas, 60 x 72 inches
(152.4 x 182.9 cm)

philip pearlstein

American, born 1924   **Two Female Models Sitting and Lying on a Navajo Rug,** 1982

At a time when abstraction was the prevailing mode of painting, a small number of artists found a way to resist its dominance and maintain a realist approach to art. Philip Pearlstein has been considered one of the leading realist painters of the twentieth century since the 1960s, when his large and stark paintings of unidealized, depersonalized nudes first startled the art world. Although Pearlstein has also done a number of more traditional landscapes rendered in a somber, Abstract Expressionist style, it is the images of the nudes, such as the Des Moines Art Center's **Two Female Models Sitting and Lying on a Navajo Rug**, that have become his signature paintings.

The Art Center's painting is both curiously frank and simultaneously unsuggestive. Pearlstein's nudes are clinical in their cool appraisal, their bodily perfections and imperfections presented equally and without prejudice. The pearly fleshtones, absence of modeling, and minimization of shadows despite the harsh, artificial light, create the notion that the specificity of the models notwithstanding, these are more like figures of marble, not flesh and blood. The composition itself is also studied and careful, as full of "art" rather than "naturalism" as is the rendering of the nudes. The composition is contrived so that the figures fill the space and are arranged, like the rug, at unusually fore-shortened and consequently dramatic angles, creating a sense of spatial dynamism at odds with the immutability of the figures. Pearlstein's title, "Two Female Models Sitting and Lying on a Navajo Rug," underscores his intention. The title makes it perfectly clear that these are models and that no psychological (or sexual) innuendo is intended, and that the elements of the composition – the sitting and reclining poses and the rug – have been carefully planned. Ironically, what becomes increasingly apparent in the work of this leading realist, is how abstract and "artful" paintings such as the Art Center's Pearlstein actually are.

A native of Pittsburgh, Pearlstein received his Bachelor of Fine Arts degree from the Carnegie Institute of Technology in 1949, and shortly thereafter moved to New York, which became his home. He also studied art history, getting his Master of Arts degree in 1955 from New York University's Institute of Fine Arts. Pearlstein has participated in numerous exhibitions beginning in the early 1950s, and has had several retrospectives. He has lectured and taught widely. TRN

Purchased with funds from the Edith M. Usry
Bequest, in Memory of Her Parents, Mr.
and Mrs. George Franklin Usry; Des Moines
Art Center Permanent Collections,
1975.34

Oil on canvas, 40 x 30 ½ inches
(101.6 x 77.4 cm)

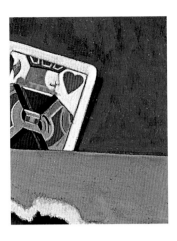

john frederick peto

American, 1854–1907   **Jack of Hearts,** c. 1900–1902

John Frederick Peto was an important figure in American trompe l'oeil painting of the later nineteenth century. The French term trompe l'oeil ("to fool the eye") is applied to images that reproduce so exactly the appearance of actual objects that they do indeed deceive the eye. Most paintings of this type depict compositions with little spatial depth, such as the door front with the attached letter rack in the Art Center's **Jack of Hearts**. Trompe l'oeil is particularly identified with American art, starting with the colonial painter Charles Willson Peale and his son Raphaelle Peale. Unlike the Peales, Peto worked most of his life in obscurity. After his death, much of his work was attributed to William Michael Harnett, partly because of their stylistic similarity, but also because Peto's signature was replaced with that of the more marketable Harnett. A photograph from the 1880s shows Peto in the studio with Harnett, so it is clear that the two men knew each other. Only in the 1940s was Peto's work distinguished from that of Harnett.

Among American trompe l'oeil painters, Peto's work is distinctive for its loose, painterly quality. The objects in his paintings are older, shabbier, and less pristine, giving the painting a more disorderly, disheveled appearance overall. Peto's softer, more luminescent color emanates a subjective, even poetic mood.

The Art Center's painting comes from late in Peto's career. The rack motif, with papers and other small objects tucked into its strips, seems to have held special importance for him. He began using it around 1879 and into the early 1880s, then discontinued it until the early 1890s. Peto had occasionally painted a popular oval engraving of Abraham Lincoln among the other objects (some of which may be references to the American Civil War) on the door or window boards depicted in his work. When he revived the rack paintings in the 1890s, the Lincoln portrait reemerged, particularly after 1894. In that year Peto's father, to whom he was devoted, died, and the Lincoln image seems to have been a sort of homage to both men.

The Jack of Hearts must also have held significance for Peto. He used it in association with Lincoln in at least two other paintings: **Lincoln and Jack of Hearts** (c. 1900; Cleveland Museum of Art) and **Hanging Knife with Jack of Hearts** (1903; private collection). In the connotation of the Jack of Hearts as a knave or sly fellow, the card may symbolize the circumstances of Lincoln's death. It may also be a condemnation of vice in general, since Peto was a religious man.

Only three other papers can be read in the painting: a Farmer Club card, the number two, and a pamphlet apparently entitled "Housekeepers Almanac." The large number two hanging askew and printed in a light color on a dark rectangular base is similar to numerals found in other paintings, notably **The Poor Man's Store** (1885; Museum of Fine Arts, Boston). The pamphlet is one of several objects that appear to be unfinished, with some letters and numbers not painted in. The other papers and pamphlets have no printing at all and, although Peto did include blank forms in other paintings, their number and prominence in the Des Moines picture are notable. Another clue that Peto intended to work further on this painting lies in the number "190" at the lower left, which may have been the start of a date whose last number Peto planned to add when he finished the painting. He worked slowly, repeatedly returning to a painting and making changes – a practice that may account for the character of this picture. It may also reflect his failing health, since he was suffering from Bright's disease, which would take his life about four years later.

Peto was born in Philadelphia, the son of a picture framer. He studied briefly at the Pennsylvania Academy of Fine Arts (1877–78), then worked in a series of studios in Philadelphia with only moderate success. In 1889 he moved to Island Heights, New Jersey, where he lived the rest of his life selling mainly to local people or tourists. He supplemented his income by playing his cornet for church services and camp meetings. LRD

Puchased with funds from the Coffin Fine
Arts Trust; Nathan Emory Coffin
Collection of the Des Moines Art Center,
1970.19

Acrylic and fabric dye on canvas,
72 x 144 inches (182.9 x 365.9 cm)

larry poons

American, born 1937   **Han-San Cadence,** 1963

Working in a broad range of styles, Larry Poons cannot be firmly categorized. His art of the early 1960s relates to several movements such as color-field, hard-edge, and Op, all of which were aspects of the dominant style, Minimalism. By the later 1960s, however, it became painterly, expressionistic, and thickly painted, and has continued to vary since then.

The Art Center's painting comes from early in Poons's career when he worked with small, sharply painted shapes such as circles and ellipses against a color-saturated background. Poons adopted and pushed the soak-stain technique developed by color-field artists Helen Frankenthaler and Morris Louis in the 1950s. The red-orange ground color is not painted on top of gessoed canvas, but is literally dyed into the fabric so that traditional figure/ground relationships are called into question. The color identifies so completely with the support that the painted elliptical shapes take on even greater intensity. The ellipses are painted either a vivid blue or brilliant green, and tilt either right or left at a forty-five degree angle.

The occasional coupling and the apparent ordering of sequences suggest some sort of pattern, but no such formula can be found in the painting. Part of the intrigue of Poons's painting is the constant search for a mathematical, predictable order in an image which, despite its precision, possesses none. The spacing, direction of tilt, and color all create an extremely rhythmic, yet, in the end, random, effect. Such a quality relates (though perhaps in a contrasting way) to the serial character of much Minimal Art.

Also related to Minimalism is the technique used in the painting of the ellipses wherein the boundary of the form is so sharp and specific that it can be described as "hard-edge," yet the paint is applied with a creamy texture that throws up a slight ridge at the edge that differentiates it even more emphatically from the dyed canvas support. Such dramatic juxtapositions of vivid colors create an active, agitated surface that is complicated further by after-images, and the sensation that its effects expand beyond the painting itself – effects that relate it to Op Art of the 1960s. A painting that starts in our perception as a predictable, controlled, easily understood image changes into a rhythmic, baffling, uncontainable visual experience. The large scale of the painting amplifies its impact on its environment and associates it with the color-field style.

The title, according to Poons, refers to **Han-San** (or **Han-Shan**), a reclusive Chinese poet who took the name of the place where he lived, Cold Mountain. Working in the late seventh-early eighth centuries, he is best known for his **Cold Mountain Poems,** which Poons read in translation in the early 1960s, and to which he referred in other paintings of the time (**Cold Mountain Breakdown, Day on Cold Mountain**). The "cadence" of the title recalls Poons's early interest in music, an important influence in his art.

Poons was born in Tokyo in 1937. The following year the family returned to the United States, where Poons grew up. He attended the New England Conservatory of Music in Boston (1955–57), but then decided to pursue a career in art. He studied at the Museum of Fine Arts School in Boston (1959). His first one-person show was at the Green Gallery in New York in 1963 and included **Han-San Cadence.** LRD

**Gift of Mrs. Charles Prendergast;
Des Moines Art Center Permanent
Collections, 1984.23**

Oil on canvas, 18 ³/₄ x 24 inches
(47.6 x 61 cm)

maurice prendergast

American, 1859–1924   **Autumn, New Hampshire,** 1912

Maurice Brazil Prendergast's paintings weave a tapestry of turn-of-the-century urban life within the parks and promenades of Boston, Paris, Venice, and New York. A crowd in a public place was Prendergast's signature theme throughout most of his life. He portrayed this subject through compositions of vibrant patterns of color, flickering light, and juxtaposed shadows. His work stands as a paradigm of the transformation of American art from late nineteenth-century Impressionism and realism to early twentieth-century Modernism.

The composition of the Art Center's painting **Autumn, New Hampshire** is linked to the majority of the artist's mature paintings. The work exemplifies Prendergast's principal interest in painting as an abstract color statement. Its dazzling, tapestrylike surface pattern of saturated oranges, purples, and reds is accented throughout by contrasting blues and greens. This pattern flattens the fall foliage, the White Mountains range (northern New Hampshire), the houses, and people so that they are only marginally dis-

tinguishable from the equally vivid multidirectional and multisized color patches. Prendergast's brush strokes are succinct, pure in color, and tightly stitched so as to intensify the painting's interwoven character. This splendid landscape shows his tendencies and how his painting was becoming increasingly fluid, increasingly expressive of the quality of his medium.

Autumn, New Hampshire is one of four works by Prendergast in the Art Center's collections. His watercolor **Surf** (c. 1900) and monotype **Roman Campagna** (c. 1902) were purchased in 1951 and 1953 respectively. The painting **Girl in Blue Dress** was purchased after being brought to Des Moines in 1958 as part of the Art Center's Tenth Anniversary Exhibition.   continued on page 229

Purchased with funds from the Coffin Fine
Arts Trust; Nathan Emory Coffin
Collection of the Des Moines Art Center,
1958.60

Oil on canvas, 18 ¹/₈ x 14 ¹/₈ inches
(46 x 35.9 cm)

maurice prendergast

Girl in Blue Dress, c. 1912

Although Prendergast did occasional portraits, **Girl in Blue Dress** stands apart from the rest of his work. This memorable image was among a small and rare group of children's portraits executed in Boston and Italy from 1910 to 1913. Its most striking aspect is Prendergast's unexpected psychological insight and expressive power. Layers of color are built up into a thick impasto surface defining the girl's cascading auburn hair, forthright gaze, and poised mouth. As in the work of Paul Cézanne, there are volumes and masses built with color, distinct brush strokes, and strong blue outlines. The pattern of firm brush strokes, a pervasively decorative expression of the dense network of minute blue and green patches, has a similarity to Vincent van Gogh's portraits.[1]

Prendergast was raised in Boston and entered the commercial and decorative arts professions. Self-taught, except for brief studio experiences in Paris, Prendergast devoted himself to the fine arts in 1891.

While in Paris he absorbed the contemporary art scene. The strongest impact on him was made by Pierre Bonnard and other Nabis, an eclectic group of artists who brought together the scientific and mystical basis of modern art, from architectural painting to book illustrations. Their preoccupation with vibrating patterns of fabrics, foliage, light, and shadow left a lasting impression upon Prendergast.

After returning to Boston in 1894, Prendergast was successful in his exhibitions and sale of his works. He gravitated toward avant-garde circles, including that of Robert Henri in New York, and was in the forefront of Modernist activity in the United States from 1900 until his death in 1924.

In 1907 Prendergast revisited Paris and was electrified by the art of Cézanne, Henri Matisse, and the Fauves. The impact of their style was immediate in his work. He devoted the next several years to the study of color and form according to the principles of early Modernism.

In addition to participating in The Eight's renowned show in 1908, Prendergast exhibited with the Society of Independent Artists in 1910, the Armory Show in 1913, and numerous other pivotal exhibitions of contemporary art in New York. He is widely recognized as one of America's first Modernists. MJR

Purchased with funds from the Coffin Fine
Arts Trust; Nathan Emory Coffin
Collection of the Des Moines Art Center,
1969.7

Oil, paper, wood, glass, and metal,
42 ⅛ x 28 inches (107 x 71.1 cm)

robert rauschenberg

American, born 1925   **Talisman,** 1958

One of the most influential artists of his generation, Robert Rauschenberg is best known for his "Combines" of the 1950s and early 1960s – distinctive mixed-media works that blend elements of painting and sculpture while belonging fully to neither category. Born in Port Arthur, Texas, the artist was christened Milton Rauschenberg but changed his name to "Bob" in 1947. After serving in the US Navy (1943–45), he studied at the Kansas City Art Institute (1947); the Académie Julian in Paris (1948); Black Mountain College in Asheville, North Carolina (1948–49 and 1951–52); and the Art Students League in New York (1949–52).

An important mentor to Rauschenberg in the early 1950s was the avant-garde composer John Cage, who taught at Black Mountain College. Opposed to the expressionist ethos then dominant in the New York vanguard, Cage sought to extinguish the artistic ego by basing his work on chance. He also embraced everyday experience as a vital source of aesthetic interest, and aimed to break down barriers between art and life. Cage's influence is felt in Rauschenberg's often-quoted statement: "Painting relates to both art and life. Neither can be made. (I try to act in the gap between the two.)"[1]

Rauschenberg's desire to work in this "gap" found perfect expression in the "Combines" he began making in the mid-1950s, which are composed not only of conventional artistic materials, but also a wide variety of ingredients scavenged from the urban environment. Rauschenberg, like Cage, saw his working process as an open-ended voyage of discovery rather than a means of arriving at a predetermined destination. "I'm opposed to the whole idea of conception-execution – of getting an idea for a picture and then carrying it out," Rauschenberg declared. "I've always felt as though, whatever I've used and whatever I've done, the method was closer to a **collaboration** with materials than to any kind of conscious manipulation and control."[2]

Conscious aesthetic decision nevertheless plays a part in Rauschenberg's work. The design of the Des Moines Art Center's **Talisman**, for example, is carefully considered. The roughly rectangular elements of the work are deployed in a gridlike arrangement that acknowledges the horizontal and vertical edges of the canvas support. Rauschenberg likewise chose deliberately to work with a Rembrandtesque palette of black, gray, yellowish-white, and warm brown, embodied both in the found materials and in the various gestural strokes of paint that punctuate the composition. The earthy color key is established naturally by the brown slab of wood that dominates the upper half of **Talisman**. Next to it, in a boxlike opening, hangs a glass jar containing an unidentified black substance of a decidedly scatological character. Incorporated into the rest of the Combine are several found images and cut-out letters: The upper register includes a photograph of industrial buildings, the letter "E," and the image of a misty shoreline and its reflection. In the lower section appear the letters "C," "E," and "RY," a magazine photograph of a baseball player and umpire, racing greyhounds, a single rose, and a hand making the sign for the number four.

While these various elements all have symbolic value, they are arranged according to no logical syntax and generate no coherent message. Nor does the title, "Talisman," which denotes an object worn as a charm to avert evil, provide much help in interpreting Rauschenberg's work. Ultimately **Talisman** is not a vehicle for fixed meanings, but an open-ended situation that invites viewer participation. "I never explain my works," wrote Rauschenberg recently, when asked about **Talisman**. "There is a how but no why and time – time is now."[3] DC

Oil on canvas, 39 1/2 x 55 inches
(100.3 x 139.7 cm)

gerhard richter

German, born 1932   **Landschaft (Landscape),** 1985

Since the early 1960s, Gerhard Richter has felt compelled to explore ways of using painting to document reality, constantly aware that reality never can be fully known or documented: "I am suspicious regarding the image of reality which our senses convey to us and which is incomplete and limited."[1] He has made widely varying abstract paintings, ranging from geometric and minimal to extremely free and gestural; and his realist paintings range from the precisely photographic to the painterly – with subjects equally diverse. And even this description does not indicate the full spectrum of his work.

Born and raised in East Germany, Richter was thoroughly schooled in traditional art-making. He moved to Düsseldorf in 1961 and sought further study at the Düsseldorfer Akademie. Richter joined the faculty there in 1971 and has been a very influential professor.

Beginning in the 1980s, Richter's work for the most part settled into two predominant types: the apparently free and gestural abstractions and works that may be called Photorealist. Most of the Photorealist works are landscapes, but there also are still lifes and, more recently, portraiture.

Ironically Richter considers the landscapes to be the more Romantic and the abstractions the more realist: "The abstraction is more real, the other more a dream."[2] The rationale is that the abstract works are a free expression of how Richter was feeling at the time he made the paintings – "my presence, my reality, my problems, my difficulties and contradictions."[3] But the landscapes are rooted in nineteenth-century German landscape painting, such as that of Caspar David Friedrich, and " … a type of yearning, a yearning for a whole and simple life. A little nostalgic."[4] It is typical of Richter's complex world view that for him the abstract paintings are more realistic. This complexity is further evidenced by his painting both realist and abstract works in the same year.

Richter belongs to a generation that experienced a great divide because of the Second World War (he was a teenager at that time): "After the war we had nothing.…We had all to build."[5] As a young artist he sought a way to stay in touch with tradition but also be contemporary: he based his images on reproductions, specifically photography, which as mechanical reproductions had the look of here and now. At first the images were taken from the media, but in 1966 Richter began taking his own photographs. Ironically even many of the abstract paintings often are underpainted with photographic landscape elements which are then painted over.

Richter made landscape paintings as early as 1967. The Art Center's painting, like many of the landscapes, has a melancholy quality – a tinge of sadness for the past that cannot be recovered. Metaphorically the uncertainty of knowing reality is underscored, especially at the bottom of the work where the foreground remains forever mysterious, wrapped in masterfully painted mist. It also is characteristic of Richter's work that his complex world view is suggested by the presence of some areas sharply focused upon and others less so. But even the focused areas are not finely resolved: reality never can be known. There also are strong contrasts between dark and light, from the shady forest to the sun. The sun itself is rare in Richter's landscapes, and creates an apocalyptic quality.

In the year he painted the Art Center's work, Richter stated: "My art has always something to do with my life and how I deal with it."[6] This painting must have had special meaning for Richter, since he kept it in his own collection for nearly ten years.

Among the cities in which this highly honored artist has had retrospectives are Berlin, Chicago, Düsseldorf, London, Madrid, Paris, San Francisco, Stockholm, Toronto, Vienna, and Washington. In 1997 he won the International Venice Biennale Prize. IMD

Purchased with funds from the Coffin Fine Arts Trust; Nathan Emory Coffin Collection of the Des Moines Art Center, 1955.12

Bronze, 78 inches high (198.1 cm)

auguste rodin

French, 1840–1917   **Nude Study (Pierre de Wiessant) for "Les Bourgeois de Calais" ("The Burghers of Calais")**, 1885–86

Auguste Rodin was a towering figure, the most famous sculptor since Michelangelo, with whom he has often been compared, since the two shared an interest in portraying the figure in all its power and humanity. Rodin, however, was the product of a later time, and his characterizations, although still idealized, have more psychological individualization than do those of his precursor.

Rodin's ability to capture the individual while simultaneously achieving universal meaning is nowhere more apparent than in his **Burghers of Calais**, completed in 1895. The French industrial port city of Calais, just opposite Dover across the English channel, wished to commission a monument honoring the six heroes who sacrificed themselves on behalf of the city in 1347. The English king Edward III, during a victorious moment in the Hundred Years War with France, agreed to spare the besieged Calais if six leading citizens were willing to come forward as martyrs. On the way to their death, Eustace de Saint-Pierre, Jean d'Aire, Jean de Fiennes, Andrieux d'Andres, and Jacques and Pierre de Wiessant, the youngest of the six, first suffered humiliation – paraded through the town in sackcloth and rope halters – but were spared beheading by the plea of Queen Philippa.

Although the figures in the final sculpture group are all fully clothed, it was Rodin's method to make small-scale nude studies, eventually full-scale nude studies, and "dress" his figures only at the end. The Art Center's sculpture is a full-scale nude study of Pierre de Wiessant, made probably around 1885–86. The bronze is unnumbered, but it was cast by Alexis Rudier, and consequently is likely to be an early cast, since this Paris foundry was responsible for the majority of Rodin's earliest and best casts; this study in fact once was part of the Rudier Estate.

Rodin worked intermittently on this commission for twelve years, revising and refining the six figures and the overall composition. As was his practice, he sought to achieve realism not through slavish imitation, but rather through distortion in the interests of emotional truth and inner states. The figure of Pierre de Wiessant underwent some adjustments in its final version, most notably in the slight raising of the upheld arm and the repositioning of the hand, opening up the space between the arm and the figure's angled and bent head. Tension and anguish are apparent throughout the figure, however, and are especially evident in the undraped Des Moines version.

Rodin was tireless in his work and in his observation of the figure in motion. He worked from life, even maintaining nude models at ease or moving about in the studio so that he could seize upon a random movement and capture it in a quick sketch or model. His affinities with Impressionism, the new style that was dominating painting in France, are apparent not only in this exploration of the fleeting moment, but also in Rodin's careful modeling of the surface of his plasters to be cast into bronze: the play of light and shadow is compelling and demands further that the works be seen from numerous viewpoints, not just from the front.

Rodin was devoted first and foremost to his work. He was born in Paris into a deeply religious family of modest means. Although he studied with French sculptors Barye and Carrier-Belleuse, it was the Italian masters Donatello and Michelangelo who were his true inspirations. Rodin's work frequently generated considerable controversy, since he often defied convention, either through applying the idea of nude studies to a historical figure, or, as in the case of **The Burgers of Calais**, turning a commission for a single figure into a group of six, dressed humbly rather than richly, and placing the life-sized figures without a pedestal so as to be perceived as "real" people, albeit made of bronze and part of history. TRN

Purchased with funds from the Gardner and
Florence Call Cowles Foundation;
Des Moines Art Center Permanent Collections,
1979.10

Acrylic and flashe on paper,
36 ¹/₂ x 36 ⁵/₈ inches (92.7 x 93 cm)

susan rothenberg

American, born 1945   **Untitled,** 1979

Born in Buffalo, New York in 1945, Susan Rothenberg received her Bachelor of Fine Arts degree from Cornell University in 1967. She spent the next two years traveling, then settled in New York in 1969 and began to work with performance artists such as Trisha Brown and Joan Jonas. This activity was important for Rothenberg's awareness of what was current: "It was just making art – it wasn't even painting or sculpture or music or dance.... It was what you were supposed to do if you were getting out of the old rules."[1] The "old rules" were those of Minimalism. Initially Rothenberg experimented with Conceptual and Process Art – influenced by artists such as Eva Hesse – but in 1971 she turned to painting and chose the horse as her subject: "I think I wasn't able or willing at that time to deal with the figure. The horse was certainly a figure – but it wasn't loaded with all the art historical weight of the human form. And also, it was powerful. I wanted a powerful image to be working with."[2]

Rothenberg's first formalist paintings (1973–77) present the horse in profile, emphasizing line, flatness, and geometry. Her first one-artist exhibition in 1975 earned her a position as one of the leading proponents of "New Image" painting, a term for young artists who were bringing painting back into the forefront of contemporary art. Challenging Minimalism without all-out rebellion; they continued to work with abstract vocabulary while reintroducing the figure.

For the next two years, Rothenberg continued to work with the emblematic horse, but presented frontally, rather than in profile. It is to this series of work that the Art Center's painting on paper, **Untitled,** belongs. In it three horses move directly toward the viewer with tremendous energy and power. It is an image not of horses, but rather of vitality, vibrancy, and strength.

In 1980 Rothenberg made an important transition in her work: she abandoned the horse for the human figure, first including only isolated parts, such as heads and hands, then gradually using the whole figure. Images of the figure in movement are especially abundant. The Art Center's collection includes forty prints by Rothenberg, dating between 1977 and 1990, thirty-seven of which were a gift from John and Mary Pappajohn, beginning in 1991. The Art Center has subsequently purchased additional prints to fill in the group. Rothenberg currently lives and works in New Mexico. DL

Purchased with funds from the Coffin Fine
Arts Trust; Nathan Emory Coffin
Collection of the Des Moines Art Center,
1975.15

Oil on canvas, 67 3/4 x 50 inches
(172.1 x 137 cm)

mark rothko

American, born Russia, 1903–1970   **Light Over Gray**, 1956

With its stacked, soft-edged rectangles of white and bluish-gray hovering against a dark red ground, **Light Over Gray** exemplifies Mark Rothko's distinctive color-field style of the 1950s. The artist was born Marcus Rothkowitz in Dvinsk, Russia, and in 1913 immigrated with his family to Portland, Oregon. Rothko attended Yale University (1921–23) before moving to New York, where he studied intermittently at the Art Students League for the remainder of the decade. In 1935 Rothko and his friend Adolph Gottlieb cofounded The Ten, an independent exhibiting group whose members generally painted in a loose, expressionistic manner. After the break-up of The Ten in 1940, Rothko and Gottlieb helped to establish the Federation of Modern Painters and Sculptors, in which they remained active until the late 1940s.

By the late 1930s Rothko had developed strong interests in European Surrealism, Greek mythology, Nietzschean philosophy, Jungian psychology, and primitive art and religion, all of which influenced his maturing art. From the early to mid-1940s, he practiced a form of abstract Surrealism, depicting strange, biomorphic creatures suspended in watery, dimensionless spaces. Rothko conceived of these mysterious organisms as actors in primeval myths and rituals, and declared his intention to express a universal "Spirit of Myth, which is generic to all myths of all times."[1]

By the late 1940s Rothko had come to see biomorphic imagery and mythic allusions as limitations, and moved towards a simpler, more abstract style that he hoped would be capable of communicating profound feelings more directly. Gradually dissolving and enlarging his figures into diffuse shapes of color drifting across the canvas, Rothko arrived by 1950 at his "classic" Abstract Expressionist format, consisting of two or three cloudy rectangles of similar width, placed one above the other and floated against a ground of another color.

While Rothko attended carefully to shape, hue, and value relationships in his classic paintings, he did not want them to be appreciated merely for their formal qualities, but hoped that they would move viewers emotionally. Rothko encouraged affective involvement with his paintings by typically making them very large and inviting the viewer to become absorbed within their vast, nebulous spaces, which seem imbued with unstated meanings and religious connotations.

While in many of Rothko's classic paintings the rectangles are placed close together and appear to merge with the ground to create a holistic field of palpitating color, in the Art Center's **Light Over Gray** the white and bluish-gray shapes remain isolated from one another and distinct from the ground. Strongly contrasting in size and value, the superposed rectangles create visual tensions between high and low, large and small, light and dark; these in turn imply fundamental dualisms such as good and evil, heaven and earth, life and death.[2] Rothko would have welcomed such associations, for he understood his art as "dealing with human emotion: with the human drama as much as I can possibly experience it," and ultimately believed that "all art deals with intimations of mortality."[3] DC

Purchased with funds from the Coffin Fine
Arts Trust; Nathan Emory Coffin
Collection of the Des Moines Art Center,
1988.13

Oil and graphite on paper on fiberglass, 46 ⅛
x 46 ⅛ inches (117.2 x 117.2 cm)

robert ryman

American, born 1930   **Cast,** 1988

By restricting himself to the color white for almost four decades, internationally acclaimed American painter Robert Ryman has achieved a body of work unparalleled in its discipline and refinement. Ryman's paintings are pure and reductivist in the extreme. His art is based on nuances of detail best perceived in white, and on subtleties of perception that become apparent only in a restricted situation. With his insistently monochromatic whiteness and generally square formats, Ryman ensures his artistic control over the viewer's perception. By denying the expected full pictorial range, Ryman guides the viewer into a sensibility of poetic calm that allows the smallest visual incident to be apprehended and appreciated. The chief functional variables in Ryman's art are brushwork and the support, including the manner in which a work is affixed to the wall.

Although Ryman's art is Minimalist, centered on the principle that the less there is, the more one can see, underlying this severe economy of means is the active influence of Abstract Expressionism. In works such as the Des Moines Art Center's **Cast**, for example, the surface constitutes the primary arena for Ryman's invention. **Cast**, done the year after he completed "The Charter Series" (1985–87), has a similarly even, smooth, hermetic surface that emphasizes the insistent two-dimensionality of painting. The artist's presence is barely detectable. Other Ryman canvases display active brush strokes that underscore the artist's touch and aerate the surface. Although all of Ryman's paintings are utterly abstract and pure, and all of them whisper, their emotional range can be considerable. This was especially apparent in Ryman's one-person exhibition at the Dia Foundation in New York in 1989, in which **Cast** was included. The artist designed the exhibition himself, and here the "…sense of significant detail – the ability to make what is usually thought of as arbitrary or secondary seem absolute and primary – spreads beyond the work and onto the wall. Ryman is capable of totalizing the entire space as art, as is seen in his current Dia installation…where the ritual progression of disparate-sized pieces climaxes in a chapel-like space with one giant work…."[1]

Ironically, despite the sophistication of his art, Robert Ryman never received any formal training as an artist. He was born in Nashville, but has lived and worked in New York for over forty-five years. After relocating to New York in 1952, he worked as a guard during the early 1950s at The Museum of Modern Art. It was at the museum that he met fellow artists Dan Flavin and Sol LeWitt and received his art education; Paul Cézanne and Henri Matisse proved to be his historical mentors and Mark Rothko a profound influence. TRN

Purchased with funds from the Edith M. Usry Bequest
in Memory of Her Parents, Mr. and Mrs. George Franklin
Usry; the Dr. and Mrs. Peder T. Madsen Fund; and
the Anna K. Meredith Endowment Fund; Des Moines Art
Center Permanent Collections, 1976.61

Oil on canvas, 60 x 69 inches
(152.4 x 175.3 cm)

john singer sargent

American, 1856–1925   **Portraits de M.E.P.... et de Mlle. L.P. (Portraits of Edouard and Marie-Louise Pailleron),** 1881

"Ask me to paint your gates, your fences, your barns, which I should gladly do, but **not the human face**." So responded an exasperated John Singer Sargent, the most successful portrait painter of his day, to an inquiry from Lady Radnor about painting portraits of additional members of her family. Sargent had recently completed a rather imposing portrayal of her ladyship's daughter, the Countess of Lathom, in 1904. Lady Radnor must therefore have been taken aback by Sargent's retort, since the artist's considerable reputation resided primarily in his portraits and not in the landscapes and genre scenes that he himself preferred. Indeed, during the course of his life, he painted well over 500 portraits. His sitters included luminaries in the arts (Auguste Rodin, Claude Monet, Ellen Terry), writers (Robert Louis Stevenson, Henry James), even presidents (Theodore Roosevelt, Woodrow Wilson), but the families of wealthy businessmen, socialites, and aristocrats made up the bulk of his commissions. In time he wearied of "painting the human face" for hire. The potboilers of the last fifteen years of so of his life, plus two murals at the Museum of Fine Arts in Boston and at the Widener Library at Harvard University, led to a sharp diminution of his reputation soon after his death in 1925. Only

in recent decades has that reputation made a substantial recovery.

Sargent had not always held portraiture in disdain. When, in the late 1870s, the young French playwright and publisher Edouard Pailleron invited Sargent to portray himself and his wife, the twenty-three year-old American was thoroughly excited by the prospect. So pleased were his patrons with the results that they also had him paint a double portrait of their children, Edouard and his younger sister, Marie-Louise.

Prior to working on that canvas, Sargent traveled to Spain and to Holland to study the paintings of his seventeenth-century artistic idols Diego Velásquez and Frans Hals, respectively. The fruits of his voyage are reflected in the heightened realism with which he imbued his youthful subjects and the bravura paint handling. Although the composition is quite conventional, his portrayal of the children's personalities is not. This is not the pair of sweet little siblings one usually finds in nineteenth-century children's portraits.

The young Edouard is clothed all in black, relieved only by the white of his broad collar and the two slivers of his sleeves. The elegant fingers of his left hand rest lightly on his thigh while he awkwardly uses the back of his right hand for support. The three-quarter profile implies that he has just turned his head to fasten his eyes on ours with a studied, haughty air, and it appears that he will grow up to be a bit of a snob, for he is almost there now.

Not haughtiness, but a seething anger characterizes Marie-Louise. According to her memoirs, Sargent had insisted that she wear this specific dress that she did not like at all; she would have preferred to be doing almost anything else than sitting for her portrait; and, worst of all, the painting required eighty-three sittings that must have been excruciating for an active, strong-willed nine-year-old who was used to having her own way.

The despised dress with its broad range of whites, and textures of buttons, frills, and lace, offered Sargent the opportunity to display his technical mastery. The sharply observed detail of the girl's gold bracelet casting a shadow on her wrist is in contrast to the impressionistic daubs of paint in her hair that suggest a satin bow. Overall the red-white-black combination that dominates the composition is not very subtle, but the freely painted abstract background provides an effective foil that further focuses our attention on the two protagonists and their serious countenances. After the painting was finally completed, Sargent reportedly danced a little jig, and then he and Marie-Louise celebrated the end of the ordeal by tossing furniture and furnishings out the window of his studio.

Sargent was born in 1856 in Florence, of well-to-do American parents. He died in London, where he had lived much of his life, in 1925.
JD

Purchased with funds from Roy Halston
Frowick; Des Moines Art Center Permanent
Collections, 1991.47

Oil and crockery on canvas and wood,
90 x 120 x 13 inches (228.6 x 304.8 x 33 cm)

julian schnabel

American, born 1951   **The Death of Fashion,** 1978

Julian Schnabel was born in Brooklyn, New York in 1951. He received his Bachelor of Fine Arts degree from the University of Houston in 1973 and entered the Whitney Museum of American Art Independent Study Program in New York in the same year. New York remains his home.

Schnabel's subjects and often the size of all his works have tended to be on a grand scale. Sources for his inspiration have included the Bible, European literature, and classical and rock music. Schnabel's idea for the "plate paintings" such as the Art Center's **The Death of Fashion** came to him when he was in Barcelona in the summer of 1978. As the artist recalled in his book, **C.V.J: Nicknames of Maitre D's and Other Excerpts from Life** (1987), p. 149: "I had had a funny idea that I could make a painting the size of the closet in my hotel room in Barcelona and that I could cover it with broken plates. My interest, unlike Gaudi's, was not in the patterning or the design of the glazed tiles, it was in the reflective property of white plates to disturb the picture plane.

The disparity between the reflectiveness of the plates and the paint were in disagreement with each other and the concept of mosaic, because they fractured its homogeneity. The plates seemed to have a sound, the sound of every violent human tragedy, an anthropomorphic sense of things being smeared and thrown. I was trying to tear the mosaic out of its own body to make a bridge to something just outside of my own body. It was that radical moment that an artist waits for. I wanted to make something that was exploding as much as I wanted to make something that was cohesive. It was an act of desperation which I needed to hurry home to realize."

Upon returning to New York, Schnabel immediately set about creating his first two plate paintings, of which **The Death of Fashion** is one. The title of the work references a media account the artist read about the death of a fashion model. He modified the title of that article for the painting's title, which bears no apparent reference to the news story.

A year after it was made, **The Death of Fashion** was exhibited at the Mary Boone Gallery in New York in a show that received enormous attention. Within a few months of its 1979 presentation, the Art Center's

painting was featured in color in two prominent art magazines, **Arts** and **Art in America**. **The Death of Fashion** and related works became emblematic of the return to acceptability of art that was unabashedly passionate rather than overtly cool and industrial like the 1960s phenomena of Minimal and Pop Art. The artist's intense feelings are communicated in a number of ways: through an energetic application of material, a surface that is fragmented rather than smoothly industrial, and also through images such as a mutilated torso. The broken plates placed around the canvas are richly suggestive of pieces of the past, like ancient plates embedded in lava. But the plates also pertain to contemporary domestic life, recalling everything from the homey chore of doing the dishes to breaking plates in the heat of quarreling and, by extension, the fragmentation of family life. IMD

Gift of the Des Moines Register and
Tribune Company; Des Moines Art Center
Permanent Collections, 1985.4

Plaster, wood, aluminum, plastic, and steel,
96 x 94 x 28 inches (243.8 x 238.8 x 71.1 cm)

george segal

American, born 1924   **Man on a Printing Press,** 1971

The leading figurative sculptor of his generation, George Segal is best known for his haunting plaster-molded representations of ordinary people set in actual environments. Born in New York, Segal grew up in the Bronx before moving with his family in 1940 to a chicken farm in South Brunswick, New Jersey. During the 1940s Segal studied at the Cooper Union, Rutgers University, the Pratt Institute of Design, and New York University, which granted him a Bachelor of Science degree in art education in 1949. In the same year Segal bought his own chicken farm across the road from his parents, and raised poultry there until 1958. From 1957 to 1963 Segal supported his family by teaching in local high schools, and in the latter year also earned a Master of Fine Arts degree from Rutgers University.

During the 1950s Segal painted large canvases of nudes in a loose, improvisatory manner derived from Abstract Expressionism. His association with the Hansa Gallery in New York brought him into contact with other young artists who were seeking

to move beyond Abstract Expressionism, including Allan Kaprow, who staged his first "happening" at Segal's chicken farm in 1958. Kaprow's conception of the work of art as a total environment encouraged Segal to venture into the realm of sculpture and eventually to place his figures in real settings.

Segal began to make sculpture in 1958, fashioning crude effigies out of wood, chicken wire, burlap, and plaster. His artistic breakthrough came in 1961 after a student provided him with some medical bandages used to make plaster casts for broken limbs. Recognizing the sculptural potential of this material, Segal began covering friends and family members in bandages soaked in wet plaster and then assembling the hollow pieces after they had dried. The rough surfaces of the resulting sculptures record Segal's gestural handworking of the liquid plaster and recall the emotion-laden brush strokes of Abstract Expressionism. But the mummylike figures themselves, with their frozen postures, closed eyes, and blank expressions, remain impassive and inscrutable.

Concerned artistically with man in his daily life, Segal supplied his figures with real furniture and fixtures, and frequently placed

them in environments extracted from actual urban structures, including a gas station, a diner, and a subway car. By situating lifelike yet ghostly figures within literal yet constructed settings, Segal generated fascinating tensions between artifice and actuality, absence and presence, art and life.

Segal's figures are sometimes shown in action, like the pressman in the Art Center's **Man on a Printing Press**. Commissioned by the Des Moines Register and Tribune Company, and originally installed in the reception area of the newspaper's executive offices, **Man on a Printing Press** appropriately celebrates the diligence and skill of the pressman and the productive power of the machinery he operates. The active pose of the pressman and the narrative of productivity he enacts are untypical of Segal's work, however. More often his figures are shown at rest, in poses that suggest lassitude or withdrawal, or they engage in mundane activities without passion or energy.

continued on page 248

Purchased with funds from the Coffin Fine
Arts Trust; Nathan Emory Coffin
Collection of the Des Moines Art Center,
1972.87

Plaster, wood, aluminum, plastic,
and lights, 96 x 144 x 90 inches
(243.8 x 365.8 x 228.6 cm)

george segal

To All Gates, 1971

Such is the case with the figures in the Art Center's
To All Gates, who are presented within
an environment that evokes a modern trans-
portation terminal. The stark palette and
severe geometry of the setting, with its
square black pillar, rectangular black wall,
and glowing red band of light, throw into
relief the spectral whiteness and craggy contours of the figures. The figures appear
almost comatose, as if wearied by travel and
alienated by their harsh surroundings.
Both face in the direction of the gates, but
neither seems able to move; the younger
woman, posed by Segal's neighbor, is frozen
in mid-step, while the older one, posed by
Segal's wife, rests heavily on her luggage.
The travelers make no effort to communicate
with one another or with the viewer; though
they share a public space, each is utterly
alone and incapable of human contact. The
ultimate subject of **To All Gates** seems to
be the loneliness and anomie of modern
urban existence – a theme that haunts much
of Segal's art. **DC**

Commissioned in Memory of Florence C. and
David S. Kruidenier, Project made
possible by the Kruidenier Family Members
and In-laws; Des Moines Art Center
Permanent Collections, 1989.5

Six granite blocks, overall, 4 1/2 x 560 x
100 feet (1.37 x 170.69 x 30.48 m)

richard serra

American, born 1939   **Standing Stones,** 1989

Richard Serra's site-specific environmental sculpture **Standing Stones** concerns itself with the rise and fall of the land and the experience of seeing the work through walking or driving past the Des Moines Art Center in a car. It is made of six rough-hewn granite blocks quarried in Sweden, each approximately five feet in height and width. The elements are intended to be human scale and to mark the elevation and distances of the land at various key points on the site. The artist was interested in the fact that the hill shifts in two directions, and the work is intended to create a kind of human measurement in the landscape. Unlike a sculptural object, this work is formed by the elements along with the space and "sculptural field" which they define, and is meant to be experienced over time and through movement within and past the sculpture.

The artist developed the work during repeated visits to Des Moines and subsequent study of the site through a model in his studio. He came to an understanding of the space through walking it repeatedly and observing it in changing seasons. In this work the sculpture consists not only of the stone elements themselves, but the spaces between them; the sculptural field is the entire area that has become more defined and clarified through the addition of the stones. In the way the building of a wall creates space, the placement of markers within a sculptural field defines a whole area and points out aspects of it that were not apparent before. In the case of **Standing Stones**, the rise and fall of the land, and its complex shift in direction, are elucidated by the sculpture. The sculpture serves to measure the space.

In a further move away from the tradition of sculpture as static object, **Standing Stones**, as with other sited works by Serra and others, is to be understood and experienced through the participation of the viewer. The work, rather than being clear in one viewing, is known from many angles and directions and only over time. This quality of experience adds the elements of duration and evolution to the understanding of the sculpture and makes the viewer an active participant in the sculptural experience.

Serra has been making sited works in landscape since the early 1970s, and his sculpture has a strong relationship to space – either to interior architecture within compressed urban sites, or within landscape. His work is concerned with the palpable weight of matter, the balance of equal or unequal forces, and energy controlled and visible. His sculpture controls and defines space and distance with volumes of expanse created through the manipulation of materials. Along with the investigation of what these materials do physically and experientially, Serra's sculptures are often concerned with the density of weight and the properties of matter and gravity centered within the sculptural elements themselves. JB

Purchased with funds from the Edmundson
Art Foundation, Inc.; Des Moines
Art Center Permanent Collections, 1964.6

Tempera on paper mounted on Masonite,
36 x 48 inches (91.4 x 121.9 cm)

ben shahn

American, born Lithuania, 1898–1969   **Integration, Supreme Court,** 1963

Ben Shahn was a pioneer of social and political art in the United States. The Art Center's **Integration, Supreme Court**, although a late work in Shahn's career, is a good representative of his advocacy and sympathy for justice.

Shahn was born in 1898 in Kovno, Lithuania in the Pale region where Jews were allowed to settle. His father, a wood carver, was a socialist and an intellectual who wrote for the Yiddish press and organized resistance to the czar. As a child, Shahn was engaged in political activism; politics and extensive religious study comprised his early education.

Shahn's family immigrated to the United States when he was eight years old, settling in Brooklyn, New York. Shahn apprenticed in his uncle's lithography shop, attended high school at night, and briefly took classes at the Art Students League. Upon completing his apprenticeship in 1917, he supported himself in lithography and studied art at New York University, City College of New York, and the National Academy of Design for five years. Shahn spent summers at the Marine Biology Laboratory at Woods Hole, Massachusetts, and soon purchased a summer home in nearby Truro.

In the 1920s Shahn traveled in Europe and North Africa. This experience spurred Shahn's interest in fine art, which was augmented by friendship with the photographer Walker Evans; in Truro they photographed and drew the bathers and fishermen.

In 1929 Shahn produced a series of watercolors of the major figures involved in the Dreyfus Affair. His next series was inspired by the Sacco and Vanzetti case in Massachusetts, another trial marked by prejudice and controversy. "Shahn chose to record the likenesses of the major characters in the case.... The combined works remind the viewer of the trial's larger significance as an example of justice gone awry."[1] With his third project, a 1932 series of gouaches on the trial of San Francisco labor leader Tom Mooney, Shahn had fully established himself as an artist and political activist.

Impressed with the Sacco and Vanzetti works, the Mexican muralist Diego Rivera asked Shahn to assist him with his Rockefeller Center mural, **Man at the Crossroads** (removed because it included an image of Lenin). Shahn himself began to be asked to submit designs for mural projects, through the various facets of the Works Progress Administration, but they were frequently rejected as too political. In the mid-1930s Shahn worked for the Farm Security Administration, taking photographs of rural life throughout the Midwest. This activity led him to focus on the more personal aspects of working life.

Shahn settled in New Jersey in 1939 and continued to be both celebrated and persecuted for his social and political art. In 1947 The Museum of Modern Art, New York presented a major retrospective of his work. In the early 1950s, however, he was investigated by the FBI and blacklisted for possible Communist sympathies and connections. Nevertheless, the Columbia Broadcasting System (CBS) hired Shahn to design advertisements for their political convention coverage, and he regularly designed covers of **The Nation**.

Painted in 1963, **Integration, Supreme Court** shows a return to Shahn's early interest in notorious trials, although this time justice triumphed. The moment selected by Shahn is the 1953–54 Warren Court, with the justices (left to right): Tom C. Clark, Robert Jackson, Felix Frankfurter, Hugo Black, Chief Justice Earl Warren, Stanley Reed, William O. Douglas, Harold H. Burton, and Sherman Minton.[2] Appointed by President Dwight D. Eisenhower in 1953, Earl Warren presided over one of the most liberal of the Supreme Courts. The specific case here is Brown vs. Board of Education of Topeka, in which Warren "spoke for a unanimous court...declaring unconstitutional the separation of public school children by race. Rejecting the separate but equal doctrine that had prevailed since 1896, he stated that 'separate educational facilities are inherently unequal.'" Shahn presented the court to viewers at an angle that also presents viewers to the court as if they are plaintiffs, leading viewers to examine their own feelings and practices. DL

Purchased with funds from the Edmundson
Art Foundation, Inc.; Des Moines
Art Center Permanent Collections, 1987.8

Wood, fir, oil, paint, and steel plate,
26 x 49 x 38 inches (66 x 124.5 x 96.5 cm)

joel shapiro

American, born 1941   **Untitled,** 1987

Joel Shapiro's **Untitled** from 1987 continues a theme that runs through his career – the human figure in movement. While seemingly abstract, Shapiro's work frequently holds a reference to the human form, held in a particular gesture that seems to contain movement as well as evoking the emotion that can be carried by a certain specific gesture. In the case of **Untitled,** the figure is lying down with legs slightly raised, as if it has just fallen to the ground. It is a work that evokes sympathy even in its stark abstraction, as the "figure" seems bare and vulnerable.

Untitled has evolved from a body of work that humanizes the austere structures of Minimal art. Shapiro has cut, sawed, and joined blocks of wood, stable and objectlike, and made sculptures that are unstable and animate.

Throughout his work Shapiro has used basic materials and simplified abstracted forms to create sculptures that hover between abstraction and representation, including both arenas of thought. His first sculpture using the figure was a small painted bronze of 1974, which appeared to be running. While static, seemingly frozen in movement, this work was his first that dealt with the figure in motion. Since that time Shapiro has made a body of work that explores this theme, in wood and metal, with the figure caught in motion at various degrees of abstraction. One sees references to Russian Constructivist sculpture, Futurism, and Cubism in Shapiro's work, both in the exploration of the breakdown and structure of

form itself, as well as the abstraction of the figure in motion.

Clearly his early work developed from a Minimalist sensibility. The properties of these abstract forms that interested him were their physical aspects, such as weight. But through the reduction of form to its most basic elements, Shapiro explored the human condition. Without using representational imagery in his work, issues of psychology, emotion, gender, and movement are articulated. His sculptures join with the actual space in which the spectator moves, poised directly on the floor. By the early 1980s, Shapiro became identified as one of the leading artists in the reemergence of figuration.

Born in New York on September 27, 1941, Shapiro studied art at the University of Colorado and New York University (1961–69), receiving Bachelor of Fine Arts and Master of Fine Arts degrees. His work has been widely exhibited in the United States and Europe, and he received a retrospective exhibition at the Whitney Museum of Art in 1982. Shapiro's work is represented in major institutions in the United States, Europe, Israel, and Japan. JB

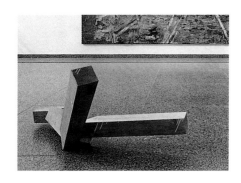

cindy sherman

American, 1954   **Untitled #90,** 1981

Cindy Sherman's revealing portraits are especially remarkable because while her subjects all look so different, Sherman herself is the person in each of the images: the artist takes photographs of herself. Through her expertise in make-up, wigs, costumes, setting, and photographic technique, Sherman is able to make the "subjects" appear different. And through her acting ability, she infuses these physical features with a personality that seems particular to that subject. The Art Center owns seven photographs representing different series the artist made between 1977 and 1990.

Sherman was born in Glen Ridge, New Jersey, in 1954. She grew up in Huntington Beach, Long Island, forty miles from New York. As a young child, Sherman enjoyed sitting in front of the television and making art; movies also were an early pleasure. Family and teachers reinforced her art interest. Not surprising to those who know how her photographs are made, she also enjoyed playing "dress up."

In 1972 the artist enrolled in the College of Art at the State University of New York at Buffalo. It was mostly from other students and from exhibitions at the Albright-Knox Art Gallery and the alternative space Hallwalls that she learned about contemporary art developments. She took two courses in photography and became enthusiastic. Soon she became attracted to the photographically based work

of artists such as Gilbert and George, John Baldessari, and Duane Michals, and to the work of William Wegman and Eleanor Antin, whose videotapes had strong performance components. While all these artists used photography, their concerns had mostly to do with issues common to contemporary painting and sculpture rather than with traditional photography. Sherman also admired the work of Hollywood photographers, such as Cecil Beaton, Milton Green, and George Platte Lynes.

After receiving her college degree, Sherman moved to New York in 1977. Early activities there included seeing numerous European films with subtitles and enlarging her collection of wigs, shoes, hats, and clothing. She became interested in what her clothing collection said about the women who wore them, and increasingly intrigued by the stereotypical roles of women projected by these clothes and the movies she saw. She was curious about the extent to which clothing affected how people saw and felt about her and how she felt about herself and others.

Sherman's first important series was the "Untitled Film Stills," made from 1977 to 1980. It brought together her interests in photography, performance, dress-up, European films, and women's roles. In most of these works, such at the Art Center's **Untitled Film Still #50** and **Untitled Film Still #56**, the image seems to be that of a female role or type from a particular 1950s or 1960s film, but in reality

the artist invented the character. In 1981–82 Sherman made a series of approximately twelve, two-by-four-foot photographs, exemplified by **Untitled #90** and **Untitled #86**. These works, rather than presenting stereotypes, are inward-looking images that allow a glimpse into a private moment in the life of an individual. Sherman continued to work mostly in series throughout the 1980s, increasingly introducing the use of prostheses – false noses, breasts, and so forth. Generally the prosthesis is visible as such – artificiality and invention are not concealed. In 1989 and 1990 the artist made a series of approximately three dozen very large photographs inspired by historical paintings seen on a European visit. These photographs of men as well as women hark back to the "Untitled Film Stills" in their representation of types.

Sherman has proven to be one of the most enduring and lively artists to have emerged in the late 1970s. Her work is important historically, signifying the return of the recognizable image to mainstream contemporary art and the continuing vitality of popular culture and media as a resource for artists. It is additionally intellectually and emotionally provocative in regard to changing attitudes towards women in recent decades. IMD

Purchased with funds from the Edmundson
Art Foundation, Inc.; Des Moines
Art Center Permanent Collections, 1995.4

Fifty panels, waterless lithography on felt,
and seventeen text panels on felt,
overall, 98 x 265 inches (248.9 x 673.1 cm)

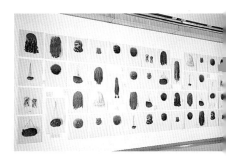

lorna simpson

American, born 1960   **Wigs,** 1994

Lorna Simpson was born in 1960 in Brooklyn, New York. She studied photography at the School for Visual Arts in New York and received a Bachelor of Fine Arts degree in 1982. In 1985 she earned a Master of Fine Arts degree from the University of California, San Diego.

Simpson's early work was documentary. In San Diego she was introduced to conceptually based photography, much of which incorporates words. Simpson came to feel that both text and image were necessary to achieve her intended meaning. Her early mature work generally consists of both elements in a visual format that owes something to the presentation in advertising design.

Simpson's art is based on her own experiences and those told to her by other black women. Often her works are about how black women become stereotyped through external attributes erroneously seen as indicative of character. Her work points up stereotyping through gender, skin color, hair type and style, and clothing. Faces are not shown, thereby focusing the viewer away from personality and toward the social and political issues addressed. The anonymity also suggests the invisibility of particular human qualities that accompanies stereotyping.

In a number of works Simpson has focused on body parts (hands, arms, heads) and articles of clothing such as shoes; since 1990 she has often addressed hair style. **Wigs** is her most direct commentary on the subject and also the largest work she has created, consisting of

fifty images of wigs printed on felt and accompanied by seventeen related text panels. Simpson has explained her interest in hair style: "It deals with the assumptions and stereotypes related to a woman's appearance, particularly black women. The way you wear your hair is supposed to say something about you, which is basically bull...."[1]

Simpson views **Wigs** as marking a transition away from the figure; the wigs are surrogate figures. She feels it also is a work that mines gender issues more fully than before.[2]

Simpson's art has earned her significant recognition. In 1990, at age thirty, she was the first African-American woman to exhibit at the Venice Biennale; she was also the first African-American woman to have a Projects show at The Museum of Modern Art, New York. In 1992 the Museum of Contemporary Art in Chicago organized a nationally traveling retrospective of her work, and a book about her art was published by The Friends of Photography (San Francisco). In the October 10, 1994 **Time** magazine cover story, "Black Renaissance," Simpson is pictured in front of **Wigs**; the work is also featured on the cover of **The New Art Examiner**, February 1995. **Wigs** has been included in museum exhibitions in the United States, Austria, and Japan.
IMD

Purchased with funds from the Coffin Fine
Arts Trust; Nathan Emory Coffin
Collection of the Des Moines Art Center,
1959.33

Oil on canvas, 24 x 32 inches
(61 x 81.3 cm)

john sloan

American, 1871–1951   **Tugs,** 1900

Although photography was beginning to encroach upon the viability of earning one's livelihood in magazine illustration, John Sloan might never have altered his career as an illustrator in Philadelphia had he not met the charismatic and highly influential American painter and teacher Robert Henri in 1892. Sloan relocated to New York in 1904 and began his long and successful career as a key member of The Eight, or "The Ashcan School," as the group was derogatorily named. Although he summered for thirty years in the New Mexico landscape, he is associated closely with New York and the important accomplishments in the early years of the twentieth century in the effort to build a genuinely American art.

In common with the other members of The Eight (Henri, Arthur B. Davies, William Glackens, Ernest Lawson, George Luks, Maurice Prendergast, and Everett Shinn), Sloan was intrigued by all things American – the landscape, the people, and the thriving commerce and industry that were everywhere evident and marked the progressive and aggressive spirit of the nation. He was anxious to play a part in that development, and served in a number of ways while continuing to pursue his own painting; by 1925 he had achieved stature as one of the country's best printmakers. Sloan was president of the Society of Independent Artists from its founding in 1918 until his death in 1951; from 1916 to 1938 he was a sought-after teacher at the Art Students League.

The Art Center's **Tugs** was painted in 1900, before Sloan settled in New York. The palette remains quite subdued, with only touches of color relieving the dominating range of grays. The setting is a wharf on the Delaware River in Philadelphia, with tugboats ranged alongside. The composition is asymmetrical, balanced by an almost mirror-image massing, the dark forms all on the right and bottom, the open air and water on the left and along the top. Despite the lack of bright color, the painting conveys a sense of life and activity, largely through the brush strokes that energize the sky and create an almost Impressionistic atmosphere. The painting was exhibited the year after it was painted at the Allan Gallery in New York, the Pennsylvania Academy of Fine Arts in Philadelphia, and The Art Institute of Chicago. TRN

Polychromed steel,
100 1/2 x 59 x 33 1/2 inches high
(255.3 x 149.8 x 85 cm)

david smith

American, 1906–1965   **Zig II,** 1961

A prodigiously talented pioneer of abstract, welded metal sculpture, David Smith created a body of work whose variety and vitality are unsurpassed in the history of American art. He was born in Decatur, Indiana, and studied art at Ohio University in Athens, Ohio (1924–25), and at the Art Students League in New York (1927–32). Although trained as a painter, Smith turned to sculpture in 1932 after seeing reproductions of the welded metal constructions of Pablo Picasso and Julio González. Applying the welding skills he had learned while working at a Studebaker plant in 1925, Smith began to create metal sculptures. In 1934 he established a studio at the Terminal Iron Works in Brooklyn, and in 1940 he moved to a farm in Bolton Landing, New York, where he built a new house and machine shop, which he named the Terminal Iron Works.

During the 1930s Smith synthesized influences from Cubism, Constructivism, and Surrealism, creating small, linear sculptures that often incorporate machine parts and pieces of scrap metal. Some of these works represent highly abstracted figures, while others are completely nonobjective. Smith also produced in 1937–40 a series of fifteen bronze medallions called the "Medals for Dishonor," whose quasi-Surrealist imagery protests the social and political injustices of the period. In the 1940s Smith continued to

create open-form sculptures, many of them conceived as abstract landscapes, which Smith rendered through a kind of fluent metal calligraphy often described as "drawing in space."

In the 1950s Smith greatly increased the scale of his sculptures and began working in series. The most impressive of these are the "Agricolas" of 1951–59, which were assembled from parts of old farm machinery; the "Tanktotems" of 1952–60, made of steel beams and boiler-tank heads; and the "Sentinels" of 1956–61, many of which were constructed of stainless-steel planes. The majority of the works in these series are distinctly anthropomorphic, and evoke primitive totems or guardian figures recast in industrial materials.

Also powerfully anthropomorphic is the Des Moines Art Center's **Zig II,** notwithstanding its membership in the series named with Smith's abbreviation for "ziggurat," the pyramidlike temple of the ancient Mesopotamians. Like the other works in the series, **Zig II** is composed of large, geometric shapes of steel, welded together and painted with bold colors. Its figurative quality arises from its vertically oriented composition, which is dominated by a large, curved plane that suggests a torso. The torso stands on three leglike elements and is surmounted by a semicylindrical neck that bears a long, rectangular "head" made from a piece of channel stock. The enormous "body" of **Zig II** rises nearly eight and a half

feet into the air, towering over the viewer and attaining a monumental presence.

While **Zig II** has an undeniably figurative character, it may also be appreciated in purely formal terms, as an engaging study in contrasts held in equilibrium. The composition incorporates such essential oppositions as horizontal/vertical, edge/surface, plane/curve, and convexity/concavity. Perhaps the most obvious contrast, here as elsewhere in Smith's late work, is that between painting and sculpture. **Zig II**'s sculptural solidity and stability seem challenged, or at least tempered, by the vigorously brushed colors that animate its surfaces, including a dark scumbled red on the top horizontal bar, bright orange over yellow on the two vertical planes farthest to the right, and black over blue on the other elements. Furthermore, even though it is fully three-dimensional, **Zig II** is meant to be viewed from the front, like a painting. As such, it exemplifies the notably pictorial quality of much of Smith's sculpture, which ultimately has its origins in his early training as a painter. DC

Purchased with funds from the Edmundson
Art Foundation, Inc.; Des Moines
Art Center Permanent Collections, 1994.333

Etching on paper, 41 3/4 x 77 1/2 inches
(106 x 196.9 cm)

kiki smith

American, born 1954   **Sueño,** 1992

Over the past twenty years, Kiki Smith's art, focusing usually on the female body or parts thereof, moved from what was thought of as the fringes of the art world to center stage. What has changed more than the artist's work is the mainstream's positive reevaluation of an approach to content and to artmaking that Smith pursues. First, content – especially with a social and political edge – has come to the fore. And second, there is renewed comfort with art in which the artist's hand is clearly revealed in making the work of art.

As early as 1976 Smith participated in the group of socially and politically directed artists in New York known as Colab (Collaborative Projects), whose members included John Ahearn, Mike Glier, Jenny Holzer, and Christy Rupp, among others. But Smith's work generally has not been driven by a social or political program. Rather it is a result of her vision regarding presentation of the human body: "I chose the body as a subject, not consciously, but because it is the one form that we all share; it's something that everybody has their own authentic experience with. I try to make my work a kind of mantra like something one can circle around, fill with their own life. It's not didactic, telling people how they should think. It's

more like opening a can of worms. All the life that happens between their tongue and the anus."[1]

Smith works most often in prints, drawings, and sculptures. Focusing on organs, systems, and the whole body, she practices a new level of realism. The realism is not in the form of heightened photographic verisimilitude, but in representing aspects of the body and its functions that have been ignored despite their fundamental importance: menstrual bleeding, urinating, weeping, ejaculating, and so forth. Sometimes her materials give a poetic quality to the work, like glass beads representing a trail of urine. The subjects often are presented in a straightforward manner, but the results can be unsettling because viewers are not accustomed to seeing such subjects addressed.

Smith was born in Nuremberg, Germany in 1954, to American parents. Art came naturally to her: her mother was an opera singer, her father the sculptor David Smith, and her sister, Seton, also is an artist. Smith was intrigued by the body early on: "I grew up in a family with lots of illness. There was a preoccupation with the body. Also, being Catholic, making things physical, they're obsessed with the body. It seemed to me to be a form that suited me really well – to talk through the body about the way we're here and how we're living."[2] In 1982 she had her first one-person show, at The Kitchen in New York, and since then she has exhibited extensively internationally.

In 1985 Smith started making drawings based on the classic anatomy text **Gray's Anatomy**. Further, she earned her certification as an emergency medical technician at Bedford Stuyvesant Brooklyn Interfaith Hospital, finding that, "It is physically very beautiful to look at the exposure of the insides and outsides at the same time."[3]

The Art Center's **Sueño** shows a reclining full figure of nondescript gender in an almost fetal position, floating in an unknown space, and seemingly asleep or dreaming (the title means "sleeper"). The figure is devoid of skin, its musculature relaxed but exposed. A second print in the Art Center's collection, **My Blue Lake** (1995), is a curious image of the human body. It actually is a self-portrait based upon a photographic image made with a very rare camera in the British Museum. It provides a 360-degree image of the sitter, in this instance the artist. It therefore shows her hair from the back, the tattoo on her shoulder, her face, and so forth. It can stand as a metaphor for Smith's description of her art: "a meandering around the body."[4] IMD

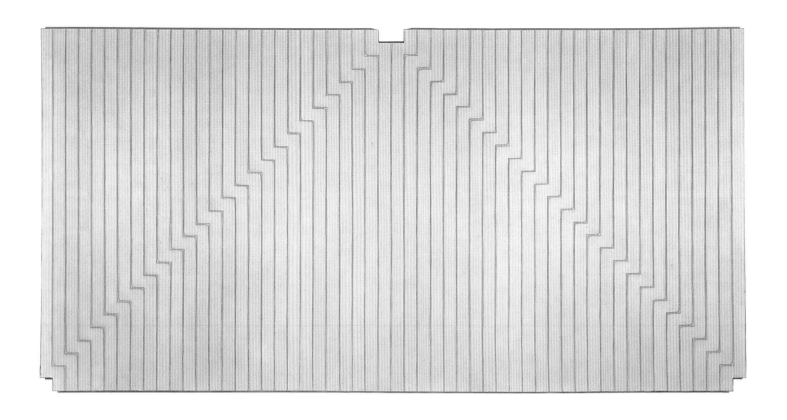

Aluminum paint on canvas,
77 1/2 x 149 inches (195.6 x 377.2 cm)

frank stella

American, b. 1936   **Union Pacific,** 1960

One of the most formally inventive painters of the modern period, Frank Stella was born in Malden, Massachusetts in 1963. He attended the Phillips Academy in Andover, Massachusetts in the early 1950s, and graduated from Princeton University in New Jersey in 1958 with a Bachelor of Arts degree in history. Stella's proximity to New York during his undergraduate years was of enormous importance, as he was able to see exhibitions of Abstract Expressionist painting, as well as work by contemporaries such as Jasper Johns. Remarkably precocious, Stella arrived at a mature approach to painting almost immediately after leaving Princeton. Although his works of 1958 are composed of colorful, softly painted bars, by the end of that year these forms had coalesced to form his signature "Black Paintings," monochromatic works featuring symmetrical compositions seemingly devoid of gesture or emotion. The clarity of Stella's forms and their apparent lack of expressive reference would characterize all of the artist's work, giving rise to his reputation as an extraordinarily gifted formalist. As he would note in an often-quoted interview in 1964: "What you see is what you see."

From the outset Stella worked in series, and after completing the twenty-four "Black Paintings," he created twelve "Aluminum Paintings" in 1960. These were the artist's first shaped canvases and within the series there exist eight distinct shapes. All feature small, rectilinear notches, the patterns of which Stella used to compose the arrangement of stripes. While the title of the Art Center's **Union Pacific** refers to the well-known railway line, other works in the series draw on Stella's love of automobiles and auto racing, for example, **Marquis de Portago** (1960), whose title derives from a Spanish aristocrat killed during a celebrated auto race in 1957.   continued on page 268

Purchased with funds from the Anna K.
Meredith Endowment; Des Moines Art Center
Permanent Collections, 1983.58

Mixed media on etched
magnesium, 128 x 120 x 18 ¹/₂ inches
(325.1 x 304.8 x 47 cm)

frank stella

Interlagos, 1983

In subsequent years Stella pursued the possibilities suggested by the shaped canvas with inventive, even breathtaking, results. Among the series that resulted were "Copper Paintings" (1960–61), "Concentric Squares" (1962–63), and "Notched V Paintings" and "Running V Paintings" (1964–65). An important breakthrough occurred in the early 1970s, when Stella began to project the stripes of his earlier work into relief planes. This began with the "Polish Village" paintings of 1970–73, and in subsequent years he developed series of painted relief constructions featuring often extravagant color applied to honeycomb aluminum panels. This continued through the 1970s in richly titled groupings such as the "Brazilian Series" (1974–75) and "Exotic Bird Series" (1976–80).

In 1980 Stella began to work on Foamcore maquettes for a large series of "Circuits" (1981–84). The series, all titled after auto racetracks, consists of sixty-eight large reliefs all expanded from an initial group of twenty-four maquettes. While some of these were fabricated of aluminum, others, such as Des Moines's **Interlagos** (1983), were composed of etched magnesium and then painted. Recalling Stella's ongoing fascination with auto racing, the titles in the series are based on celebrated racetracks, among them Silverstone, Talladega, and Zandvoort.

In many ways the "Circuits" summarize Stella's art since he began to work in relief in 1970. Extravagantly complex in their composition and applied color, the "Circuits" range from intricate, dense designs to open, sinuously graphic lines carving through space. **Interlagos** combines both aspects, for while a rectilinear outline defines the upper-right corner of the composition, a web of cacophonous color and flowing line explodes toward the lower right and culminates in a single sharp point. **NB**

Gift of Mary and John Pappajohn; Des Moines
Art Center Permanent Collections,
1998.28.a–d

Four panels, latex and tar on vinyl tiles
mounted on Masonite, each, 48 ¹/₄ x 48 x
1 ⁵/₈ inches (122.5 x 121.9 x 4.1 cm);
overall, 96 ¹/₂ x 96 x 1 ⁵/₈ inches (245.11 x
243.8 x 4.1 cm)

donald sultan

American, born 1951   **Migs,** 1984

Donald Sultan began his academic study of art in the early 1970s, a time when two of the most powerful phenomena in postwar art in the United States simultaneously made an enormous impression within the art world. Pop artists took their most characteristic images from the media, and Minimal artists took their images and materials from industrial manufacturing. Both Pop and Minimal Art appeared highly impersonal.

Sultan absorbed aspects of this heritage. Many of Sultan's paintings are based on photographs of events taken from newspapers and magazines – indeed, there exists a photograph of Sultan's studio that shows such clippings pinned to the wall above his paints. And Sultan uses industrial materials. The surface on which he makes his paintings begins with a stretcher bar onto which he bolts four-foot square sheets of plywood, adding layers of Masonite, twelve-inch squares of vinyl tiles, and then a coat of rubber. The result is nearly as much an **object** made of industrial materials as it is a painting. Pop artis Andy Warhol typically repeated the same reproduced image in a grid and likewise Minimal artist Donald Judd often serialized units of the same shape and dimensions – the repetition and grid suggesting the assembly line and manufactured objects. Similarly, Sultan's work is built upon an underlying grid of vinyl tiles and often a larger grid from butting together four of the four-foot units.

Sultan did more than absorb this industrial heritage from an earlier decade. He was among the youngest of a generation of painters such as Lois Lane, Robert Moscowitz, and Susan Rothenberg who built upon this heritage by finding ways of making paintings more explicitly personal.

The bright and cleanly finished surfaces of Pop Art paintings and much Minimal Art give way in Sultan's paintings of the late 1970s and since to captivatingly rich but dark, almost morose surfaces. Sultan's strongly worked surfaces – often scraped and burned – reveal the labor of their making and put no bloom on his bleak images of fires, warships, military planes, bombed electrical lines, and the decaying industrial rust belt. And yet despite the disturbing subjects, the potential harrowing nature of the paintings is tempered through all the formal information such as the rich and complexly worked surfaces, the bold silhouette of figure against background, and the underlying but visible grid pattern.

Sultan also is well known for his still-life paintings and drawings. While these works are beautiful by almost any standards, they are not a cheery celebration of nature's goodness. Sultan stated: "Now our landscape is all industrial and nature is receding."[1] When he made sculptures of lemons, he made them from lead because it is poisonous: "...I am involved in the idea of objects being abstract and also unnatural."[2]

The Art Center's **Migs** is characteristic of Sultan's paintings that derive from destructive events photographically recorded in the media. The three Mig jets are silhouetted against a background that recalls the paintings of fires. It is a large-format work resulting from combining four of the forty-eight-inch-square units to create the surface for the image.

Sultan grew up in Asheville, North Carolina. His father wanted to be a painter but decided he could not make a living at it. He continued painting as an avocation and took his son to art museums while making his living in the family tire business. Sultan recalls visits to that business and the smell of rubber: "It's not so very different from the rubber I use now. But you always think of these things later. He painted and he always had his place filled with pictures."[3] Sultan attended the University of North Carolina at Chapel Hill. After attempts at majoring in drama and then in film and television, he turned to art and received his Bachelor of Fine Arts degree in 1973. He subsequently attended The School of The Art Institute of Chicago from which he received his Master of Fine Arts in 1975. IMD

Gift of the Des Moines Association
of Fine Arts; Des Moines Art Center
Permament Collections, 1921.1

Oil on canvas, 51 ¹/₂ x 42 inches
(130.8 x 106.7 cm)

henry ossawa tanner

American, 1859–1937   **The Disciples See Christ Walking on the Water,** c. 1907

Henry Ossawa Tanner was born in Philadelphia in 1859. His father was an African Methodist Episcopal bishop. Tanner's interest in painting developed early, but he had few opportunities to study. In 1880, however, Tanner became the first black student to attend The Pennsylvania Academy of Fine Arts, studying for two years with Thomas Eakins. From 1882 to 1888 Tanner lived with his parents and tried to establish his career as an artist. In 1888 he moved to Atlanta and set up a photography studio. When the studio failed one year later, Tanner took a position teaching drawing at Clark University in Atlanta.

In 1890 Tanner had an unsuccessful show of his work in Cincinnati, but Bishop Joseph Crane Hartzell, who had sponsored Tanner's appointment at Clark, bought several of his works so that he could go to Europe. Settling in Paris in 1892, Tanner attended the Académie Julian under Jean-Joseph Benjamin-Constant and Jean-Paul Laurens and joined the prestigious American Art Club.

Typhoid fever forced Tanner's return to Philadelphia in 1892. He began to exhibit and sell some of his paintings, and was invited to read a paper on "The American Negro in Art" in Chicago in 1893. He returned to Paris in 1894, and began to exhibit at the Salon, frequently receiving prizes and selling his work.

In 1897 Tanner traveled extensively through Egypt, Palestine, and Italy, and thereafter religious scenes became his major focus. From 1902 to 1904 Tanner lived in Mount Kisco, New York, returning to France from 1904 to 1917, spending winters in Paris and summers at Le Touquet. It was during this time that he painted the Art Center's **The Disciples See Christ Walking on the Water**, one of his most important religious paintings.

Tanner's interpretation of this subject is very unusual. The passage is from Matthew 14:24–28: "But the ship was now in the midst of the sea, tossed with waves: for the wind was contrary. And in the fourth watch of the night Jesus went unto them, walking on the sea. And when the disciples saw him walking on the sea, they were troubled, saying, It is a spirit, and they cried out for fear. But straightaway Jesus spake unto them, saying, Be of good cheer; it is I; be not afraid. And Peter answered him and said, Lord, if it be thou, bid me come unto thee on the water."

Tanner's composition does not focus on Christ, as is customary, but rather on the disciples. Christ, who is somewhat hard to identify in the upper left corner of the painting, is rendered totally abstractly, more like an oval of light than a figure. The disciples seem caught in surprise at the moment when they first see Christ, but Peter – the tallest disciple in the center of the boat – seems to be shown at the later moment of asking to join Christ on the water. The scene is devoid

of wind and the sea is calm, allowing reflections of the mast and the lines of the boat's wake to help direct viewers' attention to Christ. The reflection of the moon in the lower left corner rendered in Tanner's reductive palette of very rich blues with violet and green also directs light up toward Christ. All of these elements combine to make this one of the most mysterious and compelling interpretations of this scene.

In 1917 Tanner was commissioned by the Iowa Federation of Colored Women's Clubs to paint a posthumous portrait of Booker T. Washington. Also in 1917 Tanner entered the American Red Cross in France, becoming a lieutenant and serving until 1919. From 1920 until he died in 1937, he established himself as the leading black American artist and regularly welcomed younger black artists to his studio. In 1922 he had a one-artist exhibition at the Des Moines Association of Fine Arts. Four paintings from this exhibition and another held in Kansas City, Kansas that same year came to the Art Center: **The Disciples See Christ Walking on the Water** (c. 1907), **Le Touquet** (c. 1910), **Near East Scene**, (c. 1910), and **Christ Learning to Read** (1910–14). DL

Purchased with funds from Rose F.
Rosenfield; Des Moines Art Center Permanent
Collections, 1988.7

Portfolio of ten lithographs with
collage and drawing, each,
30 1/2 x 22 1/4 inches (77.5 x 56.5 cm)

cy twombly

American, born 1928   **Natural History Part I, Mushrooms**, 1974

Cy Twombly was born in 1928 in Lexington, Virginia. He studied art at Black Mountain College in North Carolina, where he was a fellow student with Robert Rauschenberg. Twombly developed stylistically as an Abstract Expressionist, affirming the primacy of the painted surface as opposed to pictorial illusion. Like that of many of his contemporaries such as Rauschenberg and Jasper Johns, his work retains a connection to the visual world through the use of recognizable imagery. But instead of incorporating photographic images or real and painted objects, Twombly used handwritten words and numbers as formal elements. His work is characterized by a highly intuitive and personal use of gestural marks and script, layering and obliteration. His scribbled strokes have been likened to "the automatic writing and psychic improvisation of the surrealists."[1] Twombly moved permanently to Italy in 1957, where the eternal presence of the ancient classical cultures of the Mediterranean deeply infused his work.

Twombly's earliest prints are monotypes with images scratched into cardboard. He later began publishing editioned etchings as an outcome of visits to Rauschenberg, who was making prints at Universal Limited Art Editions on Long Island, New York, although printmaking never became a major interest for

Twombly. Most of his seventy-seven prints were produced in cycles or portfolios, executed during brief periods of work. Possibly the technical complications and indirectness of collaborative workshop printmaking were unsuited to his very private and direct way of working.

In 1974, however, Twombly created two portfolios, **Natural History Part I: Mushrooms**, and **Natural History Part II: Some Trees of Italy**. His highly personal sense of history permeates these two works. Both suites are boxed in portfolios covered in green laid paper with the title printed in dark green ink. The text pages are set in a Roman typeface printed in a warm gray ink. This elegant and traditional presentation contrasts markedly and most likely intentionally with the appearance of the prints themselves.

Mushrooms is a suite of ten prints employing from twelve to twenty-three colors printed with lithographic stones, granolithographs, and collotype, along with hand work in collage and paint stick. The untitled trompe l'oeil images appear to be collages of nineteenth-century German chromolithographs, photographs, the artist's own drawings, gummed labels, graph paper, transparent adhesive tape, jottings and scribbles with pencil and paint stick, erasures and stains. The antique images are labeled with their scientific names and comments such as "edible," "edible when cooked," or "poisonous." Some of these items are physically collaged onto the lithographs,

others are lithographically reproduced. Because active engagement is necessary to determine the real collage from printed illusion, the prints pose questions about the very illusionism that Twombly rejected in his painting. This technological tour de force was achieved thanks to the artist's collaboration with a master printer. It has been suggested that Twombly's experience in this highly complex project reaffirmed his commitment to direct work.

One print from this series bears the handwritten text "Leda and the Swan." Among its real and printed collaged elements are reproductions of two mushrooms with male and female genital characteristics, fragments of a reproduction of an Italian painting of Leda and the Swan from around 1500 which are scribbled over with paint stick, translucent graph paper, printed adhesive tape, blank labels, a sheet of lined paper with Twombly's pencil drawing of a swan, numerical notations, and lines of text.

continued on page 276

Purchased with funds from Rose F.
Rosenfield; Des Moines Art Center Permanent
Collections, 1988.8

Portfolio of eight lithographs with
collage and drawing, each, 30 ¹/₂ x 22 ¹/₄ inches
(77.5 x 56.5 cm)

cy twombly

Natural History Part II, Some Trees of Italy, 1976

These seemingly arbitrary components interact and construct meaning. The analytical elements allude to scientific inquiry. The Renaissance woodlands suggest places where mushrooms grow. The "male" and "female" mushrooms (which actually reproduce asexually) refer to the mythological sexual encounter of Leda and Zeus (the swan). The painting and theme also relate to Leonardo da Vinci's seminal painting **Leda**, known only from copies. Twombly's oblique allusion to Leonardo brings to mind that artist's notebooks, setting up a fascinating comparison with Twombly's work.

Some Trees of Italy is a set of eight prints. Aside from the title page, which incorporates collage, the series was executed in pure stone lithography with eight to thirteen colors per print. **Some Trees of Italy** presents on the title print seven old Italian chromolithographs of trees. This page is printed on a transparent overlay, and the scientific Latin names of the trees are written on each sheet. Each ensuing print is dedicated to one of the trees, and depicts, in tersely abbreviated form, its leaves and seeds. This series is reminiscent of a musical composition with a classical theme and variations. AW

Four panels, silkscreen ink and synthetic
polymer paint on canvas, overall,
32 1/8 x 32 1/8 inches (81.5 x 81.5 cm)

andy warhol

American, 1928–1987　　**The American Man – Watson Powell,** 1964

Andy Warhol, famous as a quintessential Pop artist in both work and lifestyle, was seminal in Pop's development during the late 1950s and provided American culture with some of its most enduring and revealing symbols. His work is characterized by commercial or common imagery, repetition or seriality, and the use of mechanized methods, such as silkscreen, that invest the work with an aura of anonymity. His art is focused on society, especially in its most widely known forms (whether people or products), and reveals a particular fascination with late twentieth-century celebrity and wealth. As a chronicler of American life, Warhol was sensitive to the role played by the media, not only as the producer of images, but as the creator of fame. Whether his subjects were known because of good looks, political power, business acumen, or just the vagaries of mass culture, Warhol was interested in people, and he added a distinctive chapter to the history of portraiture.

The American Man is a serial portrait of Des Moines insurance executive Watson Powell, Sr., of American Republic Insurance. It was commissioned by the company and is based on a publicity photograph of Powell. This 1964 portrait is typical of Warhol's serialized imagery carried out in a machinelike, imper-

sonal manner that parrots methods used by mass media. The portrayal of people as commodities was one of the themes Warhol explored most thoroughly during this period. But, at the same time, the repetition and the monumental scale also act as a kind of homage to success in the late modern world. Warhol was obviously fascinated by individuals who managed to separate themselves out in a huge, homogenized culture. By titling his painting "The American Man," Warhol seems to have been presenting Powell as the epitome of success in corporate America, with its blend of confidence and compromise.

Nearly every aspect of Warhol's career can be traced in the large collection of his works at the Art Center. Particularly useful in providing a context for the Powell work is another corporate portrait of a Des Moines-based business man, **Double Portrait of Gardner Cowles**, then the head of a family-owned communications company. Dated 1977, it is a more expressionistic, highly colored portrait that is consistent with Warhol's later style. Other Art Center portraits include **Marilyn, Liz, Martha Graham**, and three of Warhol's own **Self-Portrait and Skull** images (1976–78), along with examples from series such as **Campbell's Soup, Mona Lisa, Flowers**, and **Drag Queen**, many of which were gifts of the designer and Des Moines native Roy Halston.

Andy Warhol was born near Pittsburgh in McKeesport, Pennsylvania. After graduating from the Carnegie Institute of Technology in 1949, he came to New York where he quickly achieved success as a commercial designer. In the 1950s, like many younger artists, he began to react to the highly personal art of the Abstract Expressionists who then dominated the American art world. Along with Roy Lichtenstein, James Rosenquist, Claes Oldenburg, and others who would become known as Pop artists, Warhol turned to the everyday world for imagery and brought back a style of realism that reconnected American art to its traditional stylistic preference. By 1963 Warhol had added film to the media he used to explore and express contemporary life. He founded the journal **Interview** and published his diaries, autobiography, and other writings, all of which testify to his important role as a shrewd and witty commentator on the culture of his time. A celebrity himself, he was perhaps as well known to the general public for his lifestyle as for his art. **LRD**

Purchased with funds from the Edmundson
Art Foundation, Inc.; Des Moines
Art Center Permanent Collections, 1993.17.a-c

Three gelatin silver prints, a and c, 21 ¹/₈ inches
in diameter (53.7 cm); b, 21 ¹/₈ x
17 ¹/₈ inches (53.7 x 43.5 cm); overall,
20 x 60 inches (50.8 x 152.4 cm)

carrie mae weems

American, born 1953 **Sea Island Series (Thomas),** 1992

Carrie Mae Weems's visual medium is photography. Her varied formats include images of people and activities as she encounters them; people and objects that she arranges in settings; and modification of appropriated historical photographs. The images are black and white or monochromatically tinted. They sometimes are accompanied by words that contribute to both pictorial values and meaning. Often she works in a series based on a unifying concept, and a single work may include multiple images as well as text.

Weems has made series of works that focus on her own family, racist jokes, and stereotypes about African-Americans, African-American icons seen in such objects as salt and pepper shakers, issues surrounding the use of the term "colored," and family interaction around the kitchen table. The Art Center's seven works, some of which are multiple images, all come from the "Sea Island Series" made in 1991 and 1992. These works exemplify the ways in which Weems weaves together her interests and formal studies in photography, folklore, and

African-American history, which since 1984 have earned her a growing international reputation.

The source of these images is the Sea Islands off the Georgia and South Carolina coasts. In the early eighteenth century, these islands were home to thousands of African-Americans who maintained aspects of their cherished heritage while melding others with their new life circumstances. Weems reflected this mixture in images that she photographed on site, recording her impressions of surviving natural elements and artifacts such as landscapes, buildings, and graveyards, as well as more recent expressions of the culture on these islands. In some of the images, the artist herself, dressed in historical garb, interacts with history.

Of the twenty-one works in the series, three are triptychs based on daguerreotypes taken by J.T. Zealy in 1850 and in the collection of The Peabody Museum at Harvard University. In **Thomas**, Weems combined a frontal image of a male figure with two profiles, one of which she presented as originally formatted and another that has been reversed. She then tinted all three images blue. The Art Center's additional six works exemplify the full range of subject and format within this series. **Thomas** was pur-

chased with funds from the Edmundson Art Foundation and the six other works were a generous gift from The Bohen Foundation. Also part of the "Sea Island Series," but not represented in the collection, are approximately thirty ceramic plates with texts.

Born in Portland, Oregon in 1953, Weems holds a Bachelor of Fine Arts degree from the California Institute of the Arts (1981) and a Master of Fine Arts degree from the University of California, San Diego (1984). She pursued additional graduate studies in African-American folklore at the University of California, Berkeley. Weems has exhibited widely in major institutions throughout the United States and had a ten-year retrospective in 1993. IMD

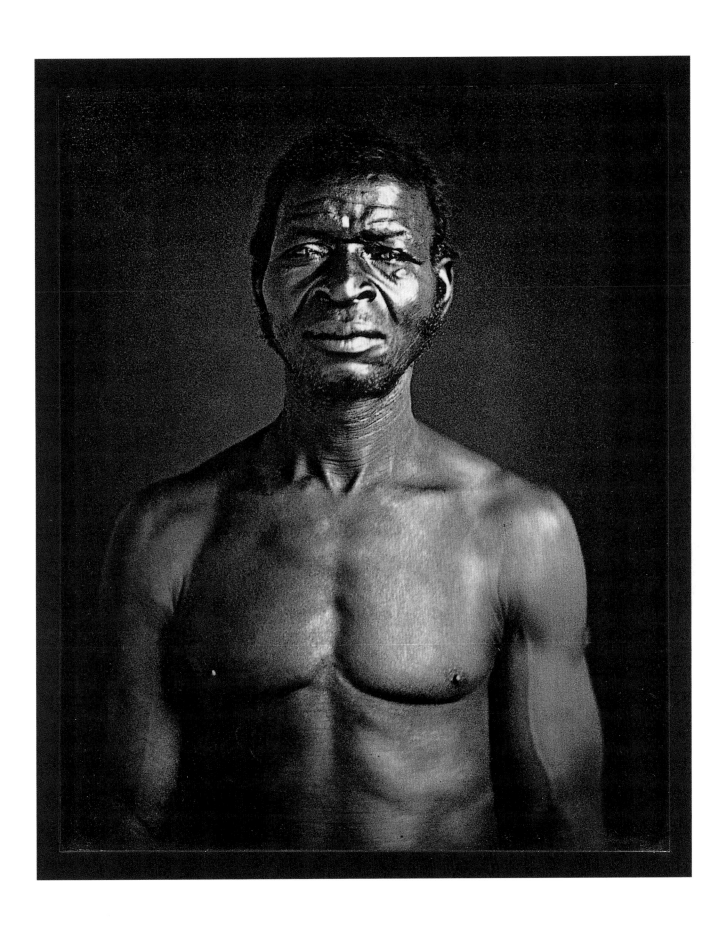

Douglas fir, pine, redwood, and
vermillian woods, 28 x 36 x 18 inches
(71.1 x 91.4 x 45.7 cm)

h. c. westermann

American, 1922–1981   **Phantom in a Wooden Garden,** 1970

H. C. Westermann, like Joseph Cornell, was an American original – an artist of great innovation who worked virtually alone and had no following, yet created distinctly personal work of enduring meaning. Both artists were also deeply self-involved, and Westermann's art in particular is chiefly autobiographical, marked especially by his war experiences as a Marine in Korea. Images of horror and humor alternate in his wood sculptures and his more cartoonlike, witty drawings.

Westermann began his adult life with military service, enlivened by a USO tour in Asia as an acrobat. Returning to the United States in 1947, H(orace) C(lifford) Westermann went to Chicago. He studied advertising and design at The School of The Art Institute of Chicago, returning to the Marines in 1951 and spending a year in Korea. He resettled in Chicago, reentered the Art Institute in 1952 on a second GI Bill, and also began working as a carpenter. Wood soon became his preferred material and he applied his considerable woodworking skills to his sculpture, exclusively fabricated from wood along with metal, glass, and found objects by 1954.

The influences on Westermann's art are varied and eclectic; all of them were transformed through his own vision into unusual and often satirical juxtapositions and personal fantasies. The Art Center's **Phantom in a Wooden Garden** shows the lighter side of his nature and consequently is in some ways more related to his drawings than to his sculpture. Moreover, **Phantom** is highly graphic, with crisply silhouetted and stylized landscape elements – a double-arching tree, a cactus, and a more architectural column surmounted by a reflecting globe – arranged friezelike on a checkerboard base. A towering, attenuated, stick figure races through the "garden," overlapping the fixed vegetal forms. On one of its arms is the word "Cliff," the name Westermann used with his friends; the implication is that the artist himself is the protagonist here. The feeling is one of mystery, however, rather than fright. In this regard **Phantom** shares affinities with certain Surrealist works, notably the enigmatic images of René Magritte, and in sculpture, with some of the early metaphysical, narrative works by Alberto Giacometti. Yet dominant in all of Westermann's sculpture is his love for wood and the perfection of his craft – aspects of his art that imbue even his most violent and disturbing pieces with a quality and even a calm beauty that transcend their immediate narrative. **TRN**

Purchased with funds from the Edmundson
Art Foundation, Inc.; Des Moines
Art Center Permanent Collections, 1997.6

Cast rubber, 27 x 30 x 34 inches
(68.6 x 76.2 x 86.4 cm)

rachel whiteread

British, born 1963   **Untitled (Plinth),** 1995–96

Although some of Rachel Whiteread's sculptures may at first appear abstract, their forms are cast from real spaces and objects, most of which are in our domestic environment. The artist was in her mid-twenties when she developed her forms. The remarkably innovative sculptures are sensuous, but also have an industrial edge.

Whiteread was born in Ilford, England – outside of London – in 1963. She studied painting at Brighton Polytechnic (1982–85) and then sculpture at London's Slade School of Art (1985–87), where the sculptor Edward Allington introduced her to casting in wax and plaster. Casting has remained Whiteread's cardinal technique. Her student work included the wrapping of furniture and making a sculpture consisting of a shirt on a hanger with a hot water bottle inside – all domestic objects.

In 1987 Whiteread cast the inside of her closet, based on fond childhood memories of its darkness and warmth. Subsequently she made plaster casts of the interiors of domestic objects such as bathtubs. **Ghost** (1990), her first work to achieve great attention, was a plaster cast of an entire Victorian room. The following year Whiteread began to cast in rubber as well, and made casts of mattresses in both plaster and rubber. She was commissioned in 1993 to make her first public sculpture, which was a concrete cast

of the interior of a three-story Victorian house. This highly controversial work received an extraordinary amount of attention in the media. The day that Whiteread was notified that **House** was to be torn down, she also learned that she had become the first women to win the distinguished Turner Prize from London's Tate Gallery.

In 1994 Whiteread added polyester resin to her materials repertoire, which now included completely opaque plaster, slightly translucent rubber, and very translucent polyester resin. The works made from polyester resin and rubber have an industrial reference because of the objects customarily produced from these materials. In 1995, for the Carnegie International, she used polyester resin to cast the space underneath 100 tables. By focusing our attention on the space beneath tables and chairs or above mattresses, Whiteread makes us aware of everyday spaces we inhabit but ignore: she makes the invisible visible. The seemingly abstract works give form to space that is quite real.

Plinth is a rubber cast of the space between the two elements that hold up a mortuary table. The amber-colored rubber creates an extremely sensuous, velvety surface. Moreover, the somewhat translucent edges appear to glow, creating an object exceptionally tempting to touch. There exists a similar version consisting of two such casts colored in an off-white that reads as more opaque (private collection).

Whiteread said, "I am making objects that are, I think, very much like tombs, the way things are incarcerated, how you know there is something inside but you never actually see what it is."[1] The choice of a mortuary table for the casting of **Plinth** is consistent with Whiteread's reference to tombs and also with a project for the international art show Documenta (1982), for which she made casts from mortuary slabs. It is noteworthy that in her youth Whiteread did maintenance work at Highgate Cemetery in North London. Yet her interest in the form of **Plinth** lies primarily in the way in which its form resembles a pedestal, hence its title.

Whiteread represented England in the 1997 Venice Biennale, the youngest English artist to have had that honor; she won the Premio 2000 Prize for outstanding achievement. She has had one-person museum shows in Basel; Boston; Eindhoven, The Netherlands; London; Madrid; and Philadelphia. **Plinth** was in an exhibition at the Los Angeles County Museum of Art (1997) that first introduced Whiteread's work to the West Coast of the United States. IMD

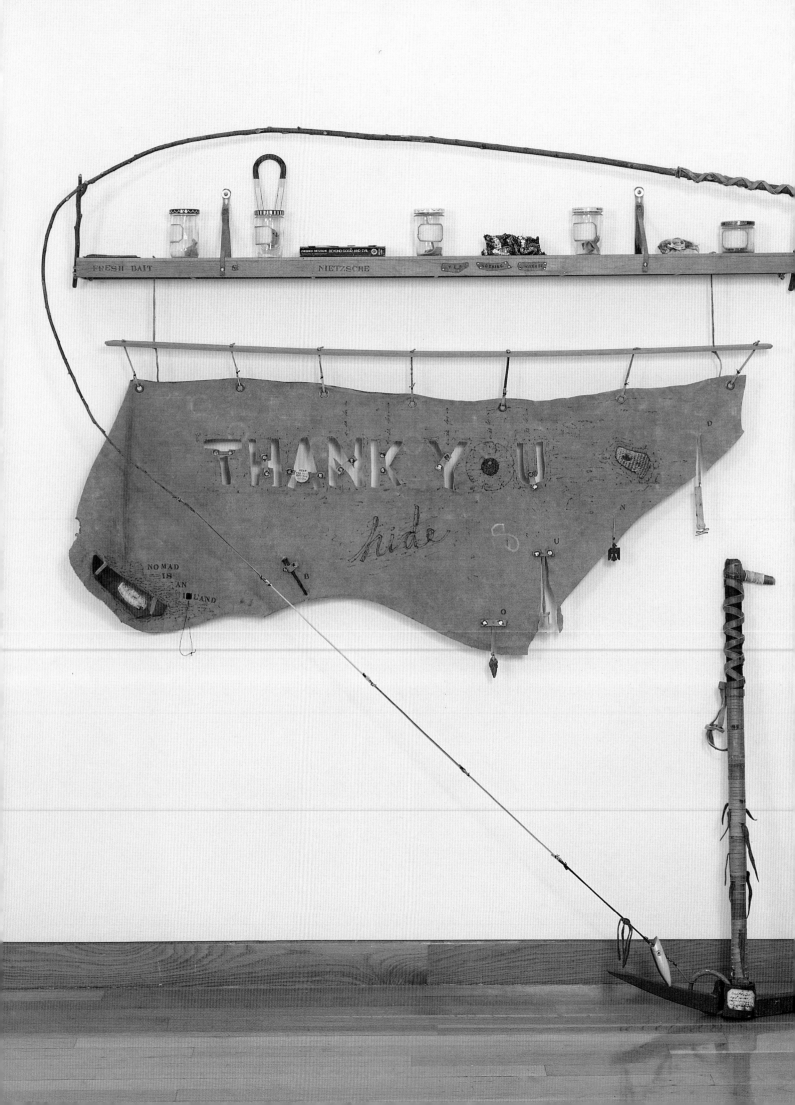

Purchased with funds from the Coffin Fine
Arts Trust; Nathan Emory Coffin
Collection of the Des Moines Art Center,
1977.9

Wood, leather, ink, and charcoal on
cowhide, with pickaxe, found objects, and six
watercolor-on-paper drawings,
74 x 160 ¹/₂ inches (188 x 407.7 cm)

william t. wiley

American, born 1937   **Thank You Hide,** 1970–71

Associated with Funk Art of the Northern California Bay Area, William Wiley's art is eccentric, confounding, and full of visual and verbal puns. His wide range of works, including prints and film, involves highly personal iconography and a tone of visual experiment. Disparate elements, whether drawn or actual objects, and enigmatic writings that seldom provide a direct clue to interpretation are typical of his art. His clear interest in the metaphysical (perhaps influenced by Zen philosophy) is combined with a high-spirited humor and irreverent but subtle wit.

The Art Center's **Thank You Hide** is a complex assemblage made up of a cowhide suspended beneath a wooden shelf bearing a series of apparently unrelated objects. Arching above the shelf is a long, thick stick that ends with a cord tied to a pickaxe resting against the wall beneath the hide. The hide has "THANK YOU" cut out and "hide" written in Wiley's distinctive script below it. Roughly the shape of the United States, the hide, according to a statement by the artist, is the central element in the overall theme of the contact between indigenous cultures and Europeans.[1] Arrowheads, leather thongs, and various tokens suggest Native American life; the handle of the pickaxe metamorphoses into a peace pipe, ornamented in Native American fashion. The phrase "No mad is an island," in the lower left

(or "Southwestern" area) of the hide is found elsewhere in Wiley's work and is typical of his punning word play.

Directly related to this piece is a series of six watercolors that, while functioning as independent works, provide studies for aspects of **Thank You Hide** and a guide to its background and possible interpretations. In the inscriptions for each watercolor, the artist gave details about the objects included in the larger piece and how they came into his possession. One describes how he bought the hide at a flea market and later, while reading a copy of Nietzsche's **Beyond Good and Evil**, he felt grateful to the person who had loaned him the book, and "When I said the words thank [you] I saw them cut into the hide." In the assemblage the book is placed on the shelf above the hide. The variety and openness of meanings in the Art Center's work are common in Wiley's art.

Born in Bedford, Indiana, Wiley moved at age ten to Washington State. He studied at the San Francisco Art Institute, receiving his Bachelor of Fine Arts degree in 1960 and his Master of Fine Arts in 1962. His earliest works were affected by the prevailing expressionist style of that school, but soon Dada and Duchamp became dominant influences. Often grouped with West Coast artists Robert Arneson and Robert Hudson as well as H. C. Westermann, Wiley taught at the University of California at Davis (1962–73) and the San Francisco Art Institute (1963 and 1966–67). LRD

Purchased with funds from the National
Endowment for the Arts and the Edmundson
Art Foundation, Inc.; Des Moines
Art Center Permanent Collections, 1975.7

Etched glass and steel, 60 x 60 x 86 inches
(152.4 x 152.4 x 218.4 cm)

christopher wilmarth

American, 1943–1987   **Blue Release**, 1972–73

Christopher Wilmarth's geometric compositions of steel and glass have their roots in Minimalism, the dominant sculptural idiom in New York during the 1960s. But while the Minimalists stressed the literal nature of their materials and avoided expressive compositions, Wilmarth found metaphorical qualities in his materials and combined them in poetic ways. The Art Center's **Blue Release** and other architectonic floor pieces of the 1970s, for example, were conceived not just as abstract structures, but as "places," replete with connotations of shelter, their elements suggesting walls and windows. The interplay of smoky glass and dark steel was intended to evoke the contrasts of light and shadow peculiar to Manhattan.

A native of Sonoma, California, Wilmarth moved to New York in 1960 and earned his Bachelor of Fine Arts degree from the Cooper Union in 1965. Following his graduation he supported himself as a cabinetmaker, and from 1967 to 1969 worked as a studio assistant to the Minimalist sculptor Tony Smith. In the last year Wilmarth was appointed professor of sculpture and drawing at the Cooper Union, and remained in

that position until 1980. He also taught as a visiting artist at Yale University, Columbia University, and the University of California, Berkeley, and received grants from the Guggenheim Foundation, the National Endowment for the Arts, and other institutions.

In the late 1960s Wilmarth drew on his cabinetmaker's skills to create elegant wood-and-glass constructions whose formal clarity was in keeping with the Minimalist aesthetic. The experience of painting Tony Smith's sculptures encouraged Wilmarth to experiment with different ways of treating his glass surfaces, and he discovered that by acid-etching the glass he could render it smoky and translucent, and bring out its natural blue or green cast. In 1970 he abandoned wood and began to tie his etched-glass elements together with steel suspension cable. Two years later he added sheet steel to his vocabulary and arrived at his signature style, epitomized by **Blue Release**.

Like all of Wilmarth's floor pieces, **Blue Release** must be viewed from every direction in order for it to be completely understood. From one vantage point the sculpture seems to consist of a square steel plate leaning impossibly against a vertical sheet of frosted glass and casting a wedgelike

shadow behind it. Only by walking around the work does one see that the steel has been cut and bent into a self-supporting, tentlike structure, and that the "shadow" is actually a piece of steel that holds the glass in place.

At this juncture of luminous, fragile glass and dark, powerful steel, a kind of alchemy occurs that transforms both materials: the glass absorbs the blackish strength of the steel, while the heavy metal, viewed through the cloudy glass, is softened, blued, and rendered almost weightless.[1] The apparent dematerialization of the steel is reflected in the work's title, which evokes the release of the soul from the body, its ascension toward the blue of the heavens, and the ultimate triumph of spirit over matter. DC

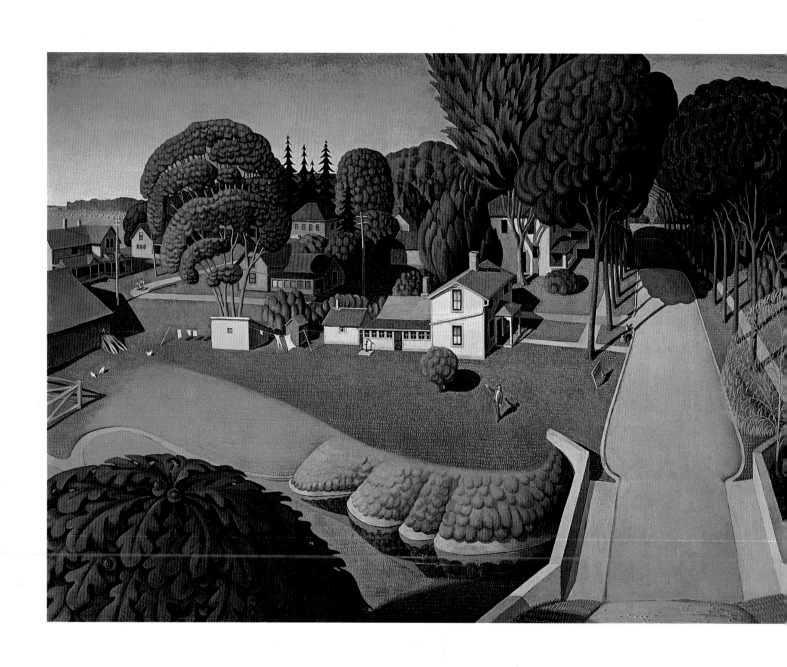

Purchased jointly by the Des Moines Art
Center and The Minneapolis Institute of Arts;
with funds from Mrs. Howard H. Frank and
the Edmundson Art Foundation, Inc., 1982.2

Oil on Masonite, 30 x 40 inches
(76.20 x 101.60 cm)

grant wood

American, 1891–1942   **The Birthplace of Herbert Hoover,** 1931

Grant Wood is without question the most famous artist from Iowa, and he chose the landscape and rural life of his native state as the main subjects of his work. His most famous painting, **American Gothic**, features a woman (Wood's sister) and a man gripping a pitchfork (Wood's dentist) in front of a house that still stands near Wood's birthplace. This painting, in the collection of The Art Institute of Chicago, is perhaps second only to Leonardo da Vinci's **Mona Lisa** as the most well-known and often parodied painting in the world.

Wood was born in 1891 on a farm near Anamosa, Iowa. He began painting at the age of fourteen and later was schooled in metal-work design in Minneapolis. In 1911 he sat in on a life-drawing class at the University of Iowa. The instructor was so moved by the young artist's talent that Wood was allowed to stay at no cost. He went on to study painting at The School of The Art Institute of Chicago, and upon returning to Iowa in 1919, taught many students at the Rosedale Country School and two public schools in Cedar Rapids. In the early 1930s Wood also founded an artists' colony and school at Stone City, near Cedar Rapids. Stone City was a vital gathering place for Midwestern artists of all generations. Wood joined the faculty of the University of Iowa, Iowa City in 1934, and taught there for the rest of his career.

In addition to teaching and creating numerous portraits and rural landscapes, Wood also traveled to France, Germany, and Italy. His ongoing study of art from different periods and cultures during these travels would prove influential to his work; although he was categorized as a regionalist because his paintings, drawings, and prints depict Midwestern rural life, much of his technique and style was influenced by European art. Cross-hatched paint application and the stylized clarity of Northern Gothic portraiture are the strongest examples of European influence on Wood's work.

West Branch, Iowa, near Iowa City, is the birthplace of another famous Iowan, President Herbert Hoover, who was in office from 1929 to 1933. In 1931 a group of Iowa businessmen asked Wood to paint an image of Hoover's birthplace as a gift for the president. Wood completed **The Birthplace of Herbert Hoover**, now in the Art Center's collection, but when the businessmen presented it to Hoover, he rejected it. The figure in the center of the painting points to the small cabin (still standing) in which Hoover was born. But Hoover "did not approve of the painting in which the actual cabin is obstructed by a house that was not there at the time of Hoover's birth."[1]

Critics also responded negatively to the painting. In the early 1930s the United States was in the midst of a vast and devastating economic depression and the Midwest and South also were subject to a drought. Wood's aerial view of exotic, stylized trees, with perfectly formed and aligned leaves, and lush, rolling hills of rich, verdant green shows no hint of the mortgage foreclosures and the dust bowls that were the reality of rural life. In her book titled **My Brother, Grant Wood**, Nan Wood relates that the critics "couldn't decide whether Grant was glorifying or satirizing President Hoover. Considering the artist, most of them decided it was satire."[2]

In 1934 **The Birthplace of Herbert Hoover** was purchased by Des Moines businessman Gardner Cowles. Over the next fifty years, it passed through the hands of many collectors and was placed on loan to The Metropolitan Museum of Art, New York. Although the Des Moines Art Center, which opened six years after Wood died in 1942, had acquired all of his prints, by 1982 it still did not have a painting. In a collaborative effort with The Minneapolis Institute of Arts, the Art Center purchased **The Birthplace of Herbert Hoover**. Both museums were interested in the painting; rather than compete, they decided to share it. The cities are only four hours apart, and the painting is rotated between the two museums every two years. TAC

Abakanowicz

1 Quoted in Chicago, Museum of Contemporary Art, **Magdalena Abakanowicz** (New York: Abbeville Press, 1982), p. 94.
2 Letter to I. Michael Danoff, November 15, 1993, Archives, Des Moines Art Center.
3 Ibid.
4 Quoted in Chicago 1982 (note 1), p. 102.

Arp

1 Quoted in Jean Arp, **Dichtende Maler, Malende Dichter** (St. Gall: Kunstverein St. Gallen, 1957), preface.
2 Quoted in James Thrall Soby, "Introduction: The Search for New Forms," in New York, The Museum of Modern Art, **Arp** (New York, 1958), p. 7.
3 Quoted in Eduard Trier, **Jean Arp, Sculpture: His Last Ten Years** (New York: Harry N. Abrams, Inc., 1968), p. xii.

Bailey

1 William Bailey to James T. Demetrion, January 5, 1982, Archives, Des Moines Art Center.

Bickerton

1 Shaun Caley, "Ashley Bickerton," **Flash Art**, November/December 1988, p. 80.
2 Ibid.

Blake

1 Marilu Knode, Interview, "Nayland Blake," **Journal of Contemporary Art**, Spring 1992, p. 20.

Boltanski

1 Effie Stephano, "Existential Art," **Art and Artists** 9, 2 (May 1974), p. 25. Quoted in Mary Jane Jacob, "Introduction," in Chicago, Museum of Contemporary Art; Los Angeles, Museum of Contemporary Art; and New York, New Museum of Contemporary Art, **Christian Boltanski: Lessons of Darkness** (Chicago, 1988), p. 10.
2 Démosthène Davvetas, Interview with Boltanski, in **From the Europe of Old** (Amsterdam: Stedelijk Museum, 1987), unpag.

Brancusi

1 A detailed analysis of the different motifs of this tale is given in A. Aarne and S. Thompson, **Types of the Folk-Tale** (Helsinki, 1928), no. 301; and in J. Bolte and G. Polivka, **Anmerkungen zu den Kinder und Hausmarchen der Bruder Grimm** (Leipzig, 1913), vol. I, pp. 503–515. The latter offers an extensive list of references from all over the world.
2 Carola Giedion-Welcker, **Constantin Brancusi** (New York: George Braziller, Inc., 1959), p. 220.
3 Athena T. Spear, **Brancusi's Birds** (New York: New York University Press, 1969).
4 One **Bird in Space** was purchased by Edward Steichen and became the subject of a famous lawsuit in New York in 1927–28, after the US Customs refused to admit it as a work of art.
5 Eric Shanes, **Constantin Brancusi** (New York: Abbeville Press, 1989), p. 33.
6 The 1913 Armory Show was the first comprehensive and accessible manifestation of Modernist art assembled in the United States.

Butterfield

1 The artist says: "I first used the horse images as a metaphorical substitute for myself – it was a way of doing a self-portrait one step removed from the specificity of Deborah Butterfield." Quoted in Winston-Salem, NC, Southeastern Center for Contemporary Art, **Deborah Butterfield** (Winston-Salem, 1983), unpag.
2 Quoted in Janet Wilson, "The Mane Event," **Connoisseur** 222 (February 1992), p. 68.
3 Quoted in Wausau, Wisconsin, Leigh Yawkey Woodson Art Museum, **Mind and Beast: Contemporary Artists and the Animal Kingdom**, text by Thomas H. Garver (Wausau, 1992), p. 25.
4 Deborah Butterfield, letter to Julia Brown Turrell, March 2, 1987, Archives, Des Moines Art Center.

Calder

1 Quoted in Curtis Cate, "Calder Made Easy," **Horizon** 14, 1 (Winter 1972), p. 57.

Cassatt

1 Elsa Honig Fine, **Women and Art, A History of Women Painters and Sculptors from the Renaissance to the 20th Century** (Montclair, NJ: Allanheld, Osmun & Co. Publishers, Inc. and Abner Schram Ltd., 1978), p. 130.
2 Adelyn D. Breeskin, letter to Louise R. Noun, August 24, 1971, Archives, Des Moines Art Center.

Chagall

1 Michel Makarius, **Chagall, The Masterworks** (New York: Portland House, 1988), p. 88.
2 Ibid., p. 35.

Corot

1 New York, The Metropolitan Museum of Art, **The Greatest Landscape Painter of Our Time, COROT**, text by Michael Pantazzi (New York, 1996), p. 141.

Crawford

1 New York, Whitney Museum of American Art, **Ralston Crawford**, text by Barbara Haskell (New York, 1985), p. 28.

Derain

1 **The Nymphes** is not included in Michael Kellerman's catalogue raisonné of Derain's works.

Dove

1 H. Effa Webster, **Chicago Examiner**, March 15, 1912.
2 Herbert J. Seligmann, **Alfred Stieglitz Talking: Notes on Some of His Conversations, 1925–1931** (New Haven, CT: Yale University Press, 1966).
3 Elizabeth McCausland, "Dove, Man and Painter," **Parnassus**, December 1937.

Dubuffet

1 The quotations are from Jean Dubuffet, "Memoir on the Development of My Work from 1952," trans. Louise Varese, in New York, The Museum of Modern Art, **The Work of Jean Dubuffet** (New York, 1962), p. 77.

Dunlap

1 Des Moines Art Center, **This is Always Finished (David Dunlap)**, text by M. Jessica Rowe (Des Moines, 1989), pp. 6–8.

Ensor

1 Stephen C. McGough, James Ensor's **The Entry of Christ into Brussels in 1898** (doctoral dissertation, Stanford University, 1981).
2 A. Croquez, **L'Oeuvre gravé de J. Ensor**, no. 114. Auguste Taevernier, **J. Ensor, Catalogue illustré de ses gravures** (Ghent, 1973), lists only three states. A fourth state has subsequently been recognized.
3 Paul Haesaerts, **James Ensor** (New York: Harry N. Abrams, Inc., 1959).

Flavin

1 Dan Flavin, "…in daylight or cool white. An autobiographical sketch," **Artforum**, December 1965.
2 **"monuments" for V. Tatlin from Dan Flavin, 1964–1982** (Chicago: Donald Young Gallery for The Museum of Contemporary Art, Los Angeles, 1989), unpag.

Gauguin

1 Austin C. Wehrwein, "Gauguin Drawing on Back of Pastel Is Major Art Find," **The Des Moines Register**, February 11, 1959, pp. 1 and 6.
2 Washington, National Gallery of Art, and Chicago, The Art Institute of Chicago, **The Art of Paul Gauguin** (Washington, 1988), p. 268.

Gilmor

1 Statement by the artist, March 1996, Archives, Des Moines Art Center.

Goya

1 Eric Young, **Francisco Goya** (New York: St. Martin's Press, 1978), unpag.

Grooms

1 This and the following comments are from Lea Rosson DeLong, "An Interview with Red Grooms," Des Moines Art Center, August 16, 1990.

Guston

1 Quoted in Jerry Tallmer, "'Creation' Is for Beauty Parlors," **New York Post**, April 9, 1977, p. 22 (review of exhibition at David McKee Gallery).

2 Ross Feld, "Philip Guston," in San Francisco Museum of Modern Art, **Philip Guston** (San Francisco, 1980), p. 32.

Halley

1 Quoted in Kathryn Hixson, "Interview with Peter Halley," in **Peter Halley**, (Bordeaux: capc Musée d'art contemporain de Bordeaux, 1991), p. 17.

Henri

1 Donelson F. Hoopes, **Robert Henri 1865–1929** (New York: The Chapellier Galleries, Inc., 1976), unpag.

2 Ibid.

3 Jan van der Marck, **In Quest of Excellence: Civic Pride, Patronage, Connoisseurship** (Miami: Center for Fine Arts, 1984), p. 96. The Des Moines Art Center's collection also contains a monoprint by John Sloan of Isidora Duncan.

Holzer

1 New York, The Solomon R. Guggenheim Museum, **Jenny Holzer**, text by Diane Waldman (New York, 1989), p. 10.

2 Ibid.

3 Ibid.

Hopper

1 New York, Whitney Museum of American Art, **Edward Hopper: The Art and the Artist**, text by Gail Levin (New York: W.W. Norton & Company in association with the Whitney Museum of American Art, 1980), p. 52.

2 Clive Gregory, ed., **The Great Artists: Their Lives, Works and Inspiration** (London: Marshall Cavendish Ltd., 1986), p. 2786.

3 New York 1980 (note 1), p. 198.

Irwin

1 Quoted in Lawrence Weschler, **Seeing Is Forgetting the Name of the Thing One Sees: A Life of Contemporary Artist Robert Irwin** (Berkeley: University of California Press, 1982), p. 104.

2 Ibid., p. 107.

Jess

1 Quoted in Buffalo, Albright-Knox Art Gallery, **Jess, A Grand Collage**, text by Michael Auping (Buffalo, 1993), p. 19.

2 Jess, letter to I. Michael Danoff, November 11, 1993, Archives, Des Moines Art Center.

3 Ibid.

4 Ibid.

Kelly

1 Ellsworth Kelly, letter to I. Michael Danoff, November 22, 1993, Archives, Des Moines Art Center.

Klee

1 Quoted in Daniel-Henry Kahnweiler, **Klee** (Paris: Braun & Cie, 1950), p. 15.

Kokoschka

1 **Hans Tietze and Erika Tietze-Conrat** (1909), **Portrait of Mr. and Mrs. John Cowles** (1949), **The Feilchenfeldt Brothers** (1952), and **The Duke and Duchess of Hamilton** (1969). There is also one triple portrait of children, **Richard, Margery and John Davis** (1958).

2 Bela Petheo, **Missions and Commissions: Oskar Kokoschka in Minnesota 1949–1957** (Collegeville, MN: Saint John's University, 1991), p. 2.

3 Ibid., p. 3.

4 Ibid., p. 15.

5 Ibid.

Koons

1 Jeff Koons, conversation with the author, January 1992.

Krasner

1 Ellen G. Landau, **Lee Krasner: A Catalogue Raisonné** (New York: Harry N. Abrams, Inc., 1995), p. 10.

2 Ibid., p. 131.

Kuniyoshi

1 Quoted in New York, Whitney Museum of American Art, **Yasuo Kuniyoshi**, text by Lloyd Goodrich (New York, 1948), p. 44.

Leslie

1 Barbara Flynn, Interview with Alfred Leslie, in New York, Flynn Gallery, **Alfred Leslie: The Grisaille Paintings 1962–1967** (New York, 1991), p. 55.

LeWitt

1 Statement in **Art Now** (New York), June 1971, reprinted in New York, The Museum of Modern Art, **Sol LeWitt** (New York, 1978), p. 169.

Lichtenstein

1 New York, The Solomon R. Guggenheim Museum, **Roy Lichtenstein**, text by Diane Waldman (New York, 1993), p. 131.

Louis

1 Quoted in James McC. Truitt, "Art – Arid D.C. Harbors Touted 'New' Painters," **The Washington Post**, December 21, 1961, p. A20.

2 The term "Veil" was first used in print by William Rubin in "Younger American Painters," **Art International** 4 (January 1960), p. 27.

3 Robert Rosenblum, "**Morris Louis** at the Guggenheim Museum," **Art International** 7 (December 5, 1963), p. 24; New York, The Museum of Modern Art, **Morris Louis**, text by John Elderfield (New York, 1986), p. 55.

MacDonald-Wright

1 Stanton MacDonald-Wright, statement, in New York, Anderson Galleries, **The Forum Exhibition of Modern American Painters** (New York, 1916); reprint, New York: Arno Press, 1968, unpag.

2 Morgan Russell and Stanton MacDonald-Wright, "In Explanation of Synchromism," in Munich, Der Neue Kunstsalon, **Ausstellung der Synchromisten Morgan Russell, S. MacDonald-Wright** (Munich, 1913); trans. and reprinted in New York, Whitney Museum of American Art, **Synchromism and American Color Abstraction, 1910–1925**, text by Gail Levin (New York: George Braziller in association with the Whitney Museum of American Art, 1978), p. 129.

3 The illustration is opposite MacDonald-Wright's statement (note 1). The same picture is reproduced in Waldo Frank et al., eds., **America and Alfred Stieglitz: A Collective Portrait** (New York: The Literary Guild, 1934), pl. XVI, fig. B, with the caption "**Synchromy** (Oil) 1914."

4 Stanton MacDonald-Wright, letter to Donald M. Halley, Jr., May 11, 1963, Archives, Des Moines Art Center. Also closely related in composition to the 1914 **Organization 5** is **Conception Synchromy** (1914; Hirshhorn Museum and Sculpture Garden, Washington).

Mangold

1 Akron, Ohio, Akron Art Museum, **Robert Mangold: Paintings 1971–84** (Akron, 1984), p. 4.

2 Ibid., p. 55.

3 Ibid.

4 Quoted in Christel Sauer and Urs Raussmüller, **Robert Mangold** (Schaffhausen, Switzerland: Hallen Neue Kunst, 1993), p. 69.

5 Christel Sauer and Urs Raussmüller, **Robert Mangold (Studio Notes)** (Schaffhausen, Switzerland: Hallen Neue Kunst, 1993), p. 77 (February 2, 1991).

Marden

1 New York, The Solomon R. Guggenheim Museum, **Brice Marden** (New York, 1975), p. 11.

2 Brice Marden, in Carl Andre, ed., "New in New York: Line Work," **Arts Magazine** 41, 7 (May 1967), p. 50.
3 Phyllis Tuchman, "Brice Marden: In the Groves of Color," **The Journal of Art (View)**, February 1991, p. 43.

Martin

1 Quoted in New York, Whitney Museum of American Art, **Agnes Martin**, text by Barbara Haskell (New York, 1992), pp. 10–12.
2 Quoted in Amsterdam, Stedelijk Museum, **Agnes Martin: Paintings and Drawings**, ed. W.A.L. Beeren (Amsterdam, 1991), p. 34.
3 Ibid., p. 13.

Matisse

1 Henri Matisse, "Notes of a Painter," 1908, in Herschel B. Chipp, **Theories of Modern Art** (Berkeley: University of California Press, 1968), p. 135.
2 Philadelphia, Philadelphia Museum of Art, **Retrospective Exhibition of Paintings, Drawings and Sculpture Organized in Collaboration with the Artist** (Philadelphia, 1948), p. 33.

Mentor

1 T.C., "Reviews: Will Mentor," **Artnews** 87, 2 (February 1988), p. 152.

Merz

1 New York, The Solomon R. Guggenheim Museum, **Mario Merz**, text by Germano Celant (New York, 1989), p. 102.
2 Ibid.
3 Ibid., p. 54.

Milles

1 Helen Boswell, "Des Moines News Letter," **The Art Digest**, August 1, 1949, unpag.
2 Joan Marter, "Sculpture and Painting," in Detroit, The Detroit Institute of Arts, and New York, The Metropolitan Museum of Art, **Design in America: The Cranbrook Vision, 1925–1950** (New York: Harry N. Abrams, Inc., 1983), p. 252.

Miss

1 This and the following comments are from an unedited video by Mary Miss about **Greenwood Pond: Double Site**, March 14, 1996, Archives, Des Moines Art Center.

Monet

1 This identification was initially made by Ellen Lawrence, a graduate curatorial assistant at Brown University.
2 Jules Michelet, **La Mer** (Paris, 1983), pp. 58–59, 83, and 288ff (originally published in Paris, 1861), quoted in Sylvie Gache-Patin and Scott Schaefer,

"Impressionism and the Sea," in Los Angeles, Los Angeles County Museum of Art; Chicago, The Art Institute of Chicago; and Paris, Réunion des Musées Nationaux, **A Day in the Country** (Los Angeles County Museum of Art and New York: Harry N. Abrams, Inc., 1984), p. 277 and n. 9.
3 Quoted in Chicago, The Art Institute of Chicago, **Claude Monet 1840–1926 Gallery Guide** (Chicago, 1995), p. 3.

Moore

1 Quoted in Kansas City, Missouri, The Nelson-Atkins Museum of Art, **Henry Moore: Maquettes and Working Models** (Kansas City, 1987), unpag.
2 John Hedgecoe and Henry Moore, **Henry Moore** (New York: Simon and Schuster, 1988), p. 501.
3 Ibid.

Munch

1 Stanislaw Przybyszewski, 1894, quoted in Patricia G. Berman and Jane Van Nimmen, **Munch and Women: Image and Myth** (Alexandria: Art Services International, 1997), p. 20.
2 Adolf Paul, "Edvard Munch und Berlin," quoted in ibid., p. 139.

Muñoz

1 Juan Muñoz and Jean-Marc Poinsot, conversation (1986), in Bordeaux, Musée d'Art Contemporain, **Juan Muñoz: Sculptures de 1985 à 1987** (Bordeaux, 1987), p. 44.

Murray

1 Elizabeth Murray, conversation with the author, October 15, 1990.

Nauman

1 Quoted in Lea Rosson DeLong Interview, in the **Des Moines Art Center News**, November 1990.

Noland

1 Unidentified viewer quoted in Thomas Wolfe, "Artist's New Technique Goes All Over," **The Washington Post**, January 5, 1960, p. A10.

O'Keeffe

1 George M. Irwin, letter to James T. Demetrion, January 4, 1984, Archives, Des Moines Art Center.

Oppenheim

1 Artist's statement, 1996, supplied by the Oppenheim Foundation, from which the works were acquired.
2 Ibid.

Oursler

1 San Diego, Museum of Contemporary Art, **A Written Conversation Between Tony Oursler and Christiane Meyer-Stoll** (San Diego, 1996), p. 9.
2 Ibid., p. 10.
3 Ibid.

Prendergast

1 Carol Clark, et al., **Maurice Brazil Prendergast, Charles Prendergast, A Catalogue Raisonné** (Williamstown, MA: Williams College Museum of Art, 1990), pp. 277–78.

Rauschenberg

1 Quoted in New York, The Museum of Modern Art, **Sixteen Americans**, ed. Dorothy C. Miller (New York, 1959), p. 58.
2 Quoted in Calvin Tomkins, **The Bride and the Bachelors: Five Masters of the Avant-Garde**, rev. ed. (New York: Penguin, 1976), p. 204.
3 Robert Rauschenberg, letter to I. Michael Danoff, November 1993, Archives, Des Moines Art Center.

Richter

1 Chicago, Museum of Contemporary Art, and Toronto, Art Gallery of Ontario, **Gerhard Richter: Paintings**, text by Roald Nasgaard and I. Michael Danoff (London and New York: Thames and Hudson, 1988), p. 9.
2 Ibid., p. 13.
3 Ibid., p. 9.
4 Ibid., p. 12.
5 Ibid.
6 Ibid.

Rothenberg

1 Quoted in Lizbeth Nilson, "Susan Rothenberg: 'Every Brushstroke Is a Surprise,'" **Artnews** 83, 2 (February 1984), p. 50.
2 Jeremy Lewison, "Form & Expression in Susan Rothenberg's Prints," in Rachel Robertson Maxwell, ed., **Susan Rothenberg – The Prints – A Catalogue Raisonné** (Philadelphia: Peter Maxwell, 1987), p. 51.

Rothko

1 From Mark Rothko's 1943 commentary on his painting **The Omen of the Eagle** (1942), quoted in Sidney Janis, **Abstract and Surrealist Art in America** (New York: Reynal and Hitchcock, 1944), p. 118.
2 See the discussion in Anna C. Chave, **Mark Rothko: Subjects in Abstraction** (New Haven, CT: Yale University Press, 1989), pp. 172–84.
3 Quoted in Dore Ashton, "Art: Lecture by Rothko," **The New York Times**, October 31, 1958, p. 26; quoted in Dore Ashton, "L'Automne à New York: Letter from New York" **Cimaise** 6, 2 (December 1958), p. 39.

Ryman

1 Donald B. Kuspit, "Red Desert & Arctic Dreams," **Art in America**, March 1989, p. 123.

Shahn

1 Francis K. Pohl, **Ben Shahn** (San Francisco: Pomegranate Artbooks, 1993), p. 12.
2 A letter from Marguerite Glass-Engelhart, Assistant Curator, Supreme Court of the United States, to Suzanne Williams Taylor, Catalog Researcher, National Portrait Gallery, January 8, 1987, in the Archives, Des Moines Art Center, identifies the justices.

Simpson

1 Deborah Wills, **Lorna Simpson** (San Francisco: The Friends of Photography, 1992), p. 58.
2 Lorna Simpson, conversation with the author, April 7, 1998.

Smith

1 London, Whitechapel Art Gallery, **Kiki Smith** (London, 1995), p. 32.
2 Ibid., p. 13.
3 Ibid.
4 Williamstown, Massachusetts, Williams College Museum of Art, and Columbus, Ohio, Wexner Center for the Arts, **Kiki Smith**, text by Linda Shearer and Claudia Gould (Williamstown, 1992), p. 75.

Sultan

1 Barbara Rose, **Donald Sultan** (New York: Random House, 1988), p. 34.
2 Ibid., p. 82.
3 Ibid., p. 20.

Twombly

1 (Julia Brown), "Permanent Collection: Recent Acquisition Cy Twombly," **Des Moines Art Center News**, March/April 1985, p. 5.

Whiteread

1 Quoted in Washington, DC, Hirshhorn Museum and Sculpture Garden, **Distemper: Dissonant Themes in the Art of the 1990s**, text by Neal Benezra and Olga M. Viso (Washington, 1996), p. 105.

Wiley

1 William T. Wiley, written statement to I. Michael Danoff, December 1, 1993, Archives, Des Moines Art Center.

Wilmarth

1 New York, The Museum of Modern Art, **Christopher Wilmarth**, text by Laura Rosenstock (New York, 1989), p. 13.

Wood

1 James Dennis, **Grant Wood: A Study in American Art and Culture** (New York: Viking Press, 1975), p. 240.
2 Nan Wood Graham, with John Zug and Julie Jensen McDonald, **My Brother, Grant Wood** (Iowa City: State Historical Society of Iowa, 1993), p. 92.

Works
on paper

Amy N. Worthen

1
Albrecht Dürer (German, 1471–1528)
The Death of the Virgin, 1510, from the "Life of
the Virgin"; Woodcut, 11 1/2 x 8 1/8 inches (29.2
x 20.6 cm); Purchased with funds from Rose F.
Rosenfield; Des Moines Art Center Permanent
Collections, 1967.10

2
Jacques Bellange (French, active 1602–1624)
Pietà, 1613–1616; Etching, plate, 12 5/8 x 7 7/8 inches
(32.1 x 20 cm); sheet, 13 1/4 x 8 9/16 (33.7 x
21.7 cm); Purchased with funds from Dr. and Mrs.
Peder T. Madsen; Des Moines Art Center Permanent
Collections, 1975.3

1

Overview of the collection. **The permanent collection
of the Des Moines Art Center contains approximately 3,000 works on paper, including prints,
drawings, pastels, watercolors, collages, portfolios, artists' books, and photographs. This group
of objects is a significant but less well-known
aspect of the museum's holdings. Chronologi-
cally and geographically, the works on paper
encompass a broader range of material than the
painting and sculpture collections, which focus
primarily on the nineteenth and especially the
twentieth century. The art on paper spans seven
centuries and ranges from fourteenth-century
manuscript pages and fifteenth-century prints to
contemporary works in all media by artists from
the United States, Latin America, Europe, and
Asia. Approximately one-third of the collection is
composed of European prints made prior to
1900; the other two-thirds are art on paper created since 1900 in a variety of media. The
strongest area of the older part of the collection
is the virtually encyclopedic representation
of nineteenth-century French printmakers. The
modern part of the collection is closely aligned
with the Art Center's primary emphasis on contemporary art. The vast majority of works are by
American artists, and most date from after 1970.**

The Art Center's works on paper collection is
a product of targeted collecting by knowledgeable
directors and curators, and by generous collectors, as well as the random accretion of fifty
years of gifts and purchases. In comparison with
many other museum collections of prints and
drawings, it is relatively small. And, like most
museums' collections, it is not unified. Many
individuals have contributed to its formation out
of their personal interests, passions, and expertise. There are several notable areas of strength
and many individual treasures. Certain artists,
periods, and countries are well represented by
important examples, other areas are under
represented. Objects of great importance, beauty,
quality, and interest coexist with items of lesser
significance.

Collections policies and criteria. **Beginning in
the 1940s, the Des Moines Art Center gradually
developed a coherent collections policy for art
on paper. The founders of the museum initially
recognized that a collection of prints and drawings would allow the Art Center to include works
by artists who worked exclusively as printmakers
and draftsmen. Prints, drawings, and watercolors
could create an enriched context for the primary
holdings of contemporary American paintings
and sculpture. A collection of European and
American prints and drawings extending back to
the Renaissance could present an alternative and**

a background to modern art. In 1971 the Art Center reaffirmed its collections policy, stating that it "should continue to build a historical collection of prints and other works on paper." That policy also discouraged the creation of a "spotty collection with gaps that are literally unbridgeable, or the acquisition of inferior examples." In 1989 the policy was amended to state that while "works representing all periods will be acquired, a particular focus on post-1945 and contemporary works on paper will be pursued to form substantial and meaningful collections. Works that can be acquired to fill in where there are gaps in the painting and sculpture collection should be particularly considered."

Although qualitative standards were not of the highest priority in determining print acquisitions for the Art Center initially, they became a greater imperative for the museum under the direction of James T. Demetrion and subsequent directors. In prints as in many other fields, there is a canon of great artists and great images. The Des Moines Art Center possesses works by many of the mostly male artists considered to be the major figures

involved in printmaking since the fifteenth century. The Art Center has few works by women of the past, but it has an adequate record for collecting work by contemporary female artists. With the museum's heightened awareness of this neglect, and thanks in part to the gifts of Louise Rosenfield Noun, significant works on paper by women artists, particularly of the first half of the twentieth century, continue to enter the collection. The new recognition of the achievements of artists from ethnic backgrounds other than those typically represented in art history, museum collections, and the art market also has had an important influence on the Art Center's recent acquisitions. Works by contemporary American artists of Native American, African, or Latino background now enter the collection in greater number.

Early on, a de facto policy evolved that the Des Moines Art Center would not collect photography. This issue has been periodically revisited, and in 1989 a revised collections policy was adopted, which stated that although the Des Moines Art Center would not attempt to document the history of photography, individual works of photography or involving the medium would be considered on a case by case basis.

History of the collection. When the Des Moines Art Center opened in 1948, a group of about 100 works transferred from the old Des Moines Fine

5

Arts Association, which had been collecting since 1923, formed the nucleus of the collection. The first prints acquired were etchings by Caroline Armington and Anders Zorn. One of the Art Center's intended roles was to encourage collecting by individuals in the community, and the strengths of the permanent collection are in large part the result of the predilections and generosity of a handful of Des Moines print and drawing collectors. Some of the most important of these were B. A. Younker (Old Master prints), Carl Weeks (modern prints and drawings), Rose Frankel Rosenfield and Louise Rosenfield Noun (Old Master and modern prints and art by women), Jennie May Gabriel (Old Master and nineteenth-century French prints), Anna Meredith (Matisse prints), Ray Halston Frowick (Andy Warhol), John and Mary Pappajohn (Susan Rothenberg prints) and John Huseby (German Expressionist and French prints of all periods).

John Huseby, museum trustee and long-time acquisitions committee member, gave his wonderfully focused and rigorously selected collection of approximately five hundred and eighty prints to the Art Center in three installments (1972, 1994, and 1995). As a young soldier during World War II, Huseby had an opportunity to buy some of his

first prints in Paris, beginning a lifelong involvement as a print collector. Collecting on a modest income, he focused on two main areas: German Expressionist and French prints. Huseby honed his sense of connoisseurship, became thoroughly conversant with print history, had totally independent taste, and found wonderful impressions of fascinating images. Landmark prints in the media interested him; his acquisition of a rare aquatint by Jean-Claude Richard de Saint-Non, inventor of that medium in the eighteenth century, was a thrill. Nineteenth-century French prints were Huseby's special passion, and he had one or more works by nearly 100 different French artists of the period. He also collected works by contemporary American printmakers, including artists from Iowa. The detailed records of his collection came to the Art Center along with his bequest of prints in 1994. A number of works not included in the bequest were purchased from his estate in 1995.

Although the Des Moines Art Center did not have a separate curatorial department for prints and drawings until 1998, many of the directors have had a significant impact on the collection of works on paper. During the 1950s Dwight Kirsch attracted numerous gifts of contemporary drawings and prints to the Art Center from his artist friends and colleagues around the country. Many of these works were given in memory of Kirsch's wife, the artist Truby Kelly Kirsch. Many of the works reflect Dwight Kirsch's own sensibilities as an artist, with his openness to abstraction, his interest in Oriental art, and his love of ink, wash, and watercolor.

In 1960 the first fund specifically designated for art on paper was established through the bequest of Rose Frankel Rosenfield. The income was used first by Director Thomas Tibbs and then by James T. Demetrion to purchase many fine older and contemporary prints and drawings. During Demetrion's directorship, the Art Center increased its collecting of contemporary prints, especially by major contemporary artists newly attracted in the 1970s to work in lithography. Demetrion also purchased important drawings by European artists of the late nineteenth and first half of the twentieth century, as well as Old Master prints and drawings of high quality and splendid condition. Among the important older works on paper that entered the collection during his directorship are drawings by Burne-Jones, Gauguin, Klimt, Schiele, and Wölfli, and superb prints by Callot, Canaletto, Fantin-Latour, and Goltzius.

Director Julia Brown Turrell showed her commitment to works of art on paper through her acquisition of several important portfolios, books, and suites of prints by Marcel Duchamp, Cy Twombly, and Francesco Clemente. Director I. Michael Danoff brought a new direction to the collection by acquiring art that uses photography, such as the works of Cindy Sherman and Carrie Mae Weems, and experimental prints by artists exploring new media, such as Kiki Smith and Lorna Simpson.

Use and exhibition of the collection. During the 1930s and 1940s, the idea that prints were a "democratic" art form paralleled the kind of thinking that led to the formation of community art centers such as the Des Moines Art Center. The concept in which museum, art school, and community had mutual interaction and common purpose also influenced the way the Des Moines Art Center would collect and exhibit prints.

Prints and drawings were envisioned as relatively small in size and inexpensive. Eliel Saarinen's plan for the Des Moines Art Center's print exhibition area reflects this common conception of the appropriate size of works on paper. His wood-paneled print corridor, adjacent to the lobby entrance, provides for the exhibition of

small, matted artworks which could be propped on a continuous molding. The mats would be protected by plate glass set into the molding and secured above with turnbuckles. This system offered a certain amount of flexibility, but it was designed for works that did not exceed fairly modest dimensions. Subsequent changes in the scale, aesthetics, and display requirements of art on paper made Saarinen's original design less useful as time went on. The Art Center usually mounts three to six print exhibitions a year, each containing about thirty works, and has also organized a number of major exhibitions featuring or including works on paper from the permanent collection. In addition, several major traveling shows organized by the Des Moines Art Center included significant amounts of work on paper.[1]

Sometimes an exhibition organized by the Art Center has occasioned an acquisition. Examples include the purchase of Jacques Bellange's Pietà (1613–1616), and the 1986 gift of Giorgio Morandi's important etching Large Still Life with Coffee Pot (1933), in honor of retiring Assistant Director Peggy Patrick, who had worked extensively on the Morandi exhibition (fig. 10).

The Des Moines Art Center has never had a proper print study room; a table in the registrar's office was used on an ad hoc basis. When Richard Meier remodeled parts of Saarinen's building in conjunction with the construction of his own addition in 1985, a print study and storage facility was, in fact, designed and built. Due to the increased staff and support space required by the enlarged museum, however, the Art Center could not afford to utilize the space for its intended purpose, and it reverted to office area.

Still, despite the relative inaccessibility of large parts of the collection, there has long been an enthusiastic audience for prints and drawings at the Des Moines Art Center. The education department has always offered classes in printmaking and sometimes on print history and print collecting. In 1981 the Des Moines Art Center Print Club was formed as a museum support and study group. The Print Club donates a work to the permanent collection annually, and since 1991 has published a print each year by an artist with an Iowa connection.

6

Max Klinger (German, 1857–1920)
Entführung (Abduction), 1880–81; from the portfolio "Ein Handschuh (A Glove)"; Etching and aquatint, plate, 3 1/2 x 8 5/8 inches (6.4 x 21.9 cm); sheet, 17 3/4 x 25 1/4 inches (45.1 x 64.1 cm); Purchased with funds from the E.I. Sargent Family; Des Moines Art Center Permanent Collections, 1974.21.9

Description and highlights of the collection: Non-Western art. The overwhelming majority of the works on paper in the Des Moines Art Center are by European and American artists. Nevertheless, a small group of works from Japan and India are part of the collection, although they are catalogued separately from the Western collection. There are Japanese woodcuts by about fifty artists, dating from the eighteenth to the twentieth century, including Harunobu, Shunsho, Toyokuni I, Utamaro, Kiyonaga, Hokusai, Kuniyoshi, Hiroshige, Keisai, and Toyokuni III. Probably the finest work is Kuniyoshi's block print Asahina and the Little Samurai (1852–53). Prints by thirty twentieth-century artists provide a fascinating glimpse of how modern Western art was adopted in Japan, and interacted with traditional Japanese printmaking techniques and imagery. Works on paper by Japanese-Americans are classified with American art.

The Art Center's six lovely Mughal and Hindu miniature paintings on paper from India are probably even less well known to the public than the Japanese prints. Dating from the sixteenth to the nineteenth century, they entered the collection in 1948 as part of the Coffin bequest.

Western art. Other than illuminated, printed book pages from the second half of the fifteenth century, the earliest prints in the Art Center are by artists who began working in the 1490s. Albrecht Dürer is represented by twelve engrav-

ings and woodcuts, including fine impressions of the Cook and His Wife (the Magpie Gossiping about the Eel) (c. 1497), the large Hercules (c.1500), the Sea Monster (c. 1501), and a beautiful impression of The Death of the Virgin (1510) (fig. 1). Notable woodcuts by his followers and contemporaries include a magnificent impression of Hans Sebald Beham's Holy Family (1521), four Scenes from Christ's Passion (1515) by Albrecht Altdorfer, and a beautiful impression of Esther before Ahasuerus (n.d.) by Hans Schauffelein. The Crucifixion (c. 1510) by Daniel Hopfer is an early example of etching.

Early Italian printmaking includes sixteenth-century engravings by Marcantonio Raimondi and Giorgio Ghisi's Death of Procris (c. 1540) after Giulio Romano. The highlight of the seventeenth-century Italian prints is Giovanni Benedetto Castiglione's Circe (c. 1640), in addition to etchings by Simone Cantarini, Stefano della Bella, Salvator Rosa, Francesco Grimaldi, and Pietro Aquila. Eighteenth-century Italy is represented by Giovanni Battista Piranesi's Carceri d'Invenzione (Imaginary Prisons), plate III (1745–50); Antonio Canaletto's double-plate

7

Wassily Kandinsky (Russian, 1866–1944)
Zwei Reiter vor Rot (Two Riders Against Red), 1911
Woodcut, plate, 4 ³/₁₆ x 7 inches (10.7 x 15.8 cm); sheet,
11 ¹/₈ x 10 ¹³/₁₆ inches (28.3 x 27.5 cm); John C. Huseby
Print Collection of the Des Moines Art Center, through gift;
Des Moines Art Center Permanent Collections, 1972.54

etching of Padua, Santa Giustina in Pra' della Valle (c. 1740); and etchings by Giovanni Battista Tiepolo and his son Giandomenico.

Flemish and Dutch sixteenth-century prints include Pieter Brueghel the Elder's fascinating allegory The Combat Between Money Bags and Strongboxes (1563) and a very beautiful impression of Hendrick Goltzius's Captain of the Infantry (1587). Dutch seventeenth-century prints include twenty-nine Rembrandt etchings, such as a rich impression of Christ and the Woman of Samaria (1658) (fig. 4). There are twenty-one etchings by Adrien van Ostade, and numerous individual works by Dutch landscape artists such as Jacob van Ruysdael, Karel Dujardin, Herman Swanevelt, and Anthony Waterloo; by artists specializing in animal subjects, such as Paul Potter; and many others. Seventeenth-century Flanders is best represented by a number of Anthony van Dyck's etched portraits of artists from his Iconography (n.d.).

British prints are less well represented in the Art Center's collection than might be expected. From the eighteenth century are William Hogarth's Four Stages of Cruelty (1751), and chiaroscuro woodcuts by John Baptist Jackson. There are several hand-colored satires by James Gillray, such as Harmony before Matrimony and Matrimonial Harmony (1805).

A wonderful example of mid-sixteenth-century French regional printmaking is the Last Judgment (c. 1550) by Georges Reverdy, an engraving with dark tonalities and a dense figural composition. There are works by twenty-six French printmakers of the seventeenth century, including the late Mannerist painter Jacques Bellange's Pietà (1613–1616), one of the real rarities of the collection (fig. 2). Jacques Callot's The Temptation of St. Anthony (c. 1634), one of his most striking and imaginative images, is an excellent impression (fig. 3). Among additional Callot works in the museum are a working proof impression of La Carrière à Nancy (n.d.) and the complete "Prodigal Son" series (1631). Other etchers from Lorraine represented in the collections are Claude Lorrain and Sebastien LeClerc. From seventeenth-century Paris is Abraham Bosse, who published exquisite etchings illustrating biblical, literary, allegorical, and moral themes, as well as documenting the crafts and life of the rising bourgeoisie, as in The Sculptor in His Studio (1642). There is a selection of engravings by Claude Mellan, including his masterful single spiral-line St. Joseph (n.d.), which carry engraving to its most conceptual and virtuoso level. There are also definitive examples of French Baroque

engraving by Robert Nanteuil and his Parisian contemporaries. About twenty French printmakers illustrate late Baroque and Rococo styles. Technical innovations are represented by a rare aquatint, Venus and Love (1766), by the medium's inventor, Jean-Claude Richard de Saint-Non, and a beautiful color aquatint, The Cake Merchant (1772), by Jean-Baptiste Le Prince.

The nineteenth century is heavily represented, thanks in great part to the detailed coverage of the period provided by French prints from the Huseby collection. John Huseby had an intense interest in the early history of lithography, frequently collecting lithographs dealing with the bitter experience of Napoleonic veterans, images of Romanticism, and urban rebellions in France. Among the most important examples are Pierre-Paul Prud'hon's Une Lecteur (1822), nineteen images by Eugène Delacroix, and eight lithographs by Théodore Géricault. Nicholas Charlet, Honoré Daumier, Achille Deveria, Guillaume Gavarni, Eugène Isabey, Eugène Lami, and Carle Vernet (see fig. 5) and Horace Vernet are represented in quantity. There are disturbingly imaginative works by Eugène Blery, Charles Meryon, Rodolphe Bresdin, Gustave Doré, Grandville, and Odilon Redon. Thanks to John Huseby, the Art Center also has works by the Fontainebleau etchers and the peintre-graveurs of the Parisian etching revival, such as Félix Buhot and Félix Bracquemond. Huseby also gave color lithographs by Pierre Bonnard, Edouard Vuillard, Henri Rivière, Henri de Toulouse-Lautrec, Ker Xavier Roussel, and Paul Signac.

Other examples of nineteenth-century printmaking are less inclusive. Max Klinger, the most gifted and influential German etcher of the period, is represented by the complete series of his important, fetishistic etched narrative "A Glove" (1880–81) (fig. 6), as well as by individual etchings. Another fascinating and beautiful German portfolio is Hans Meyer's "Dance of Death" (1892), containing a suite of twelve etchings. One of the Art Center's most important treasures is the hand-colored lithograph Vampire (1895) by the Norwegian Edvard Munch, who was active in the 1890s in Berlin, where he made prints that influenced the development of German Expressionism. Among Swiss artists are several prints by Félix Vallotton, who worked in Paris. Prints from Britain include an early color lithograph by Thomas Shotter Boys, etchings by Joseph Mallord William Turner, and drypoints by Sir Francis Seymour Haden. The great Spanish artist Francisco Goya is represented by a few

8

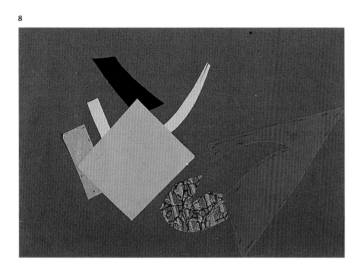

prints from his various series: "Caprichos" (1798), "Disasters of War" (1810–1814, published 1863), "Disparates" (c. 1816, published 1848), and one lithograph from "Tauromaquia," The Way the Ancient Spaniards Baited the Bull in the Open (1816). There are only a few nineteenth-century works from the Low Countries. Among them are etchings by Félicien Rops and James Ensor, including a hand-colored impression of the latter's Christ's Entry into Brussels (1898). The work of James Abbott MacNeil Whistler, whose career was spent in England, France, and Italy, dominates the selection of nineteenth-century American prints. Whistler's work includes etchings from his "French Set" (1859), "Thames Set" (1858–61), "Venice Set" (1879–80), portraits, a few transfer lithographs, and the beautiful lithotint Across the Thames (1896). There is also a wonderful monotype, Roman Campagna (c. 1900), by Maurice Prendergast.

Although prints certainly dominate the older part of the collection, there are some fine early drawings. There are two highly finished wash portraits of a man and woman by the Flemish artist Frans Pourbus the Younger, and a lovely red chalk drawing, Head of a Young Woman, attributed to Rubens's colleague Jacob Jordaens. The highlight of the British drawings is a superb black chalk Woman's Head (1890) by Edward Burne-

Jones. French drawings include a conté crayon Sheep (n.d.) by Rosa Bonheur, Louis Léopold Boilly's pastel Head of a Woman (1830), Gustave Doré's wash drawing Cavalier Talking with Father Time (n.d.), and one of the Art Center's most important treasures, Paul Gauguin's pastel Standing Tahitian Nude (Eve) (1892–94). There are also a few choice American drawings in the Art Center collection, among them, Winslow Homer's outstanding watercolor Banana Tree (1885), Maurice Prendergast's watercolor Surf (c. 1900), and Mary Cassatt's pastel Nicolle and Her Mother (c. 1900), a lovely portrait of a family who lived near her chateau in the Oise valley in France.

The Art Center's holdings of works on paper from the twentieth century are more extensive. Rich holdings of German Expressionism and art of the post–World War I period include prints by about forty artists, especially those active in Munich and Berlin during the first three decades of the century. Eight works by Ernst Ludwig Kirchner span nearly thirty years of his career, from 1900 to 1929. The collection features a very strong pencil and wash drawing, Untitled (Female Nude) (c. 1913), by Egon Schiele; a fine watercolor, Chinese Head (1916), by Emil Nolde; and fourteen watercolors by Jeanne Mammen. George Grosz, an internationally acclaimed German artist who emerged around 1915, taught painting and drawing in 1957 at the Des Moines Art Center as artist-in-residence. The Art Center has several of his biting satires from 1918

through 1949, among them a stunning watercolor Mother and Daughter **(1933) (fig. 9). More recent works on paper by German artists include a gouache** Portrait of Max Beckmann **(1948) by Karl Zerbe; a pencil drawing,** Untitled **(1969), by Joseph Beuys; and Anselm Kiefer's** Untitled **(1983), a watercolor and collage image of a dark, threatening, museumlike space. There are few works by Russian artists, but almost every piece is significant.** Two Riders Against Red **(1911) is a particularly beautiful color woodcut by Wassily Kandinsky, made in Munich when he was a leader of Der Blau Reiter group** (fig. 7). **An important group of works of avant-garde Russian art include Olga Rozanova's suite of twenty-three watercolored lithographs, "A Duck's Nest of Bad Words" (1913–1914), and twelve editioned collages, "Universal War" (1916), both collaborations with the poet Nicholas Kruchenykh** (see fig. 8). **The Art Center also has a lithograph,** Half-length Female Figure **(1922–23) by Natalia Gontcharova, and a drawing,** Meditation 68 **(1937), by Alexei Jawlensky, active in Germany and Switzerland. A recent work, the large fantastical etching** The Dwelling House of Winnie the Pooh **(1990), is by the contemporary Russian team Alexander Brodsky and Ilya Utkin, who in 1992 created an extraordinary architectural installation using chainlink fencing and a pool of black ink at the Art Center as part of a traveling exhibition.**[2]

Swiss artists are represented by a 1910 lithograph by Ferdinand Hodler; Adolf Wölfli's graphite drawing Schaggi in the Grass **(1923); prints and a monotype,** Memorial to the Kaiser **(1920), by Paul Klee; lithographs by Alberto Giacometti; and Franz Gertsch's monumental Photorealist woodcut** Natascha IV **(1987–88). British early twentieth-century printmakers include Robert Bevan, Muirhead Bone, Frank Brangwyn, Gerald Brockhurst, D. Y. Cameron, and James McBey. Post-1945 British artists represented include Stanley William Hayter, who was to have a great impact on printmaking in Iowa through his student Mauricio Lasansky; Henry Moore; Pop artist Richard Hamilton; and Bridget Riley, who has an ink drawing in the collection. One of the Art Center's most interesting items is an impressive watercolor of a ceramic vessel (c. 1950) by Bernard Leach, one of the most important ceramists of this century. Mid-century Spanish art is represented by several etchings by Pablo Picasso from the "Suite Vollard" (1933), and some additional prints, as well as prints by Salvador Dali and Antoni Tapies. Belgian and Dutch artists with significant work in the collection are Pierre Alechinsky with sixteen prints, and Anton**

Heyboer with his etching End of the Search for Knowledge; Starting to Think from Knowledge; Limit of Consciousness **(1966). Twentieth-century French works on paper combine the scholarly interests of the Huseby collection with Modernist prints acquired from a variety of other sources, which include well-known artists and styles from Cubism to post–World War II abstraction. There are some extraordinary watercolors, such as André Derain's** The Nymphes **(c. 1905–1906); Sonia Delaunay-Terk's** Contrastes simultanés; **Paul Signac's** Lac d'Annecy **(c. 1919), and a splendid gouache,** The Lovers **(1926), by the Russian-French artist Marc Chagall. Henri Matisse is well represented with several drawings, lithographs, and the complete portfolio "Jazz " (1947). There are two important multiples by Marcel Duchamp:** The Green Box **(1934) and** The Box in a Valise **(1955–68).**

The heart of the collection is American art of the twentieth century, with over 500 artists of the United States, Canada, and Latin America. Prints and drawings of about eighty artists with connections to Iowa are a special strength of the collection. American drawings and watercolors from the early years of the century include works by Robert Henri, Jerome Myers, William Glackens, six works by Arthur B. Davies, George Bellows, Everett Shinn, ten by Abraham Walkowitz, George O. "Pop" Hart, Charles Demuth, Diego Rivera, José Clemente Orozco, and John Sloan. Among Sloan's works are several drawings for magazine illustrations and a beautiful monotype, Isadora Duncan Dancing **(1915). There are also several of his etchings, including the haunting** Memories **(1906). There are etchings by Edward Hopper and lithographs by George Bellows. The Canadian artist Caroline Armington, who settled in Des Moines, is represented by a group of nineteen etchings.**

In the 1920s and 1930s, many artists and critics believed in an art for the people that was comprehensible, accessible, and affordable; they held a devotion to representational figuration, were indifferent or antagonistic to abstraction, and had a purist preference for black-and-white as opposed to color printing. Such prints were seen

by critics and artists alike as distinctively American, and the subject matter often reflected social themes. American Regionalist lithographs in the collection include prints by Thomas Hart Benton, John Steuart Curry, and Grant Wood. The Des Moines Art Center owns a complete set of Wood's twenty prints (see fig. 11). Other printmakers of the period include Peggy Bacon, who is also represented by a wonderful late drawing (1949), Reginald Marsh, Adolph Dehn, Louis Lozowick, the wood engraver Thomas Nason, and several lithographers associated with the WPA.

Among the Art Center's best watercolors of the 1930s are works by Arthur Dove, White Table in Snow (1932); Charles Burchfield, Snow Remnants (1932); John Marin, Outer Sand Island, Maine (1936); Edward Hopper, The Forked Road (Wellfleet) (1934); Ralston Crawford, Pennsylvania Barn (1937); and Karl Mattern, who is amply represented in the collection by twenty-seven prints, watercolors, and drawings.

Figurative imagery and social themes continued during the 1940s in the work of Raphael Soyer and Irving Norman, whose graphite drawing Labour (1946) is one of the more remarkable images in the collection. There are works by American Realists who continued to work figuratively, including Russell Cowles and Marsden Hartley; and by German Expressionist refugee artists such as Albert Block, Lionel Feininger, George Grosz, and Karl Zerbe. Ben Shahn's works on paper include a large and masterful ink drawing, National Pass Time (1955); a watercolor, ABC (1953); Patterson No. 1 (n.d.), a screenprint; and the famous wood engraving collaboration between Shahn and Leonard Baskin, Beatitudes (1954).

The works in the collection from the 1940s also reflect the changing stylistic trends in the decade during which the Des Moines Art Center was founded. Among the examples of 1940s abstraction are Mark Rothko's watercolor Abstract Composition (1945) and Ann Ryan's watercolor Untitled (1947). Abstract Expressionism, which came to dominate American art during the 1950s, is represented by important figures of the first generation of painters, such as Lee Krasner's Black and White Collage (1953), two of William De Kooning's lithographs, and Robert Motherwell's Orange Suchard Bitra #4 (1973), an acrylic with collage on board.

In 1940 Stanley William Hayter, a British artist active in Paris, transferred his Atelier 17 workshop to New York, infusing fresh ideas into the American printmaking scene. Hayter's workshop promoted refreshing new attitudes of experimentation and sharing, as opposed to craft secrecy, and an openness to abstraction. At Atelier 17 many American artists came in contact with European refugee artists. In 1946 the Argentinean artist Mauricio Lasansky, who had worked with Hayter in New York, arrived to teach at the University of Iowa, bringing with him the innovative approach to printmaking he had learned in the stimulating environment of Hayter's workshop. Lasansky founded a highly influential program in intaglio techniques that endures to this day, and for a time in the 1950s and 1960s, Iowa City was one of the most important centers of printmaking anywhere. The Art Center has over twenty examples of Lasansky's work spanning his early years in the 1930s in Argentina to the 1970s. Sol y luna (1945) reflects the strong influence of Picasso. By the 1950s Lasansky's prints such as España (1956) (fig. 12) and Self-Portrait (1957) had become very large and technically complex, competing with the scale and appearance of paintings. Printmaking activity in Iowa has been related closely to the medium's academic connections. The Art Center has collected the works of Iowa artists, and artists with Iowa connections, providing a continuous fifty-year survey of activity. Approximately eighty Iowa artists are represented, some in depth. Des Moines and Iowa City have long been the two most important centers for art in the state, and Fairfield is a more recent center of activity. Many of the state's leading artists have been associated as faculty members or students with art and educational institutions of the state, including the Des Moines Art Center.

The collection reflects how in the 1950s printmaking training in the United States generally shifted to academia, and was taught by influential artist-teachers such as Leonard Baskin at Smith College, Karl Schrag at Cooper Union, Gabor Peterdi at Yale University, Rudy Pozzatti at Indiana University, Garo Antresian at the University of New Mexico, and Dean Meeker and Warrington Colescott at the University of Wisconsin. Generations of their students became teachers in their own right, spreading out to schools around the country. The collection also shows how printmakers such as Leonard Baskin, in prints such as his Man of Peace (1952), took on the challenge of Abstract Expressionism, adopting its grand scale and gestural qualities but affirming the necessity for figurative imagery.

11

By the late 1950s, with the institution of collaborative printmaking, practice outside the academic world began to undergo drastic changes. Around 1957 lithography was greatly altered through the efforts of Tatyana Grosman, founding director of the Universal Limited Art Editions lithography workshop in West Islip, New York. Grosman invited artists associated with the second generation of Abstract Expressionism, such as Robert Rauschenberg, Larry Rivers, and Jasper Johns, to come to ULAE and make prints. These artists were not trained printmakers, but they were invited to see the process with fresh eyes, participate in it, and essentially reinvent color lithography. The spontaneity they injected into the medium was unparalleled. Johns's Decoy **(1971) and** (Savarin Can) Paint Brushes **(1967–69)** were produced at ULAE. Jim Dine, also invited to ULAE, created an extraordinary body of prints. Braid **(1972)** is a fine example of his impressive accomplishments in etching. The collection includes prints by additional Abstract Expressionists who worked at ULAE, including Sam Francis and Helen Frankenthaler.

About the same time as ULAE began publishing, the California artist June Wayne created The Tamarind Workshop, to which she also invited artists of international repute, such as Joseph Albers and Iowa's Ulfert Wilke. In the 1960s Tamarind began to exert a powerful influence on lithography, when its trained printers spread out all over the country to found print shops of their own. The most famous and innovative of the second-generation shops was Gemini G.E.L., a print and multiples editioning workshop in

Los Angeles, with master printer Ken Tyler, who later founded Tyler Graphics in Bedford, New York. Tyler helped create some of Jasper Johns's most important prints, such as the color edition of his numerals "0–9" (1968), of which the Art Center has #6. Also produced at Gemini were Roy Lichtenstein's Rouen Cathedral #3, #4, and #6 **(1969); and Frank Stella's first screen print,** Pastel Stack **(1970).**

The scale of prints and the use of color began to rival paintings. Publishers funded expensive print projects, bringing hundreds of painters to collaborative relationships with print workshops. New complexity brought vastly increased costs, intensive marketing, and problems of storage and presentation. Instead of being the 1930s "democratic" art form, characterized by technical simplicity, availability, and inexpensiveness, the new collaborative prints were technically complex and had breathtaking prices.

The Art Center collection contains examples of prints and drawings by many artists associated with the Pop Art movement. Screen printing, a method developed in WPA workshops during the Depression, was revived in the 1960s. It was well suited to Pop Art imagery, with its hard edges and flatness, as in Lichtenstein's Sweet Dreams Baby **(1965). The Art Center has over forty prints spanning the career of Andy Warhol, including** Liz

12
Mauricio Lasansky (American, born 1914)
España, 1956; Intaglio, 31 7/8 x 20 7/8 inches
(81 x 53 cm); Purchased with funds from the
Edmundson Art Foundation, Inc.; Des Moines
Art Center Permanent Collections, 1957.7

12

(1964), and complete series such as "Electric
Chairs" (1971), "Mao Tse-Tung" (1972), "Ten
Portraits of Jews of the Twentieth Century" (1980);
"Real Diamond Dust Shoe" (1980). Other Pop Art
prints in the collection include James Rosenquist's
four-part lithograph F-111 (1974), and works
by Claes Oldenburg, Wayne Thibaud, Mel Ramos,
Ernest Trova, Richard Lindner, Red Grooms, and
Robert Indiana.

In addition to prints the Art Center has works in
other media on paper from the 1960s. Among them
are a large ink drawing by John Altoon, Untitled
(1966); Alfred Leslie's charcoal drawing Jane Elford
#3 (1968); and Claes Oldenburg's Late Submission
to the Chicago Tribune Architectural Competition of
1922: Clothespin (Version Two) (1967). There is a
beautiful group of six dreamlike collages by Joseph
Cornell from around 1960.

The largest groups of works on paper in the collection dates from the 1970s, with hundreds of prints
by many of the leading artists who collaborated
with the major print workshops and publishers that
flourished during these years. Tax laws encouraged
donation of works of art to museums and tax-shel-
tered investments by corporations and individuals
fueled much of the explosive growth in print publishing and artistic experimentation of the time.
Print portfolios of the 1970s that entered the collection serve as great anthologies of the artists
of that decade. Among them are EAT's "New York
Collection for Stockholm" (1973), with work by
thirty leading painters, sculptors, and Conceptual

artists; and the "Spirit of Independence" bicenten-
nial portfolio (1974–75). There are also portfolios
and suites by many individual artists, including
Robert Rauschenberg's Surface Series (1970), from
"Currents"; Cy Twombly's mixed-media "Natural
History Part I, Mushrooms" (1974) and "Natural
History Part II, Some Trees of Italy" (1976); and
Philip Pearlstein's color aquatint portfolio "Ruins
and Landscapes" (1979).

West Coast artists came to prominence, and works
by numerous Californians began to enter the Art
Center's collection. Works on paper include the
quirky vision of H. C. Westermann's watercolor
Oasis (1970), William T. Wiley's watercolor Hide as
a State of Mind (1971), Robert Arneson's ebullient
self-portrait Clown (1978), prints and drawings by
Ed Ruscha, a monotype by Joseph Goldyne, and
many others. There are numerous prints and drawings by artists associated with Minimalism.
Sol LeWitt is represented by his "Five Silkscreen
Prints" portfolio (1970), as well as the full color
ink drawing for his wall drawing at the Des Moines
Art Center. In addition the collection has works
by Ellsworth Kelly, Larry Zox, Frank Stella, Jackie
Ferrara, and Joel Shapiro.

Conceptualism, practiced by artists from Duchamp
to Johns to Arakawa to Beuys, is represented in the

collection by Joseph Kosuth's photostat Definition: Abstract (Art as idea as idea) (1967); Bruce Naumann's Raw War (1971); lithographs by Robert Morris, Vernon Fisher, Terry Allen, Pat Steir, and others. There are three prints by Shusaku Arakawa, who was highly influential after his arrival in New York in the 1960s. His etchings, such as The Signified or if (1975–76), with stenciled lettering, hand-work, and geometric forms, explore language, semantics, and meaning. Environmental artists include Christo, represented by the drawing and collage Valley Curtain Project (Rifle, Colorado) (1972). Richard Serra's monolithic oil crayon drawing, Mary Miss' collage "photodrawing" of Orvieto Cathedral, and her untitled digital collage Iris print commissioned by the Des Moines Art Center's Print Club in 1996. Photorealism is represented by prints of Robert Cottingham and Richard Estes, and by Chuck Close's etching Self-Portrait (1977) and Vija Celmins's drypoint Ocean Surface (1985). One of the most accomplished etchers of the 1970s was Peter Milton, whose widely admired masterpiece Daylillies (1975), is in the Art Center's collection. There is a magnificent pastel landscape drawing, Kaye's Farm (1982), by William Beckman.

In the 1980s in printmaking there was great interest in the monotype, a revival of the woodcut, experiments with computer-generated imagery, a new freedom in mixing diverse print media in the same print, and the printing of variant editions with hand-worked interventions. Artists were concerned, too, about issues of consumerism, identity, gender, race, and ethnicity, and the impact of AIDS. Artists and images of the decade in the collection include Michael Mazur's richly layered, human-centered narrative drawings and monotypes; John Buck's woodcuts with their primitive-looking human shapes inscribed with graffiti; Richard Bosman's aggressively bad draftsmanship, jarring colors, and cavalier treatment of violence and disaster; and Susan Rothenberg's visions of emaciated, totemic figures, bones, and horses. The Des Moines Art Center owns forty prints by Rothenberg – a virtually complete collection of her printed work in a variety of media, thanks in large part to a gift from John and Mary Pappajohn. Robert Longo's silhouetted lithograph Mark (1983), from "Men in the City," evokes the crisis of anonymity, and Cindy Sherman's photographs articulate the artist's concerns about the role of social situation, appearance, and gender in the construction of identity. Louisa Chase, Jennifer Bartlett, Nancy Spero, and T. L. Solien are other artists represented in the collection whose activity in printmaking contributed to the excitement of the decade.

Many artists of the 1980s pursued their private visions apart from the dominant trends. The Art Center has Ann McCoy's large drawing on paper mounted on canvas Osiris for Patsy O'Hara (1981), a drawing and prints by William Bailey, works by Nancy Graves, and about twenty monotypes and etchings by Matt Phillips. Bruce Nauman's photo-collage Animal Pyramid (1989) is an amazing image in itself, and reveals part of the process of how the artist designed his bronze sculpture in Greenwood Park.

Print publishing activity slowed during the late 1980s in response to an economic downturn in the art market. Works on paper of the 1990s reveal intensification of a number of developments whose seeds were planted in the previous decade. Some of the same political issues of race and gender continued to inform content. Feminism assured the recognition of many important women artists who had been ignored for much of their career. The Art Center acquired works such as Dorothea Rockburne's folded paperwork White Angel #3 (1982), and Louise Bourgeois's portfolio of etchings "Anatomy" (1991). The intellectual methodologies of deconstruction and post-Structuralism impacted art and art criticism. Diversity became an imperative consideration in the selection of works for the collection, in order to give due recognition to artists and to build new audiences for art. Works made and acquired in the 1990s include Glenn Ligon's remarkable fictive book title-page series "Runaways" (1993) and "Narratives" (1993); and Carrie Mae Weems's photography and text constructions, including her "Sea Island Series" (1992) and portraits. Kiki Smith's Sueño (1992) and My Blue Lake (1995), and Lorna Simpson's Wigs (1994), printed in waterless lithography on felt, employed new print technologies.

Conclusion. The founders of the Des Moines Art Center, convinced of the importance of contemporary drawing and printmaking as well as of the past, chose to collect works of art on paper from all periods. Yet they could hardly have anticipated the revolution in scale, technique, and style in contemporary art, nor the changes in availability of historic works that were to take place over the following half-century. Fortunately, the Art Center has kept pace with these changes, and today this collection of thousands of works of art on paper from seven centuries forms a notable resource for exhibition, study, and enjoyment.

1   **Egon Schiele and the Human Form.**
    Drawings and Watercolors,
    September 20–October 31, 1971. Also
    shown at The Columbus Gallery of Fine
    Arts, Ohio and The Art Institute of
    Chicago.**The Etchings of Jacques**
    Bellange, October 7–November 13,
    1975. Also shown at the Museum of
    Fine Arts, Boston, and The Metropol-
    itan Museum of Art, New York.
    Giorgio Morandi, February 1–March
    14, 1981. Also shown at the Museum of
    Modern Art, San Francisco, and The
    Solomon R. Guggenheim Museum,
    New York.
    Robert Arneson: A Retrospective,
    February 8–April 6, 1986. Also shown
    at The Hirshhorn Museum and
    Sculpture Garden, Smithsonian
    Institution, Washington, and the
    Portland Art Museum, Oregon.
    Lewis Baltz: Rule without Exception,
    July 13–September 15, 1991. Also
    shown at the Institute for Contem-
    porary Art, P.S. 1 Museum, New York;
    the John and Mable Ringling Museum
    of Art, Sarasota, Florida; Mills College
    Art Gallery, Oakland, California; and
    the Los Angeles County Museum of Art.
    Three Berlin Artists of the Weimar
    Era: Hannah Höch, Käthe Kollwitz,
    Jeanne Mammen, April 23–July 17,
    1994. Also shown at the Galerie St.
    Etienne, New York.
2   "Between Spring and Summer: Soviet
    Conceptual Art in the Era of Late
    Communism," organized by the
    Tacoma Art Museum, Washington,
    and the Institute of Contemporary Art,
    Boston.

Tribal

arts

Christopher D. Roy

The Des Moines Art Center is in the enviable position of being able to display one of Iowa's most important assets for the study and understanding of other people's culture. The African art collections at the Art Center have been growing since the early 1960s and numbered until recently almost 300 objects, the great majority of which have come through the generosity of the late Julian and Irma Brody, of Des Moines (see figs. 1 and 12).[1] Recently the Art Center had the collection evaluated by two scholars – me and Mary Jo Arnoldi. It has been reduced to just under one hundred first-rate works, with the remainder being sold. The funds from sales will be used exclusively for additional quality acquisitions of African art.

The Brody collection was first shown at the Art Center in 1975, in an exhibition guest-curated by Roy Sieber, a distinguished professor of African art history at Indiana University, with the assistance of a graduate student, Theodore Celenko. In evaluating the collection, Sieber discovered that there was a great deal of variation in the quality of the objects. When Brody asked how he could improve his collection, Sieber responded that he should dispose of much of it – a response that might have discouraged other collectors, but not Julian Brody. In the years that followed,

he made a careful effort to improve the caliber of the pieces he purchased, with considerable success. He also was generous enough to cooperate with Professor Sieber in his efforts to teach his students the differences between "fine," "authentic," and "traditional" pieces, and lesser work. Several Brody objects were even subjected to x-ray examination at the Indiana University Health Center in Bloomington, so that alterations could be discovered and studied. Brass sheets that covered a Kota reliquary figure had been cut into strips with modern tin snips – a tool that nineteenth-century Kota did not own. A Dan mask with round eyes had been filled in with plastic wood to form slit eyes – which fetched more on the market. A Kongo nail figure (nkisi nkonde) had round holes, predrilled with an electric drill, into which square masonry nails had been inserted by some disreputable dealer to transform an ordinary object into a "valuable" one. Throughout all this scrutiny of his beloved collection, Brody maintained an engaging sense of humor and enthusiasm, still memorable to Roy Sieber today, a quarter-century later. During his visit in 1974, Brody showed Professor Sieber a beautiful, leather-bound book, with Everything I Know About African Art stamped in gold on the cover. Inside were bound page after page of blank paper.

In 1993, following the death of Brody, the bulk of the collection was donated to the Des Moines Art Center, forming the core of a small but valuable

2

2
Igala, Nigeria; **Helmet Mask**, n.d.
Wood, metal, and pigment, 12 inches high (30.4 cm)
Gift of Irma and Julian Brody; Des Moines Art
Center Permanent Collections,1978.28

3
Ijaw, Nigeria; **Masquerade Headdress (Egbukele)**, n.d.
Wood, pigment, and metal, 17 ¹/₂ x 40 x 8 inches
(44.5 x 101.6 x 20.3 cm); Gift of Irma and Julian Brody
Des Moines Art Center Permanent Collections, 1997.73

3

collection. Among the real masterpieces is
a superb Igala helmet mask (fig. 2), carefully
carved by an accomplished artist, detailed,
refined, symmetrical, thin, light, old, and truly
dignified. Another remarkable object is a mask
(fig. 3) worn on top of the head rather than over
the face, representing a pangolin or scaly ant-
eater, from the Ijaw people in southern Nigeria.
Astonishingly graceful, considering the subject
matter, this piece is carefully constructed of
small, rounded strips of wood nailed in place and
painted red, yellow, and green. It is sufficiently
rare that it traveled the United States as one of
the highlights of an important exhibition,
"Animals in African Art," curated by University
of Iowa professor Allen F. Roberts. The mask
exemplifies the African artist's genius at distilling
the shape of a human being or an animal into its
most essential and expressive parts.

In addition to their sheer aesthetic value, both
the Stanley Collection of African Art at the
University of Iowa in Iowa City and the Brody
(now Des Moines Art Center) collection are
important cultural treasures for Iowa, especially
because the State is so homogeneous culturally.
The collections are important for Iowa's African-
American residents as documents of their own
cultural heritage, and to the population at large
as a means of understanding the creative genius,
as well as the systems of thought, of diverse peoples. The African art collections are significant
because the objects are beautifully carved, pow-

erful compositions, with unusual and stimulating
shapes, and also because they are a means to
understanding the people who made and used
them. The context of these works is relevant to
appreciating their value, since African works of
art, like all works of art, have been created for a
purpose: to communicate a message, to embody
meaning, and to reflect important ideas. For
Africans in particular, art objects are valued tools
for marking key passages in life, for overcoming
adversity and solving problems. Art objects
appear at important occasions throughout the
lives of most African peoples. Roy Sieber has
often said that Africans do not make art for art's
sake, instead they make art for life's sake. An
examination of how some of the outstanding
objects in the Des Moines Art Center were actually used will lead to a better understanding
of how important such objects have been to
Africans and how much they can instruct us
in African cultural history.

Birth. On a continent where people must deal
with an environment that is often very unfriendly,
where human life is threatened by disease,
accident, famine, and strife, and where there are
very few countries with any system of social
security, it is important to have a large family. For

4   5

enough children to survive into adulthood to
care for their elderly parents when they are too
infirm to work in the fields, it may be necessary
for a woman to bear a dozen children. The result
is that human fertility is an important concern,
and in fact, most of the questions addressed to
traditional healers and religious leaders revolve
around child-bearing and infant health. Many of
the most beautiful and appealing works of art
from Africa are figures of mothers bearing children on their backs or nursing infants. These are
placed on shrines in the home as a means of communicating with God to ask for healthy children.

Perhaps the most abundant of African art objects
in public and private collections around the
world are the paired small figures, either male or
female, with what appear to be peaked caps
and beads around their necks (fig. 4). These are
images of twins, ere ibeji, commissioned by a
Yoruba woman from southwest Nigeria on the
instructions of her diviner/pastor/priest in
response to the death of twins she has borne.
The Yoruba have the highest rate of twinning in
the world, in great part because twins are considered to bring good fortune to their parents and
to anyone who honors them. In contrast to other
peoples around the world who abandoned twins
and encouraged women who bore twins to have

more children. But twins are fragile, their mortality rate is especially high. If one twin dies, its
mother may have one figure carved; if both die,
two figures are carved. Twin figures may be collected singly, if only one infant dies, or in pairs, if
both die. The artist carves the figures with marks
of status and honor, including prestigious head-
wear and sandals, the scarification patterns of
the group into which they were born, and gender. The mother then honors the spirits of the
deceased twins in an effort to bring to herself
and her family the good fortune they would have
provided had they lived. She applies to their
bodies a cosmetic of oil mixed with a red dye
made of the powdered pith of the dyewood tree,
just as she would to a living child, and she dyes
their hair blue-black with indigo, a color associated with prosperity and well-being. She may
dress the small figures in expensive clothes, even
jackets of colored beads or cowry shells, an old
form of currency. Finally, she feeds them small
servings of their favorite foods, beans and palm
oil; when their faces become soiled, she washes
them carefully with a handful of clean sand.

Education. Among the most important steps or
passages in life for all human beings is the
process by which we acquire the skills necessary
to function and thrive as respected members of
adult society. In our own society, as in contemporary Africa, these skills may include reading,
writing, history, and arithmetic, as well as computer science and the arts, and are acquired in
school. In traditional rural communities in Africa,

4
Yoruba, Nigeria; **Figures (Ibeji)**, n.d.
Wood, pigment, and glass beads, each 12 1/2 inches high
(31.8 cm); Bequest of Irma and Julian Brody; Des Moines
Art Center Permanent Collections, 1997.50 .a–.b

5
Mende, Sierra Leone/Liberia; **Mask**, n.d.
Wood, 15 1/2 inches high (39.4 cm)
Gift of Irma and Julian Brody; Des Moines
Art Center Permanent Collections, 1973.36

6
Makonde, Tanzania; **Mask (Mapiko)**, n.d.
Wood, beeswax, hair, pigment, and metal; 10 1/4 x
7 1/2 x 10 1/4 inches (26 x 19 x 26 cm); Gift of
Irma and Julian Brody; Des Moines Art Center
Permanent Collections, 1988.19

6

the school system is administered by local families, and includes such skills as farming, trade,
crafts, child-rearing, cooking, and sex education.
The history of the family and the community,
and the religious laws that provide social cohesion
are also studied. When young people leave modern schools, they go through graduation and
wear special clothing, including a cap and gown,
often in the school colors. When young men and
women in rural African societies have completed
their education, they are "initiated," and their
graduation may include the wearing of special
clothing, including prestige cloth, body paint,
and jewelry. The initiation may be accompanied
by the wearing of masks.

Another excellent work is the helmet mask from
the Mende people of Sierra Leone (fig. 5). This is
a powerful, expressive carving of a human face,
with tiny eyes and a puckered, protuberant
mouth. The neck is covered by layers of tele-
scoping creases, as if the head had been drawn
down into the shoulders. The back of the head
is covered by a marvelous pattern of braids that
gives the shape a unique texture. Such masks are
made for and used by women. They are commissioned by middle-aged women based on dreams
they have experienced of spirits that watch over
them and over the young women of the community who are undergoing the important "rite of

passage" from childhood to adulthood. Featuring
Mende ideals of feminine beauty, the mask is also
loaded with references to Mende belief about
the spirit world. The facial type – small with a
high, noble forehead – is admired by the Mende,
and the elaborate hairstyle reflects the importance of personal grooming among a people who
will not appear in public unless they are perfectly
coifed, their clothing neat and clean, and their
bodies washed and perfumed. The neck rings
or creases represent a condition of prosperity and
well-being that all Mende aspire to. The three
lobes at the top of the hairstyle are references to
female genitalia, and make it clear that the mask
is the exclusive property of women.

A spectacular mask from the Makonde people
in East Africa was also worn at the end of the long
period of initiation, to represent spirits called
midimu (fig. 6). Makonde men carve masks that
represent heroes in their battles with the colonial
powers and characters that they see around
them. Most of these take the form of caricatures,
and many are quite comical. They have been
described by a Portuguese scholar who studied
for decades in northern Mozambique, where
the Makonde live:

"The mapiko, although still shrouded in mystery,
today dances in the village square during the
feasts associated with masculine and feminine
initiation rites. Although the men continue to
have nocturnal mapikos, with animal frames and
stilts, and the women have their own dances,

7

Chokwe, Angola; **Throne**, n.d.; Wood,
leather, and brass tacks, 24 1/2 x 9 1/2 x 9 5/8 inches
(62.2 x 24.1 x 24.4 cm); Bequest of Irma and Julian Brody
Des Moines Art Center Permanent Collections, 1997.24

8

Arowogun of Osi-Ilorin (1880–1956); Yoruba, Nigeria
Door, c. 1925; Wood and pigment, 62 x 32 inches
(157.5 x 81.2 cm); Purchased with funds from the
Coffin Fine Arts Trust; Nathan Emory Coffin Collection
of the Des Moines Art Center, 1971.2

7

there is a certain degree of collaboration during the feasts. The women form a large circle and dance slowly, beating their feet and moving their arms and shoulders to the rhythm of the drums. When the mapiko enters the square, with rapid and frantic movements, doing his staccato tap dance to the accompaniment of the rattles which he has on his body, the women bow and lower their heads, as if they cannot bear the terrible aspect of this supernatural figure."[2]

The performer's body is covered with cloth, and the climax of the dance is the rapid agitation of the entire body accompanied by a crescendo of drumming.[3] Each spirit character is unique and is identified by particular accouterments, including fly whisks, staffs, weapons, and costume.

"These utensils either had a symbolic character or simply emphasized the dancer's movements. The midimu were descriptive dances – named after the midimu spirits in which mask, costume, music and dance could illustrate particular personified characters or certain aspects of communal life. Different dances were consequently connected to different mask forms or types. In some cases it was enough to exchange the characteristic implements or to change the song and rhythm."[4]

Rule. Art has been used to express political power and validate rule among all cultures for millennia. Portraits of George Washington and Thomas Jefferson in the National Portrait Gallery are reminders of political history in the United States. Portraits of kings of France and England have reminded generations of the long and dis-

tinguished lineage of their royal houses. In Africa, where centralized forms of government, with kings, ministers of state, and complex government bureaucracies, had been in place for centuries before the arrival of the first European visitors in the fifteenth century, art has been used for at least 6,000 years to communicate ideas about political power and to confirm the right of an individual or small group to exercise that power.

Among the most recognizable symbols of political authority around the world are thrones, which embody symbols of kingship and which validate power. The Chokwe chair in the Des Moines Art Center is an example of a type that was modeled on seventeenth-century Iberian prototypes that the Chokwe saw European (principally Portuguese) colonials using (fig. 7). Because these square-backed chairs were associated with Europeans who held power, the Chokwe adopted them as symbols of power for their own leaders. This chair bears two carved representations of masks named chikunza which were worn by performers to impersonate the chief. These rise vertically from the side rails. In the center of the back is another mask that represents the chief himself, chihongo, complete with his distinctive chief's hat, called chipenya mutwe. The two small figures on the lower stretcher represent the spirits of royal ancestors, who watch over the chief and his subjects and

9
Igbo, Nigeria; **Figure (Ikenga)**, n.d.
Wood, 23 inches high (58.4 cm); Bequest of
Irma and Julian Brody; Des Moines Art Center
Permanent Collections, 1997.10

10
Baule, Ivory Coast; **Gong**, n.d.; Wood,
iron, and cotton cloth, 23 5/8 inches high (60 cm)
Purchased with funds from Dr. and Mrs. Peder T.
Madsen; Des Moines Art Center Permanent
Collections, 1973.19

9   10

protect them from harm. Because such chairs were ceremonial, chiefs rarely sat on these small thrones, but more often reclined in a comfortable chair while the carved throne was displayed nearby.

Among the finest objects in the collection is the Igala mask, which was described in the first catalogue of the Brody collection as a royal mask similar to one Roy Sieber saw and photographed in Idah, the capital of the Igala kingdom. The mask is of the helmet type, used by performers in royal ceremonies among both the Igala and their neighbors to the east, the Jukun, from whom the Igala trace their descent. There are nine different types of royal masks used in the Igala court. These are intended to protect the royal family and to validate their rule. The mask here in Des Moines most closely resembles the type called Odumado, which appears on the fifth day of the royal Ocho festival, and walks ahead of the king as he returns to his palace following the Ocho ceremonies, held once a year.

The wonderful door carved for a Yoruba palace is among the largest and most impressive objects in the collection, and is one of the earliest African acquisitions, having been purchased in 1971 (fig. 8). It is particularly important because it was carved by an artist whose name is well known in the history of African art: Arowogun of Osi-Ilorin (1880–1956). Arowogun was an extremely productive artist who carved important commissions

all across the northeast Yoruba area. He is well known in this country for the large and elaborate palace doors he carved for a northern Yoruba palace, now in the UCLA collection. The smaller but equally complex panel in Des Moines is arranged in four registers, each with about five figures, including musicians and men and women holding pistols in the top panel, a seated king with attendants in the second, an honored man riding a horse in the third, and two women pounding cassava and a man on a bicycle in the lowest. Many of these motifs occur repeatedly in Arowogun's work, and several, including the woman with two men, the bicyclist, and the women pounding cassava, are included in both the Des Moines panel and the UCLA doors.

Status. Just as art may represent the power of a ruler, it may communicate the status of a wealthy person, a person of position and influence, or a person who has attained a special place in the community. In this country persons of good taste and wealth may be recognized by an original painting or sculpture displayed in their home. The role people play in society may be identified by the clothing they wear. In Africa art also may even reflect a person's role in the community, and may, as in the case of the Igbo people, assist the owner in achieving his goals.

The ikenga figure (fig. 9) was made by the Igbo people of southern Nigeria, a people for whom status is achieved, not ascribed. A young man who is smart, aggressive, works long and hard, and takes advantage of opportunities presented, can rise in wealth, power, and social standing quite far and quite fast. The Igbo are in fact so aggressive and so successful in their efforts to achieve that they are both looked down upon and envied by other Nigerians. Their aggressiveness, their tendency always to push ahead, whether in line for a bus or in the business world, is quite logically associated with the aggressiveness of a ram – which explains the figure's horns, a metaphor for aggression. Such figures were owned by every Igbo male, and were kept on personal shrines to each man's "right arm." They represented for their owner the abilities, talents, and the spirit that would help him achieve. Sacrifices of raw egg were made on them to honor and feed the spirits, and to bring the owner success and good fortune. The vertical lines on the forehead are the scars, called ichi, that identify a man who has been so successful that he has accumulated the fortune that is required to purchase membership in an Igbo titled society, much like buying membership in an expensive country club, and thereby earning the right to wear the club's seal.

Healing. For people all over the world, disease has both a physical and a spiritual dimension. Sufferers may resort to prayer, or be prayed over. In Africa, where the equipment and drugs to effect a cure might be unavailable or too costly, a healer might emphasize the use of spiritual healing, including the use of art objects as the representations of the spiritual beings who hold the power to heal.

One of the most appealing objects in the Art Center's African collections is a small male figure made by the Baule people of the Ivory Coast (fig. 10). The figure, standing with knees flexed, elbows bent, and hands on each side of the umbilicus, has an elaborate and beautifully carved hairstyle, a short twisted beard, and fine scarification patterns on head, chest, arms, and abdomen. This type and style of African art was collected avidly in the early part of this century by French colonial officers and artists who bought them at the Paris flea market. Although its elegance and smooth, polished surface suggest that this was an ancestor figure, it is, in fact, a spirit spouse or spirit lover – the spouse the Baule believe each individual had in the spirit world before birth. Each man had a woman who was his spirit lover, and each woman had a man. When a Baule man or woman fails to fulfill his or her idealized role in the community, when a man

fails in love or business, when a woman fails to marry or bear the children that guarantee the survival of her husband's lineage, a diviner/pastor/ priest may discover, by speaking with God, that it is the person's own spirit spouse that has caused the affliction. A local artist is commissioned to carve a figure with all of the marks of respect, honor, and beauty the Baule value, which will serve as a dwelling place for the client's spirit spouse. Gifts, prayers, and offerings are made to the figure/ spirit, which in turn ceases to cause the sexual dysfunction that was the cause of concern. If the figure is not made beautiful, the spirit will ignore it, refusing to take up residence and, dishonored, make matters worse.

Power. In our own culture electrical power, gasoline power, solar power, are all part of our daily lives. Political power and spiritual power, less tangible and more abstract, are just as real and important. In Africa spiritual power may be used for both positive and negative purposes – it can both heal the sick and destroy those who have committed an offense against their neighbors or against God. This power is too abstract to be seen, or handled, unless a work of art is created that embodies the power, and allows it to be put to use. In Africa such power may be embodied in figures, which make it visible, or in masks, which bring the power to life and permit it to participate in the life of the community.

The wooden mask from the Ijaw people of Nigeria is over three feet long, with a surface made up of what appear to be tiny rounded shingles painted red, yellow, and green (fig. 3). A long, broad tail curls downward on one side, while a small head and two long legs project from the opposite end. The only visible evidence about how the object was worn is the cylindrical base that extends downward from the abdomen, forming a sort of socket that could be placed over the head of the performer. This is a horizontal mask, worn on the performer's head rather than on his face, by Egbukele masqueraders of the Ijaw people of the Niger River Delta. The Niger Delta is a hot, watery, humid place, covered with mangrove swamps that are in turn interlaced with creeks, lagoons, and occasionally broad rivers. Masks such as this one represent creatures from the spirit world that take the form of natural animals and beings. In Africa the pangolin serves as a symbol of many things for many people. For the Lega people of Zaire, the animal represents the value of marrying outside one's group rather than committing incest. (The Lega are exogamous, believing that to marry someone from one's own village or corporate group, not just one's

11
Ashanti, Ghana; **Memorial Head**, n.d.
Clay, 11 ¼ inches high (28.6 cm); Gift of Irma
and Julian Brody; Des Moines Art Center
Permanent Collections, 1968.35

12
Ibibio (Eket), Nigeria; **Mask**, n.d.
Wood and pigment, 13 inches in diameter
(33 cm), 2 ½ inches deep (6.3 cm); Gift
of Irma and Julian Brody; Des Moines Art Center
Permanent Collections, 1986.11

11

family, is incest.) For the Yoruba the animal celebrates Ogun, the god of iron and hunters, and
one's ability to protect oneself from attack and
threats, both natural and supernatural. The pangolin
is one of dozens of creatures that are represented by
masks among the Ijaw during important ceremonies
when water spirits from the creeks and lagoons
that surround Ijaw communities enter the towns
and participate in annual festivals. The emphasis
in these masquerades is on spectacular feats by
which the masks dash from the town and swim out
into the lagoon at a great rate of speed, smashing
into miniature boats, coiling around palm trees,
and consuming great quantities of sacrificial
gin and chicken. These water spirits live in a spirit
world parallel to that of the Ijaw, but beneath
the surfaces of the rivers, where they build towns,
organize markets, and hold their own spirit festivals.

Death. The last great passage in life is death, the
final moment in the key moments of life. For people
who think of life as a cycle, it is both an ending
and a beginning, for death leads to rebirth: in the
natural world, as the next generation born to a
family, or in the spiritual world of the ancestors.
For many people around the world, death is
accompanied by a need to remember the character and accomplishments of the deceased, and at
the same time send the soul of the deceased on his
or her way to the afterworld – giving rise to the

phrase "dearly departed." In Africa the dead may
be remembered through ancestor portraits, their
spirits may be asked to provide for the well-being
of those who remain behind in the world of the living, and their spirits may be sent on their way to
the land of ancestors by the appearance of masks
or the performance of sacrifices and prayers, which
mark the breaking of the ties between the living
and the dead. Some of these African ancestral
objects have been purchased with great enthusiasm by European and American collectors. The
Art Center's collection includes an outstanding
Ashanti memorial head (fig. 11).

In addition to the works discussed above, the Art
Center's collection also includes numerous objects
of personal adornment and use, such as bracelets,
combs, and an apron. These works are made with
the same attention and appreciation as those of
spiritual significance. Also, in addition to imagery
related to people's spiritual lives, the personal
objects often include imagery found through colo-
nization, such as bicycles and watches known
from Western sailors.

In the early half of the twentieth century, European artists such as Picasso collected and were
influenced by African art. The Art Center's African
collection is a great companion to the contemporary painting and sculpture collections, inviting
viewers to learn about art-making outside of their
immediate heritage and to see the connections
between modern Western art and African art.

12

1   See, for example, Des Moines Art Center, **Selections from the Julian & Irma Brody Collection**, text by Christopher D. Roy (Des Moines, 1988).

2   Antonio Jorg Dais, "The Makonde People: History, Environment and Economy," in **Portuguese Contribution to Cultural Anthropology** (Witwatersrand: Witwatersrand University Press, 1961), pp. 59–60. Volume 2 of Publications of the Ernest Oppenheimer Institute of Portuguese Studies of the University of Witwatersrand, Johannesburg.

3   Carlos Carvalho, "Histoire et Traditions des Malcondes," in **Art makonde: tradition et modernité** (Paris: Association française d'action artistique, 1989), p. 24.

4   Giselher Blesse in Jens Jahn, ed., **Tanzania: Meisterwerke Afrikanischer Skulptur** (Munich: Verlag Fred Jahn, 1994), p. 436.

Index

Abakanowicz, Magdalena, 42–43
    Flock II, 42–43pl
Abstract Expressionism, 17, 78, 112, 128,
    145, 153, 164, 172, 175, 210, 215, 221,
    241, 247, 275, 309, 311
    "classic," 238
    second generation; 168, 311
Abstract painting, 96, 100, 233, 309
    geometric, 131
    hard-edged, 153
African art collection, 33, 34, 316–28
    examination of, 316, 319
    importance of, 319
    Makonde masks, 321
    Mende masks, 321
    theme of birth in, 319–20
    theme of death in, 326
    theme of healing in, 325
    theme of polical power in, 322, 324
    theme of skill/education in, 320–22
    theme of spiritual power in, 325–26
    theme of status in, 324–25
    twin images in, 320
    understanding, 319–26
Albers, Joseph, 44–45
    Study for Homage to the Square,
    44–45pl
American Mimimalism, 36
American Realism, 309
American Regionalism, 309
Aquila, Pietro, 303
Arakawa, Shusaku, 313
Architecture. **See** Des Moines Art Center,
    Architecture
Armington, Caroline, 301, 308
Armory Show, 1913, 54, 66, 142, 229
Arneson, Robert, 46–47
    Klown, 46pl, 47
Arnoldi, Mary Jo, 316
Arowogun of Osi-Ilorin, 324
    Door, 323fig
Arp, Jean, 48–49
    Torse Gerbe (Torso Sheaf), 33, 48–49pl
Art Brut, 103

Art in the Park, 39
Arte Povera, 189
The Arts Club, Chicago, 132
Ash, Margaret Ann Dubie, 39
The Ashcan School, 260
Ashanti, Memorial Head, 326fig
Atelier 17, 309

Bacon, Francis, 50–51
    **Study after Velásquez's Portrait of
    Pope Innocent X**, 50, 51pl
Bailey, William, 52–53
    Head, 53
    Head and Torso, 53
    Migianella Still Life, 52pl, 53
    Still Life No. 4, 53
Barr, Alfred H., Jr., 48
Baskin, Leonard, 309
Baule
    Gong, 324fig, 325
Bellange, Jacques
    Pietà, 299fig, 302, 305
Bellows, George, 54–55
    Aunt Fanny (Old Lady in Black), 28, 54,
    55pl
Benezra, Neal, 34
Beuys, Joseph, 56–57, 63
    Energie Plan for the Westman, 56, 57pl
    Eurasia, 56
Bickerton, Ashley, 58–59
    **Tormented Self-Portrait (Susie at
    Arles) No. 2**, 58pl, 59
Blake, Nayland, 60–61
    Untitled, 1933, 60–61pl
Body Art, 217
Bohen, Mildred Meredith, 34
The Bohen Foundation, 280

Boltanski, Christian, 62–63
    Les Bougies (Candles), 62–63pl
Bonnard, Pierre, 229
Bosse, Abraham, 305
Bourgeois, Louise, 64–65
    "Femme Maison" paintings, 65
    The Blind Leading the Blind, 64–65pl
Brancusi, Constantin, 66–67
    Bird in Space, 66
    Golden Bird, 66
    Maiastra, 66, 67pl
Brody Collection, examination of, 316, 319
Brody, Irma and Julian, 34, 316
Brooks, John Woolson, 29
Brown, Julia. **See** Turrell, Julia Brown
Buck, John, 69
Bucksbaum, Carolyn and Matthew, 36
Bucksbaum, Melva and Martin, 35, 36
Butler, Cornelis, 36
Butterfield, Deborah, 68–69
    Untitled (Hoover), 68–69pl

Cage, John, 230
Cain, Michael Peter, 70–71
    **Nature Takes Delight in Nature: Seed
    of the World – Forming Process –
    #s 10, 15, 23, 20, 35, and 46**, 70–71pl
Calder, Alexander, 72–73
    Black Spread, 32, 72–73pl
Callot, Jacques, **The Temptation of St.
    Anthony**, 300fig
Canaletto, Antonio, 303, 305
Cantarini, Simone, 303
Carnegie International, 1995, 284
Carpenter, Florence, 28, 38
Carpenter, J. S. (Sanny), 26, 28
Cassatt, Mary, 74–75
    Nicolle and Her Mother, 74pl, 75
Castiglione, Giovanni Benedetto, 303
Celenko, Theodore, 316
Chagall, Marc, 76–77
    Les Amoureux (The Lovers), 76, 77pl
Chamber of Commerce, 26
Chamberlain, John, 78–79
    Vandam Billy, 78–79pl
Charlot, Jean, 39
Chase, William Merritt, 80–81
    Still Life with Fish, 80pl, 81
Chicago Tribune Competition, 10
Chokwe, Throne, 322fig
Coffin Memorial Funds, 32
Coffin Trust, 33, 34
Coffin, Nathan Emory, 31
Coffin, Winnie Ewing, 31
    photo of, 31fig
Colab (Collaborative Projects), 264
Color-field painting, 210, 238
Conceptual Art, 35, 163, 171, 217, 312–13
Constructivism, 73, 263
Cornell, Joseph, 82–83, 312
    Habitat Group for a Shooting Gallery,
    84pl, 85
    Untitled (Pour Valéry), 82, 83pl
Corot, Jean-Baptiste-Camille, 86–87
    **Ville-d'Avray – L'Etang et les maisons
    Cabassud (The Pond and the Cabassud
    Houses at Ville-d'Avray)**, 86pl, 87

Courbet, Gustave, 88–89
    **La Vallée de la Loue (Valley of the
    Loue)**, 88, 89pl
Cowles Sculpture Court, 33–34, 35
Cowles, Florence Call, 32, 34
Cowles, Gardner, 34, 291
Cowles, John and Elizabeth Bates, 33
    portrait of, 158, 159pl
Cowles, Russell, 28
Cranbrook Academy, Michigan, 10,
    12–13fig, 15
Crawford, Ralston, 90–91
    Worth Steel Plant, 90pl, 91
Cubism, 65, 192, 263

Dadaism, 48, 73
Danoff, I. Michael, 36, 38, 302
Darling, Jan N., 29
Daumier, Honoré, 92–93
    Le Liseur (The Reader), 92, 93pl
Deconstruction, 313
Degenerate Art, 1937, 158
della Bella, Stefano, 303
Demetrion, James T., 33–34, 35, 300, 302
Der Blau Reiter group, 308
Der Sturm Gallery, Berlin, 76
Derain, André, 94–95
    The Nymphes, 94pl, 95
Des Moines Art Center, Architecture,
    10–23
    additions to, 12, 17–23
    auditorium, 18–19, 19fig
    balcony of, 18
    debate on design of, 12
    education wing, 10–11fig, 15, 36–37fig
    exhibition halls, 22
    footbridge, 18
    foyers, 15, 15fig
    integrity of designs, 12, 22–23, 23fig
    interiors, 18, 19fig, 23fig
    International elements of, 13
    Lannon stone in, 13, 19
    layout of, 13fig, 14, 15fig, 17–18, 20, 22
    main galleries, 15
    original plans for, 29
    print exhibition area, 302
    reflecting pool, 15, 17, 18fig
    site, 13, 22, 29, 36
    stairways, 18, 23fig
Des Moines Art Center, Collections,
    298–328
    African art collection, 33, 316–28
    American works, 308–309, 311–13
    Belgian and Dutch works, 308
    British prints, 305, 308
    collections policies/criteria, 32–38, 298,
    300
    Des Moines Fine Arts Association
    collection transferred to, 26–29,
    300–301

directors' impact on, 28, 31, 32–38, 301–302
early drawings, 306
engravings, 303
Flemish and Dutch prints, 305
French prints (19th C), 298, 301, 305
French works (20th C), 308
German Expressionism, 306
history of, 32–38, 300–302
Huseby collection donated, 301, 305
Italian prints, 303, 305
Japanese woodcuts, 303
Mughal and Hindu miniature paintings, 303
nineteenth-century prints, 298, 301, 305–306
printmaking and, 309, 311–13
Russian works, 308
Spanish works, 308
Swiss works, 308
twentieth-century works, 306, 308
use and exhibition of, 32–38, 302
watercolors, 309
woodcuts, 303
works on paper, 298–313
see also Des Moines Association of Fine Arts
Des Moines Art Center, History, 26–42
acquisitions and exhibitions, 32–38, 302
Des Moines Art Center Association, 29
Des Moines Association of Fine Arts, 26–29
directors, acting/interim directors, 28, 31, 32–38
Edmundson bequest/trustees, 28, 29, 31, 33
education department, 38, 39, 302
member activities, 39
purchasing controversies, 31
WPA and, 29
works on paper collection, 38, 298–313
see also Des Moines Art Center, Architecture; Des Moines Art Center, Collections; Des Moines Association of Fine Arts
Des Moines Art Center Association, 29, 31
Des Moines Art Center Print Club, 39, 302, 313
Des Moines Association of Fine Arts, 10, 26–27fig, 28, 29, 272
depression and, 28
early acquisitions, 26, 28
early exhibitions, 26, 28
establishment of, 26
Walnut Street gallery, 28fig
WPA and, 29
Des Moines Chamber of Commerce, 26
Des Moines Founders Garden Club, 36
Des Moines Junior League, 38
Des Moines Parks and Recreation Department, 36

Des Moines Public Library, 39
Des Moines Public Schools, 39
Des Moines Women's Club, 26
Dia Foundation, New York, 241
Diebenkorn, Richard, 96–99
Ocean Park No. 70, 98, 99pl
The Table, 96, 97pl
Director's Discretionary Fund, 34
Documenta, 1982, 284
Dove, Arthur, 100–101
Corn Crib, 100, 101pl
Dubuffet, Jean, 102–105
Le Villageois aux cheveux ras (The Villager with Close-Cropped Hair), 103pl, 104
Paysage métapsychique (Metapsychical Landscape), 104, 105pl
Duchamp, Marcel, 63
Dunlap, David, 106–107
D-a-i-l-y P-a-i-n-t-i-n-g, 106–107pl
Dutch still-life painting, 81
Dwan Gallery, New York, 217
Dürer, Albrecht, 303
The Death of the Virgin, 298fig

EAT, "New York Collection for Stockholm," 312
Earthart, 217
Edmundson acquisitions funds, 28, 33
Edmundson Art Foundation, Inc., 29, 280
Edmundson Memorial Foundation, 29
Edmundson trustees, 31
Edmundson, James D., 10, 26
bequest of, 29
plaque, 26fig
The Eight, 54, 136, 229, 260
Ensor, James, 108–109, 306
Entry of Christ into Brussels, 108, 109pl
Environmental art, 313
Environmental sculpture, 36, 194–95, 251
Evans, Walker, 252
Exhibition of Independent Artists, 1910, 54
Expressionism, 154
figurative, 36
German, 132, 305, 306, 308
see also Abstract Expressionism

Farm Security Administration, 252
Fauvism, 95, 184, 192
Federation of Modern Painters and Sculptors, 238
Ferus Gallery, Los Angeles, 145
Figurative Expressionists, 36
Fingerman, Lois and Louis, 39
Flavin, Dan, 110–11
Untitled (For Ellen), 110–11pl
Fluxus, 63
Forum Exhibition of Modern American Painters, 1916, 176
Francis, Sam, 112–113
Summer No. 2, 112, 113pl
Frankenthaler, Helen, 175, 210
Mountains and Sea, 175
French avant-garde, 192
French Impressionism, 115, 135
Frieseke, Frederick Carl, 28, 114–15
The Hour of Tea, 28, 114pl, 115

Frowick, Ray Halston. See Halston, Ray
Funk Art, 287

Gabriel, Grace E., 38
Gabriel, Jennie May, 301
Galerie René Drouin, Paris, 103
Gardner and Florence Cowles Foundation, 34
Gauguin, Paul, 116-17
Reworked Study for Te Nave Nave Fenua (The Delightful Land), 116, 117pl
Gemini G.E.L., 311
Geometric abstract painting, 131
George Olmsted Foundation, 33
German Expressionism, 132, 305, 306, 308, 309
Gertsch, Franz, 118–19
Natascha IV, 118pl, 119
Ghisi, Giorgio, 303
Giacometti, Alberto, 120–21
L'Homme au doigt (Man Pointing), 120, 121pl
Gilmor, Jane, 122–23
Windows, 122–23pl
Goya y Lucientes, Francisco José de, 124–25, 305–306
Don Manuel Garcia de la Prada, 124, 125pl
Majas on a Balcony, 204
The Mannequin, 204
Greater Des Moines Committee, 26
Green Gallery, New York, 225
Greenberg, Clement, 175, 210
Greenwood Park, 29
Friends of Greenwood Park, 36
Greenwood Pond: Double Site, 36, 194–95
Grimaldi, Francesco, 303
Grooms, Red, 126–27
Agricultural Building, 126–27pl
Grosman, Tatyana, 311
Grosz, George, 306
Mother and Daughter, 307fig
Guston, Philip, 128–29
Friend – To M.F., 128, 129pl

Halley, Peter, 130–31
Fire in the Sky, 130pl, 131
Halston, Roy, 279, 301
Happenings, 127
Harnett, William Michael, 222
Harris, Paul, 28
Hartley, Marsden, 132–33
Mont Saint Victoire, 132, 133pl
Hassam, Childe, 134–35
Bridge in Snow (Brooklyn Bridge in Winter), 134pl, 135
Hayter, Stanley William, 309

Henri, Robert, 136–37, 260
    Ballet Girl in White, 28, 136, 137pl
Herbert, Charles, 33
Hesse, Eva, 138–39
    Untitled, 1970, 138–39pl
High Museum of Art, Atlanta, 20, 22fig
History painting, 154
Holzer, Jenny, 140–41
    Selections from Truisms, 140–41pl
Hopper, Edward, 142–43
    Automat, 32, 142, 143pl
Howard, Richard F., 32
Huseby, John, 34, 38, 301

Ibibio, Mask, 327fig
Igala
    Helmet Mask, 318fig
    Mask, 324
Igbo, Figure (Ikenga), 324fig
Ijaw, Masquerade Headdress (Egbukele),
    319fig
Impressionism, 75, 81, 88, 115, 142, 196,
    226
    French, 115, 135
Indépendants, 75
Iowa artists, 36, 308, 309
Iowa Arts Council, 122
Iowa Natural Heritage Foundation, 36
Irwin, Robert, 144–45
    Untitled, 1968–69, 144–45pl

Jess (Burgess Collins), 146–47
    **"A Panic That Can Still Come Upon
    Me": Salvages II**, 146, 147pl
Johns, Jasper, 148–49, 275, 311
    Tennyson, 148pl, 149
Judd, Donald, 139, 150–51
    Untitled, 1976–77, 150, 151pl

Kandinsky, Wassily, **Zwei Reiter vor Rot
    (Two Riders Against Red)**, 304fig, 308
Kelly, Ellsworth, 152–53
    Yellow Blue, 152pl, 153
Kiefer, Anselm, 154–55
    Untitled, 1987–88, 154, 155pl
Kirsch, Dwight, 32–33, 301–302
    photo of, 32fig
Kirsch, Truby Kelly, 33, 302
Klee, Paul, 156–57
    Anchorage (Anlege Platz), 156pl, 157
Klinger, Max, **Entführung (Abduction)**,
    303fig, 305
Kokoschka, Oskar, 158–59
    Portrait of Mr. and Mrs. John Cowles,
    158, 159pl
Koons, Jeff, 160–61
    Jim Beam – J.B. Turner Train, 160
    The New Shelton Wet/Dry Decker,
    160–61pl
Kosuth, Joseph, 162–63
    **Definition: Abstract (Art As Idea As
    Idea)**, 162pl, 163
    Five Words in Blue Neon, 163
    One and Three Chairs, 163
Krasner, Lee, 164–65
    Black and White Collage, 164, 165pl
Kress Foundation, 33
Kruger, Barbara, 259

Kruidenier, Florence Cowles, 29, 33
Kruidenier family, 35–36
Kuba, Mask, 316–17fig
Kuniyoshi, Yasuo, 166–67
    Amazing Juggler, 32, 166pl, 167
    Asahina and the Little Samurai, 303

Lasansky, Mauricio, 309
    España, 312fig
Leach, Bernard, 308
LeCorbusier, 18, 19, 20
Lee, Rose, 35
Lee, Ted, 38
Les XX (Les Vingts), 108
Leslie, Alfred, 168–69, 312
    grisaille paintings, 168
    Jane Elford #3, 168, 169pl
    Small Iron Picture, 168
Leveton, Deborah, 36, 38
Levitt, Jeanne and Richard, 34
LeWitt, Sol, 170–71
    **Wall Drawing #601, Forms Derived
    from the Cube (25 Variations)**, 170pl,
    171
Lichtenstein, Roy, 172–73, 311
    The Great Pyramids, 172, 173pl
Lithography, 311
Louis, Morris, 174–75
    Untitled 1–89, 1959, 174pl, 175

MacDonald-Wright, Stanton, 176–77
    **Abstraction on Spectrum
    (Organization 5)**, 33, 176, 177pl
Madsen, Peder and Ellen Maytag, 34
Makonde, Mask, 321fig
Mangold, Robert, 178–79
    Circle Painting No. 5, 178pl, 179
Marden, Brice, 180–81
    Range, 180, 171pl
Marin, John, **Mid-Manhattan**, 33
Martin, Agnes, 182–83
    Untitled #3, 1974, 182pl, 183
Mary Boone Gallery, New York, 245
Matisse, Henri, 184–85
    **Dame à la robe blanche (Woman in
    White)**, 184, 185pl
    Head of a Girl, 184
    Jazz, 184
Matthew Marks Gallery, New York, 60
Meier, Richard, 12, 20–22, 23, 34, 302
    Des Moines Art Center, 20–21fig, 23fig
    High Museum of Art, Atlanta, 20, 22fig
    interiors, 23fig
Mende, Mask, 320fig
Mentor, Will, 186–87
    A History of Agribusiness, 186–87pl
Meredith, Anna K., 34, 301
Merz, Mario, 188–89
    Untitled, 1989, 188pl, 189
Milles, Carl, 190–91
    Europa and the Bull, 15
    Man and Pegasus, 15, 32, 190–91pl

Milton, Peter, 313
Minimalism, 36, 111, 139, 150, 179, 183,
    225, 237, 241 , 255, 271, 312
Miró, Joan, 192–93
    **Femmes, Oiseau, Etoiles (Women,
    Bird, Stars)**, 192, 193pl
Miss, Mary, 194–95
    Greenwood Pond: Double Site, 36,
    194–95pl
Mixed-media assemblies, 127
Modernism, 17, 100, 226, 229
    debate over, 12
Monet, Claude, 196–97
    **Rocher du Lion, Rochers à Belle-Ile
    (Lion Rock)**, 196, 197pl
Monotypes, 313
Moore, Henry, 198–99, 200–201
    Seated Woman (Thin Neck), 198pl, 199
    Shelter Sketchbook, 199
    Three Way Piece No. 1: Points,
    200–201pl
Morandi, Giorgio, **Grande Natura Morta
    con la Caffettiera (Large Still Life with
    Coffee Pot)**, 302, 310fig
Munch, Edvard, 202–203
    Attraction, 202
    Femme Fatale, 202
    In a Man's Brain, 202
    Lust, 202
    Madonna, 202
    Vampyr (Vampire), 202, 203pl, 305
Muñoz, Juan, 204–205
    Piggyback (Left), 204–205pl
Murray, Elizabeth, 206–207
    Sad Sack, 206, 207pl
Myers, Dennis Peter, 33

Nabis, 229
National Center for Atmospheric Research,
    Colorado, 17, 17fig
National Endowment for the Arts, 35
Nauman, Bruce, 208–209, 313
    Animal Pyramid, 35, 208–209pl
Neo-Dadaism, 47
Neo-Expressionism, 127
New Image painting, 237
Noland, Kenneth, 175, 210–11
    Whirl, 210, 211pl
Noun, Louise Rosenfield, 34, 38, 164, 300,
    301
Nouveau Réalism, 63

O'Keeffe, Georgia, 212–13
    From the Lake No. 1, 212pl, 213
Old Masters, 124
Oldenburg, Claes, 214–15, 312
    **Three-Way Plug, Scale A (Soft),
    Prototype in Blue**, 214–215pl
    Three-Way Plug, Scale A, Brown, 215
Op Art, 225

Oppenheim, Dennis, 216–17
    Theme for a Major Hit, 216–17pl
    Tooth and Nail, 217
    Wishing the Mountains Madness, 217
Oursler, Tony, 218–19
    Pressure Blue/Green, 218–19pl
Outsider Art, 107

Panama-Pacific International Exposition,
    San Francisco, 26
Pappajohn, John and Mary, 38, 237, 301,
    313
Parker, Paul, 29, 31, 32
Patrick, Peggy, 34, 35, 302
Pearlstein, Philip, 220–21
    **Two Female Models Sitting and Lying
    on a Navajo Rug**, 220pl, 221
Pearson, William and Edith King, 28, 33
Pei, I. M., 12, 17–19, 23, 33
    Des Moines Art Center, 16–17fig, 18fig,
    19fig
    interiors, 18, 19fig
    National Center for Atmospheric
    Research, Colorado, 17, 17fig
Peto, John Frederick, 222–23
    Jack of Hearts, 222, 223pl
Photorealism, 233, 313
Piranesi, Giovanni Battista, 303
Political art, 252
Polk County Conservation Board, 36
Pollock, Jackson, 164
Polydoran, Anastasia and Paul, 38
Pomerantz, Marvin, 35
Poons, Larry, 224–25
    Han-San Cadence, 224pl, 225
Pop Art, 17, 63, 172, 271, 279, 311, 312
Postmodernism, 124
Post-Structuralism, 313
Powell, Watson, Jr., 38
Precisionism, 91
Prendergast, Maurice, 226–29
    Autumn, New Hampshire, 226, 227pl
    Girl in Blue Dress, 226, 228pl, 229
    Roman Campagna, 226
    Surf, 226
Principal Financial Group, 35
Print publishing, growth of, 311, 312
Printmaking, 309, 311
Process art, 139
Pulsa, 70

Raimondi, Marcantonio, 303
Rauschenberg, Robert, 230–31, 275
    Talisman, 230, 231pl
Realism, 221, 233
Redfield, Edward, **Woodland Brook**, 26
Reed, Sue Welsh, 34
Rembrandt van Rijn, **Landscape with a
    Cow Drinking**, 300fig
Richter, Gerhard, 232–33
    Landschaft (Landscape), 232pl, 233
Roberts, Allen F., 319
Rodin, Auguste, 234–35
    **Nude Study (Pierre de Wiessant) for
    "Les Bourgeois de Calais" ("The
    Burghers of Calais")**, 234–35pl
Rosa, Salvator, 303
Rosenfield, Rose Frankel, 33, 38, 302, 303

Rothenberg, Susan, 236–37, 313
    Untitled, 1979, 236pl, 237
Rothko, Mark, 238–39
    Light Over Gray, 238, 239pl
Rowe, M. Jessica, 35, 36, 38
Rozanova, Olga, 308
    Battle of the Futurist and the Ocean,
    306fig, 306
Russell, Morgan, 176
Ryan, David, 34
Ryman, Robert, 240–41
    Cast, 240pl, 241

Saarinen, Eliel, 10fig, 10–15, 23
    Chicago Tribune Competition, 10
    Cranbrook Academy, Michigan, 10,
    12–13fig, 15
    Des Moines Art Century, 10–11fig,
    12fig, 14fig, 15fig
    print exhibition area, 302
    Smithsonian project, 10, 12fig, 28
Saint-Non, Jean-Claude Richard de, 301
Salon d'Automne, 1905, 184
Salon des Indépendants, 1905, 95
Sargent, John Singer, 242–43
    **Portraits de M.E.P. ... et de Mlle. L.P.
    (Portraits of Edouard and Marie-
    Louise Pailleron)**, 34, 242, 243pl
Schnabel, Julian, 244–45
    The Death of Fashion, 244–45pl
Schneider, Louis E., 38
Schramm, James and Dorothy, 33
The Science Center of Iowa, 36
Screen printing, 311
Segal, George, 246–49
    Man on a Printing Press, 246–47pl
    To All Gates, 248–49pl
Serra, Richard, 250–51
    Standing Stones, 35, 250–51pl
Shahn, Ben, 252–53, 309
    Integration, Supreme Court, 252,
    253pl
Shapiro, Joel, 254–55
    Untitled, 1987, 254, 255pl
Sherman, Cindy, 256–57
    Untitled #90, 1981, 256, 257pl
Sieber, Roy, 316, 319, 324
Simon, Joan, 34
Simpson, Lorna, 258–59
    Wigs, 258pl, 259
Sloan, John, 260–61
    Tugs, 260, 261pl
Smith, David, 34, 262–63
    Zig II, 262–63pl
Smith, Kiki, 264–65
    My Blue Lake, 264
    Sueño, 246, 265pl
Smith, Tony, 288
Social Realism, 128
Society of Independent Artists, 260
Solomon R. Guggenheim Museum,
    New York, 78

Sonnabend Gallery, New York, 59
Stanley Collection of African Art, 319
Stella, Frank, 266–69, 311
    Interlagos, 34, 268–69pl
    Marquis de Portago, 267
    Union Pacific, 266pl, 267
Sultan, Donald, 270–71
    Migs, 270pl, 271
Surrealism, 120, 263, 283
    abstract, 238
Swanson, J. Robert F., 13
Symbolism, 202
Synchromism, 176

Taeuber, Sophie, 48
The Tamarind Workshop, 311
Tanner, Henry Ossawa, 272–73
    Christ Learning to Read, 272
    Le Touquet, 272
    Near East Scene, 272
    **The Disciples See Christ Walking on
    Water**, 26, 28, 272, 273pl
Tatlin, Vladimir, 111
The Ten, 135, 238
Tibbs, Thomas, 33, 302
Tiepolo, Giovanni Battista, 305
Trompe l'oeil painting (American), 222
"Truisms," 140
Tudor-Hart, Ernest Percyval, 176
Turrell, Julia Brown, 28, 35, 36, 302
Twombly, Cy, 274–77, 312
    Natural History Part I, Mushrooms,
    274pl, 275
    **Natural History Part II, Some Trees of
    Italy**, 275, 276, 277pl
Tyler, Ken, 311

Universal Limited Art Editions, 311
Usry, Edith M., 34
Van Rysselberghe, Théodore, **A Path at
    Ste. Brelade**, 28
van Weeren-Griek, Hans, 38
Velásquez, Diego, **Las Meninas**, 204
Venice Biennale, 48
    1948, 199,
    1980, 154,
    1990, 259,
    1997, 284
Vernet, Carle, **Rearing Horse**, 301fig, 305
Voulkos, Peter, 47

Warhol, Andy, 278–79
    The American Man – Watson Powell,
    278pl, 279
    Campbell's Soup, 279
    Double Portrait of Gardner Cowles, 279
    Drag Queen, 279
    Flowers, 279
    Liz, 279
    Marilyn, 729
    Martha Graham, 279
    Mona Lisa, 279
    Self-Portrait and Skull, 279
Wayne, June, 311
Weeks, Carl, 301

Weems, Carrie Mae, 280–81
    Sea Island Series (Thomas), 280, 281pl
Westermann, H. C., 282–83
    Phantom in a Wooden Garden, 282pl,
    283
Whistler, James Abbott MacNeil, 306
Whitechapel Art Gallery, London, 164
Whiteread, Rachel, 284–85
    Ghost, 284
    Untitled (Plinth), 284, 285pl
Whitney Studio Club, 142
Wiener Werkstätte, 158
Wiley, William T., 286–87
    Thank You Hide, 286–87pl
Wilmarth, Christopher, 288–89
    Blue Release, 288–89pl
Wood, Grant, 290–91, 309
    American Gothic, 291
    The Birthplace of Herbert Hoover, 34,
    290pl, 291
    Sultry Night, 311fig
    Birthplace of Herbert Hoover
Worthen, Amy N., 34
WPA, 128, 164, 175, 252, 309, 311

Yoruba, Figures (Ibeji), 320fig
Younker, Benjamin A., 38, 301
Zorn, Anders, 301